HAMPSHIRE COLLEGE
WORKING PAPER NUMBER ONE

# THE MAKING OF A COLLEGE

*Plans for a New Departure in
Higher Education*

by Franklin Patterson, *Kessel 1916—*
and Charles R. Longsworth

DECEMBER 1966

THE M. I. T. PRESS
Massachusetts Institute of Technology
Cambridge, Massachusetts and London, England

# ACKNOWLEDGEMENT

H AMPSHIRE COLLEGE is grateful for permission to quote from the following: LITERATURE AND THE AMERICAN COLLEGE: ESSAYS IN DEFENSE OF THE HUMANITIES, by Irving Babbitt, published by Houghton Mifflin Company; "The New Man in the Arts," by Jacques Barzun, published in THE AMERICAN SCHOLAR; "The Disjunction of Culture and Social Structure: Some Notes on the Meaning of Social Reality," by Daniel Bell, published in DAEDALUS, Journal of the American Academy of Arts and Sciences; THE REFORMING OF GENERAL EDUCATION, by Daniel Bell, published by Columbia University Press; article by Kingman Brewster, Jr., published in VENTURES, Magazine of the Yale Graduate School; "Quo Vadis," by P. W. Bridgman, published in DAEDALUS, Journal of the American Academy of Arts and Sciences; "Changes in American Education in the Next Decade: Some Predictions," by James M. Cass in INNOVATION IN EDUCATION, ed. by Matthew B. Miles, copyright © 1964 by Teachers College Press, Columbia University, and used by permission; AN ESSAY ON MAN, by Ernst Cassirer, published by Yale University Press; "Social, Political, Economic, and Personal Consequences," by Henry Steele Commager in UNIVERSAL HIGHER EDUCATION, ed. by Earl J. McGrath, copyright © 1966 by McGraw-Hill, Inc., and used by permission of McGraw-Hill Book Company; "Quality vs. Quantity in the Colleges," by Robert C. Cowen, published by THE CHRISTIAN SCIENCE MONITOR; "The Changing Uses of the City," by John Dyckman, published in DAEDALUS, Journal of the American Academy of Arts and Sciences; EDUCATION AT BERKELEY: REPORT OF THE SELECT COMMITTEE ON EDUCATION, published by University of California, Berkeley, Academic Senate; SELF-PERCEPTION IN THE UNIVERSITY: A STUDY OF SUCCESSFUL AND UNSUCCESSFUL GRADUATE STUDENTS, by Edgar Z. Friedenberg and Julius A. Roth, published by The University of Chicago Press; "The Master Speed," from COMPLETE POEMS OF ROBERT FROST, copyright © 1936 by Robert Frost, copyright © 1964 by Lesley Frost Ballantine, and used by permission of Holt, Rinehart and Winston, Inc.; MEGALOPOLIS, by Jean Gottmann, published by New York Twentieth Century Fund; article by Stephen R. Graubard in DAEDALUS, Journal of the American Academy of Arts and Sciences; "The Economic Aspects," by Algo D. Henderson, in UNIVERSAL HIGHER EDUCATION, ed. by Earl J. McGrath, copyright © 1966 by McGraw-Hill, Inc., and used by permission of McGraw-Hill Book Company; EDUCATION AT AMHERST: THE NEW PROGRAM, ed. by Gail Kennedy, and used by permission of Harper & Row, Publishers, Inc.; ANTHROPOLOGY, by Alfred L. Kroeber, published by Harcourt, Brace & World, Inc.; PHILOSOPHY IN A NEW KEY: A STUDY IN THE SYMBOLISM OF REASON, RITE AND ART, by Susanne K. Langer, published by Harvard University Press; LIBRARIES OF THE FUTURE, by J. C. R. Licklider, published by The M. I. T. Press; "Anglo-Saxon Attitudes," by P. B. Medawar, published in ENCOUNTER; "The Ethos of the American College Student: Beyond the Protests," by Martin Meyerson, published in DAEDALUS, Journal of the American Academy of Arts and Sciences; "The Psycholinguists: On the New Scientists of Language," by George A. Miller, published in ENCOUNTER; MEN, MACHINES, AND MODERN TIMES, by Elting E. Morison, published by The M. I. T. Press; INTREX: Report of a Planning Conference on Information Transfer Experiments, September 3, 1965, ed. by Carl F. J. Overhage and R. Joyce Harman, published by The M. I. T. Press; "The Campus Climate: A Reminder," by James G. Rice, in HIGHER EDUCATION: SOME NEWER DEVELOPMENTS, ed. by Samuel Baskin, copyright © 1965 by McGraw-Hill, Inc., and used by permission of McGraw-Hill Book Company; THE AMERICAN COLLEGE AND UNIVERSITY: A HISTORY, by Frederick Rudolph, copyright © 1962 by Frederick Rudolph, Vintage Books 1965, and used by permission of Alfred A. Knopf, Inc.; THE AMERICAN COLLEGE: A PSYCHOLOGICAL AND SOCIOLOGICAL INTERPRETATION OF THE HIGHER LEARNING, ed. by Nevitt Sanford, published by John Wiley & Sons, Inc.; LANGUAGE: AN INTRODUCTION TO THE STUDY OF SPEECH, by Edward Sapir, published by Harcourt, Brace & World, Inc.; THE TEACHING OF SCIENCE (AS INQUIRY), by Joseph J. Schwab and Paul F. Brandwein, copyright © 1964 by the President and Fellows of Harvard College, published by Harvard University Press; "The Undergraduate and His Culture," by Richard B. Sewall, published by VENTURES, Magazine of the Yale Graduate School; A UNIVERSITY IN THE MAKING: THE BBC REITH LECTURES, 1963, by Albert E. Sloman, published by Oxford University Press; article by Susan Sontag in THE NATION; "Extend our Vision . . . to All Mankind," by Adlai Stevenson, in THE NATIONAL PURPOSE, copyright © Time, Inc., 1960, published by Holt, Rinehart and Winston, Inc.; "The Contemporary University: USA," by Julius A. Stratton, published in DAED-

ALUS, Journal of the American Academy of Arts and Sciences; TO-WARD EXCELLENCE IN PHYSICS, by Committee on Physics Faculties in Colleges, published by American Institute of Physics; PRIMITIVE CULTURE, by Edward B. Tylor, published by John Murray (Publishers) Ltd.; UNIVERSITY OF OXFORD: REPORT OF COMMISSION OF INQUIRY, used by permission of The Clarendon Press, Oxford; RELI-GION, POLITICS, AND THE HIGHER LEARNING, by Morton White, copyright © 1959 by the President and Fellows of Harvard College, published by Harvard University Press; review by Morton White of THE UNIVERSITY IN TRANSITION, by James A. Perkins, in BOOK WEEK, used by permission of WORLD JOURNAL TRIBUNE; THE AIMS OF EDUCATION, AND OTHER ESSAYS, by Alfred North Whitehead, copyright © 1929 by The MacMillan Company, copyright renewed © 1957 by Evelyn Whitehead, Mentor edition 1929, used by permission of The Macmillan Company; ABBOTT LAWRENCE LOWELL, 1856-1943, by Henry Aaron Yeomans, copyright © 1948 by the President and Fellows of Harvard College, published by Harvard University Press.

Specific citations appear in the notes to this volume.

# CONTENTS

# PREFACE

B EFORE COMING TO HAMPSHIRE, I had thought about schools and colleges from many points of view, but I had never faced head-on the whole question of what a college in this era should be and do. Suddenly, at the beginning of the summer of 1966, I found myself deeply involved in such a confrontation.

The experience was exhilarating and consuming. It was also more than a little humbling, as I began to realize the full reach of the question. This realization grew as I became more familiar with the careful planning that had gone into the conception and revision of the *New College Plan* from 1958 onward. It increased as I talked with faculty and administrators from Hampshire College's sponsoring institutions: Amherst, Mount Holyoke, Smith, and the University of Massachusetts. It was compounded by consultation with other scholars, artists, scientists, foundation officers, government officials, and architects. And everything that I read in the literature of higher education confirmed that the question of undergraduate liberal education was, to put it mildly, an open one. Out of all this, in two short but enormously full months, came this Working Paper and its framework of basic policy recommendations.

The preparation of the Working Paper would not have been possible without the collaboration of Charles R. Longsworth, Vice-President of Hampshire College. In addition to co-authoring Chapter VIII, writing Chapter IX, and preparing all projections and appendices, Mr. Longsworth gave thoughtful counsel which is reflected in the whole Paper.

A.

As the summer began, I found that the question of making a college, in the case of Hampshire, must be asked in three different, principal ways. One needed to ask again, even though eight years earlier

ix

the *New College Plan* had given an answer: what should Hampshire College be as an undergraduate institution? One needed to ask further: what should the Connecticut River Valley complex of Massachusetts institutions be, and what role should Hampshire College play within the complex? And because the new college would inevitably affect and be affected by its non-academic environment, one needed to ask: how should Hampshire College participate in the changing community life around it?

The Working Paper seeks to answer the basic question as it is asked in these three ways. It recommends that undergraduate liberal education at Hampshire College be even more thoroughly restructured, in terms of ends as well as means, than the *New College Plan* of 1958 suggested. It recommends that, as Hampshire College is established, the four sponsoring institutions and Hampshire take a giant step forward in interinstitutional cooperation, so the Valley complex may become one of the great coordinated centers of higher education in America. And it recommends that Hampshire College, hopefully in close collaboration with its sister institutions, play an active part as a corporate citizen in helping shape the rapid, inevitable urbanization of the Valley.

Taken together, these recommendations of the Working Paper present a model for a total enterprise in higher education. They are designed not only to enlarge and strengthen higher education in the Valley, but to provide a major demonstration which would contribute to educational development in the New England region and the nation as a whole.

A bold demonstration of this order is sorely needed. Undergraduate liberal education in the United States faces social, curricular, and financial pressures that will not be denied. The fiscal base and academic viability of the private liberal arts college are everywhere precarious. Except for a few institutions whose endowments and achievements still insulate them, the independent colleges and many of the university undergraduate colleges are as much in curricular disarray as they are in chronically difficult financial shape. Strong, coherent interinstitutional collaboration—perhaps the main hope for adequate quality, balance, and fiscal efficiency in higher education for the era just beginning—

lags far behind what is needed in the last third of the 20th century.

The Working Paper is directed at these needs. The design for Hampshire College calls for a redefinition of the purposes, structure, and operations of liberal education, to bring it in line with a new era. The College will explore ways the private liberal arts institution may regain a full relevance in American culture generally and higher education in particular, and do so within its own economic means. Hampshire's pursuit of answers about its own proper role as a college, about the nature of cooperation among Valley institutions, and about institutional responsibility in an urban society may be of service to higher education as a whole.

The establishment of Hampshire College means that a host of practical problems must be met and solved. The range of these problems, in their size and complexity and number, is very great. Meeting and solving them will test the full resources of initiative and imagination that a new Board, a new faculty, and new administrative leadership can bring to bear. More than this, establishing Hampshire College will test the meaning of interinstitutional cooperation in the Valley. There is always the possibility de Tocqueville wrote of, that men may "refuse to move altogether for fear of being moved too far," that they may not make, "when it is necessary, a strong and sudden effort to a higher purpose." The establishment of Hampshire and the strengthening of the Valley complex will require many hands and much time. Most of all, it will require in the beginning "a strong and sudden effort" by men and women who are convinced that such a venture is worth the boldness and energy it costs.

B.

The Working Paper deals principally with plans for Hampshire College. It examines the present context of circumstances in which a new college will be built, projects Hampshire's role as an agent of change, defines an organized vision of liberal education for a new era, establishes the groundwork of the College's academic program, outlines in provisional but illustrative detail the nature of the Hampshire curriculum, specifies *language* as a major new component of liberal education content, describes the community of Hampshire College, and forecasts the financial requirements and operations of the new institution. We have treated the College further in a series of appendices which add information about its earlier planning, its present site, its potential resources, and the like.

What emerges is as accurate an approximation of Hampshire College as its present leadership can manage. I regard the word *approximation* as essential to emphasize, since the report is not a precise blueprint, but one in a series of successive approximations of what Hampshire will be and do. Other approximations will follow, as the faculty and staff of the College grow, and as experience further informs its planning. The College cannot be given a static definition, since it will embody, as well as speak for, change.

Hampshire College, as the trustees intend, will be built on a campus of 450 acres of land in South Amherst, Massachusetts. The Working Paper recommends that Hampshire be a coeducational undergraduate institution of approximately 1440 students and 90 faculty. It will be residential, but, as the 1958 *New College Plan* suggested, it will have neither fraternities nor sororities. It will have ample provision for intramural sports and recreation, but it is not likely to enter into intercollegiate athletics. Its academic program will be distinctive in its ends as well as in its means. And it will demonstrate that, through innovation, it is possible for a new private undergraduate college to achieve high quality without a heavy, continuing subsidy of its operations.

## C.

The first chapter of the Working Paper deals with changing circumstances which affect all of higher education today, including Hampshire College. Revolutionary current changes in higher education and the general culture present problems which a new institution cannot afford to ignore. Severe economic questions of unlimited demand and limited resources haunt higher education, particularly challenging the viability of the private undergraduate college and demanding new solutions. A radical expansion of knowledge and the rapid emergence of new intellectual strategies and technologies for handling it call into question the capabilities of liberal arts colleges as they now are. Urbanization and community change likewise profoundly affect today's colleges and universities, and call for new responses. Specifically, these changing circumstances of society and culture, of the economics of education, of knowledge and intellectual technology, of urbanization and community, challenge us:

> To reconstruct liberal education so that young men and women may find acceptable meaning in social order and acceptable order in the freedom of an increasingly subjective culture.

> To put the private college in a strong cooperative relationship with other institutions, as well as economizing within itself, so that instruction will be adequate in quality and variety.

> To reconstitute the context of liberal education to include greater attention to the *language* of knowledge, both in terms of processes of inquiry and technologies of information transfer.

> To reorient the college as a corporate citizen, active in the civic problems and processes of its surrounding community.

In responding to these challenges, as the second chapter emphasizes, Hampshire College will seek to be an agent of change, both an undergraduate institution of excellence and a laboratory for experimenting with ways the private liberal arts college can be a more effective intellectual and moral force in a changing culture.

## D.

The vision of liberal education taken by Hampshire College is one of hospitality to the possibilities of contemporary life: the task of the College is to help its students learn to live their adult lives fully and well in a society of intense change, immense opportunity, and great hazards. As the third chapter suggests, the College should:

> give students, for whatever use they themselves can make of it, the best knowledge new and old that we have about ways man may know himself and his world. This means that the College must help them acquire the tools with which it looks as though men in the future may be most likely to be able to build lives and a society they consider worthy. The most continually experimental thing about Hampshire College will be its constant effort, in collaboration with its students, to discern what these tools are and how best they may come to fit one's hand.

The College is committed to a view of liberal education as a vehicle

for the realization of self *in* society. To this end, it will try to help each
student gain a greater grasp of the range and nature of the human condition, past, present, and possible future. It will aim at assisting each
student toward a greater sense of himself in a society whose meaningfulness and quality *depend in significant degree on him.* It will seek to
strengthen his command of the uses of intellect to educate and renew
himself throughout life. And it will try to enhance his feeling for the
joy and tragedy that are inherent in life and art, when both are actively
embraced. The total college program through which Hampshire will
pursue these ends emphasizes intellectual inquiry, artistic experience, engagement with the non-academic world, and a college culture that will
support these things.

### E.

I have suggested the general organization of the Hampshire College
academic program in the fourth chapter of the Working Paper. The
principal element the academic program of the College will depend
upon for coherence and continuity will be *conceptual inquiry.* This
central organizing principle means that education at Hampshire will be
unsatisfied with *knowledge about,* which Whitehead described as pro-
ducing inert ideas. Conceptual inquiry follows Whitehead's definition
of education as "the acquisition of the art of the utilization of knowledge." It means exercising the intellect to learn, use, test, and revise
ideas, concepts, theoretical constructs, propositions, and methodological
principles in active inquiry. This process is at the heart of Hampshire's
intention and program.

One of the basic propositions the College will test, as I have noted
earlier, is that an academic program of good quality can be organized
in a private college collaborating with nearby institutions, with its costs
met principally out of tuition income.

Academic planning toward this economic end, as well as toward the
ends mentioned earlier, begins with certain base-points. Among these
are the following principles: that curriculum development at Hampshire must be a continuous process in order to avoid academic obsolescence as much as possible; that this means continuing institutional self-
study and the provision of ways an innovative climate can be maintained;
that the "academic" program must be actively connected with student

experiences in the "real" world; that cooperation with other Valley institutions is essential; that the Hampshire academic program should have a highly flexible organization; and that students should have preparation and experience in teaching both themselves and others.

The College will not be departmentalized. It will be organized instead by major fields of disciplines and subjects into four Schools, designated as:

The School of Humanities and Arts
The School of Natural Sciences
The School of Social Sciences
The School of Language Studies

Students will have a substantial introduction to each of these four fields, and they will have intensive experience in at least one of them before they graduate. Schools, in Hampshire's sense, will be fields of study in which to enter, *not* places of residence and study.

Hampshire students will progress through a three-phase divisional sequence in their academic work, rather than through the usual four-phase freshman-senior sequence. Division I will introduce students to the intentions of liberal education at Hampshire and to the fields its Schools deal with. In Division II, students will enter (i.e., concentrate in) one of the four Schools for preparation in the concepts and methods of a single discipline, after having explored the School fields further. Division III will occupy students with advanced studies in their chosen field and integrative studies across disciplines and fields. In the divisional sequence, students will move steadily toward greater independence in study.

*No* courses in the three-phase divisional sequence will be required in the literal sense, and no fixed accretion of course-credits will be held to for graduation. Most students will be likely to spend one academic year in Division I, two academic years in Division II, and a year in Division III. Most will take three courses in each of eight terms. But it will be possible for students to vary all of these arrangements with the advice and sanction of the College. The only absolute requirements for graduation from the College are that the student:

Pass the basic field and integrative examinations for Division I.

Pass the intermediate School examination, field examinations, and integrative examination for Division II.

Pass the advanced School and integrative examinations for Division III.

Complete and have accepted a Division III advanced study or project, and

Pass a foreign language examination, demonstrating competence in understanding and speaking a language other than English.

In principle, if not in any but the rarest practice, a student could receive his degree at Hampshire as soon after matriculation as he could accomplish these requirements and might, in the process, take no courses at all. What may happen, much more usually, is that students will move through the divisional sequence at different rates. Some may take less than four years, while other students may take longer, particularly if they are given sanctioned leaves for work, travel, military service, or other purposes.

Examinations may be given in courses where faculty find them useful. In any case, only three categories of grades will be given: fail, pass, and distinction. No grades will be more than advisory, except for those on the divisional field and integrative examinations, and on Division III studies and projects.

Foreign language offerings in the Hampshire program will be limited during the regular academic year. Course work will be supplemented by an excellent language laboratory, to which individual students and groups may have ready access. During the summer term, on the other hand, Hampshire College will conduct intensive foreign language institutes. These will not resemble "summer schools"; their character will be that of *total-culture simulations*, in which students will live with a language and its culture day and night for a period of six to eight weeks. Such institutes, making use of native-speaking teachers and aides, will provide an instructional service of use to students from the other Valley institutions, will aid Hampshire students, and will move the College facilities in the direction of full use in the summer period.

## F.

The fifth chapter of the Working Paper offers provisional models of curriculum for the Hampshire divisional sequence. To compress these models in a preface would distort them beyond recall. I should like only to underline several points about the Working Paper's discussion of curriculum. One point is that the course examples, while detailed in some cases, are offered simply as illustrations of ways the general intentions of the College might be expressed. A second point is that the curriculum for Division I marks a deliberate break in content and structure from what is usually the work of the freshman year. The Division I curriculum is intended to do several things: to serve as a controlled decompression chamber after the high-pressure information-ingesting, test-scoring period of high school; to enable students to begin to see the meaning of liberal education in Hampshire's terms; to use a structured sequence to introduce students to the fields and educational procedures of the College; and to give them preparation for greater independence in their studies. A third point is that, in Division II and Division III, independent study shifts from a minor proportion of the program to a major proportion.

The curriculum outlined in chapter five's discussion would concentrate faculty heavily in Division I, as the 1958 Plan suggested for its freshman year. The total faculty (or full-time faculty equivalents) that the College would require for all Divisions at a full strength of 1440 students would be approximately 90, a faculty-student ratio of 1 to 16. This is not quite the "ideal" ratio of 1 to 20 suggested in 1958; detailed calculations and discussions lead us to conclude that a ratio of 1 to 16 approaches the limits of practicability within the kind of program the College desires to offer. Even so, such a ratio is very considerably higher than that at most private colleges of high quality and still represents a workable figure from the point of view of ultimate fiscal independence for the institution.

## G.

I have recommended in the sixth chapter of the Working Paper that a new principal field be added at Hampshire to the usual three found in the academic programs of liberal arts colleges. In addition to the humanities and arts*, the natural sciences, and the social sciences,

---

* The report emphasizes the lively and expressive arts as being integral to Hampshire's view of the humanities.

Hampshire College will introduce a fourth field, that of *language*. This should not be taken to mean simply foreign language studies, although these would be subsumed in the field. The School of Language Studies at Hampshire will comprehend within it the study of "language" in its many aspects, through analytic and linguistic philosophy, psycholinguistics, the historical development of natural languages, the study of symbolism, structural linguistics, mathematics as a language, computer language evolution, and other approaches.

In addition, the School of Language Studies will have a principal responsibility for leadership in the improvement of information transfer capabilities in the College. As the Working Paper says, "Hampshire College is far from committed to any idle notion that gadgetry will do the job in liberal education." But neither does it propose to repeal the 20th century nor revive the 12th. A concentrated emphasis on the human uses of the new technologies or information transfer means simply that Hampshire intends to exploit them for the ends of liberal education and economy wherever it is sensible to do so. In addition, I hope that Hampshire's internal emphasis on the improvement of information transfer capabilities may be orchestrated with external developments in this field from which all of the Valley institutions could profit.

### H.

The seventh chapter of the Working Paper discusses the community and campus of Hampshire College.

As its main constituency, the College community will seek students of diverse backgrounds who are as able as those attending the other major institutions of the Valley. Hampshire will be an innovative, "experimenting" place, giving its students an approach to liberal education that emphasizes understanding self and society through fields in which inquiry and expression are the central concern of study. The College's intention is to equip students as well as possible to handle their own education and their own realization as people. Such preparation cannot usefully be given in wholly abstract terms. From the beginning, therefore, students at Hampshire will have a good deal of experience with self-direction in their studies and campus life. They will face, in consequence, the responsibilities that go with increasing degrees of freedom for a mature person. While Hampshire will be innovative, innovation will not be an end in itself, and its students will not be those who are simply attracted by "experimentation" for its own sake. Hampshire's students will have to be abler to handle responsibility, abler to learn discipline of self in study and campus life, than most students at most colleges are expected to be. At their best, they will be like the best of American students today—neither privately disaffiliated "achievers," technocratic conformists, nor deviants. I hope they will be questioning themselves and the society they find themselves in. I hope they will look for honesty in the values of society, be contemptuous of fraud when they are sure that is what it is, be willing to go down hard roads that make genuine sense, and be unafraid to laugh.

Hampshire will build a faculty devoted as much to teaching in the terms the College stands for, as to scholarship and art. The Hampshire faculty will have, as its largest group, very able young men and women who are still relatively close to college age themselves. The second largest group will be senior faculty members, men and women of professor's rank, with mastery of their fields and a right to the title of master teacher. The third and smallest group will be faculty in mid-career, in touch with the frontiers of their fields and with teaching. Faculty salaries, tenure, and similar matters will be governed by standards comparable to those at other undergraduate institutions of high quality. Within the College's general framework of purposes and its accent on the centrality of method in disciplines of inquiry and expression, faculty will have unusual freedom to teach in terms of their own principal intellectual or artistic interests.

The organization, government, and administration of the College will be committed, as will the campus design, to building an academic community where intellectual and artistic discourse is as easy and natural outside the classroom as it is inside. The College will be guided by the basic policy decisions of its trustees and the leadership of the president, who serves at their pleasure. But the internal governance of the College will be shaped by all of the community's constituencies. The major governing bodies of the community will be few, but students will have representation on each of them. Faculty will have at least as much voice in shaping the academic affairs of the College as they have at

Hampshire's sister institutions. Over-administration, as well as over-committeefication, will be avoided like the plagues they are. Presidential leadership will not be equivocal, but will articulate alternatives, project goals, and mobilize the energies a vigorous institution requires.

The community of the College, not only in residential terms but in many academic and administrative ways as well, will be decentralized. The design of the College will feature a series of residential-academic clusters, each of about 360 men and women students, grouped loosely around a central College and library complex. These clusters will be known as Houses. Each will have its unique identity in architecture and in the qualities given to it by students and faculty. Each House cluster will combine student residential units with related academic facilities, including individual office-studies for at least sixteen faculty members from the four Schools. The House in each case will have a Master, a senior faculty member provided with a commodious residence, who will give approximately half of his time to administrative responsibility for the House. Each House will have, as well, a full-time Proctor or executive associate of the Master, also with a separate residence. Provision is made in each House cluster for the separate residence of two younger faculty members and their families.

Master planning of the whole campus is being done by Hideo Sasaki, a noted landscape architect, and his colleagues in the firm of Sasaki, Dawson, and DeMay. The design and development of the House clusters and the central College complex are in the hands of Hugh Stubbins, one of America's most distinguished architects. In addition, the trustees and the College administration are advised on general architectural questions by Pietro Belluschi, former Dean of Architecture at the Massachusetts Institute of Technology. I trust that we may create a campus that will not be a walled tower but an open city, that will allow for individuality, for unity, for urban intensity and rural serenity, for a sense of connection and a sense of detachment. Among other things, we want to create a campus which will respect the great natural beauty of the land as the setting of its human community.

## I.

I have urged two considerations in the eighth chapter that directly involve Hampshire's sponsoring institutions. One of these concerns the strengthening of interinstitutional collaboration in the Connecticut River Valley of Massachusetts. The other emphasizes the role that Valley institutions of higher education could play as corporate citizens of the larger community, shaping the form that urbanization takes as it continues to develop here.

The major importance of interinstitutional cooperation and its enlargement was touched upon at the beginning of this Preface. From the 1958 *New College Plan* on, the evolution of Hampshire College has been premised on the notion that economy and quality in higher education are most possible through cooperation among institutions. *All* institutions, even the most well-endowed and powerful, need the benefits of interinstitutional cooperation today, and will need them urgently in the near future. New England is relatively backward in recognizing this, as it has been in recognizing the need for strong support of public higher education. The institutions of the Valley constitute an exception; the beginnings of interinstitutional cooperation have been made here in the past twenty years. Because this is the case, the Valley institutions have a rare opportunity now to make a strong and sudden effort toward much greater collaboration. In so doing, as noted earlier, they would benefit themselves and present a model that could have a profound effect on higher education in New England and elsewhere.

To this end, Hampshire College proposes the creation of a Valley Center for Cooperative Development in Education, with its own corporate governance representing at the highest level the academic and other interests of the four colleges and the University. The Valley Center should have its own adequate headquarters, its own chairman or director and small but full-time professional staff, its own funding and budget. A principal purpose of the Center would be to assist the participating institutions in the active development of cooperative services, ventures, and programs, sometimes only coordinating these, sometimes undertaking partial or complete responsibility for their operation. Such a Center should be established simultaneously with the establishment of the College. We propose, therefore, that land for a Center be donated by Hampshire to Five Colleges, Inc., a corporation representing the Valley institutions, that funds be sought for Center construction and an initial operating budget simultaneously with the seeking of a major foundation grant for Hampshire College, and that funds be sought to enable the participating institutions to enlarge their cooperation substantially during the next ten years.

The financial projections for Hampshire College, and for a rapid strengthening of the cooperative institutional environment in which the College will be set, are presented in the ninth chapter. From these it is apparent that given support to meet its capital requirements and initial operating deficits, Hampshire College could thereafter manage mainly on its own. In doing so, it would demonstrate the proposition put forward by the 1958 *New College Plan:* that a private institution of academic excellence can be organized to function principally on its tuition income. It is also apparent from the projections what would be required to demonstrate the advantages of active, serious collaboration among an important group of public and private institutions.

These projections together make clear the dimensions of "the strong and sudden effort" which I recommend as the proper course for Hampshire College and the institutions which have helped bring her into being. The delivery of the new College into the world is not an event discrete from the needs and purposes of the Valley community of institutions. As the first conception of the New College in 1958 was an expression of the linked interests of institutions, the birth of Hampshire College is a time to strengthen the family of which it is a part.

While the Working Paper represents valuable ideas and assistance from many quarters, shortcomings or errors in it are my responsibility alone.

An appendix lists individuals who, in various ways, have contributed to the evolution of ideas about Hampshire. I owe a special debt to Professor Daniel Bell of Columbia University, whose thinking about general education in the present period has substantially influenced my own. I am deeply grateful, too, to Mrs. Virginia H. Aldrich and Mrs. Ruth G. Hammen, whose devotion and care in the preparation of the manuscript made its early publication possible.

FRANKLIN PATTERSON
*President*

December, 1966

# 1

## ISSUES AND PERSPECTIVES
## IN UNDERGRADUATE EDUCATION

*As new schools are founded, we shall, if we exert our options, be able to develop them with new educational philosophies, or with known ones, newly clarified. We have shown relatively little innovation in recent years either in the ends or in the means of higher education. A few small liberal arts colleges, such as St. John's or Antioch, continue to be our sports. New schools such as Hampshire College . . . may help revitalize the thinking about how new schools can create a special character.*

MARTIN MEYERSON
*Daedalus,* Summer, 1966

HAMPSHIRE COLLEGE intends to pick up the glove that Martin Meyerson says the times have cast down for it. The elision in the prefatory quote from President Meyerson says correctly that the founding of Hampshire was prefaced "by asserting that it was concerned primarily with new means rather than ends in education. . . ." This separation in the College's conception of itself is no longer true. Hampshire is vitally interested in new means in higher education and proposes to demonstrate its interest by positive action. But it is equally interested in new and older ends for education in an epoch of radical growth and change. The discussion that follows is premised on the idea that ends and means are in reality inseparable.

Hampshire College begins its existence as an institution in the midst of enormous change and growth in American society. Undergraduate education as a whole is caught up in this total social flux, but for a new private college the present situation is especially, and understandably, momentous. New private undergraduate colleges encounter conditions of unprecedented change alongside a range of opportunities for creative response which appears unlimited. They also confront remarkable hazards. The very existence and character of the private liberal arts college, new or old, are called into question by social and economic imperatives of the developing American scene.[1]

Hampshire College, even so, begins committed to the idea that there is a persisting need for excellent private liberal education in the mix of alternatives available to American youth. Further, Hampshire College stands for a belief that the private undergraduate institution must become again a force for needed redefinition and innovation in the whole field of higher education. The present current of immense change and growth does contain hazards, but many of these merit and demand more than avoidance. Properly considered, they may teach us new ways for the private college to contribute to the quality of education and life.

A reconnaissance shows at least four major sets of circumstances that provide private undergraduate education with the potential of disaster or of significant new points of departure. Without a creative and vigorous response, each of these sets of circumstances will operate on its own to constrict and distort the role of undergraduate education. Contrariwise, each presents extraordinary opportunities for a restatement of the function of undergraduate education in terms of positive relevance to our time. As such, the establishment of Hampshire College begins with attention to them.

### 1. Issues of Institutional and Social Change

Social structure in the following discussion refers to the roles, relationships, and institutions of organized social life. Culture connotes the ways people feel, think, and act within a society. In America today, social structure is changing in some ways and in many others is under great stress. The culture, of which social structure should optimally be the consonant patterned expression, is changing with breathless speed and in directions which produce stress and conflict in the social structure. Higher education is enmeshed in this congeries of social and cultural change and is itself changing. All of these circumstances tend to affect the undergraduate college.

a.  *The Consequences of Change in Higher Education*

Clearly observable change in higher education, as Daniel Bell has pointed out, includes a massive increase in research operations, a great expansion in the variety of roles of the professor, a heightened orientation to the disciplines, and the emergence of a very active national job market for the academic professional.[2]

Growing emphasis on research operations has substantially increased the power of graduate schools, magnifying both their funds and their prestige. In the academic status system, one who teaches only graduate students and participates in the graduate school's opportunities for research stands higher than one who is wholly occupied with teaching undergraduates. The increasing variety of professorial roles (in research, consultation, public policy, educational development) has required a lessening of the time professors spend in teaching. In an elite institution, a professor may teach only two courses, with one a research seminar, and expect frequent leaves for research and his other work. The heightened orientation of faculty to particular disciplines as the real community of their interest also has functioned to diminish the status and resources of undergraduate teaching. Able young faculty find research money available, so that teaching lower level courses is not always the economic necessity it once was. And they find that within their disciplines the road to recognition, advancement, and higher pay is through research and publication rather than through teaching. They aspire, therefore, to move out of the college and on into the more elevated world of the graduate school: the rewards and the research money are there. Their disciplines, through national professional associations, have become ideal national job markets through which to pursue this aspiration.

The consequences of all this for the undergraduate college, as the foregoing suggests, are profound. For many students, especially the more able ones in the better undergraduate institutions, college tends to become an anteroom to graduate school, to the real thing. A more serious impact on the small private liberal arts college is that an increasing number of the most able students choose not to go there at all, preferring instead to take their undergraduate instruction in university colleges, where contact with graduate school may be more easily and swiftly made. Many of the offerings of the undergraduate college, independent or university-related, in any case are shaped by what the graduate school requires as preparation. And the small private college, as preceding discussion implied, finds it increasingly hard to acquire and hold first-rate younger faculty who will be content to stay in undergraduate teaching.

The net general result of such current changes in higher education is to erode the vitality and resources of undergraduate education, particularly in the independent liberal arts college.[3] The erosion of undergraduate education by developments in the total structure of higher education is complicated by phenomenal growth of the college population. College enrollment was one and one-half million in 1941. In 1966, a quarter century later, it stands at five and one-half million. All present projections are provisional; most past ones have proved much too conservative. One recent responsible estimate projects fifteen million college students in 1991, a quarter century ahead.[4] Whatever the case, growth of awesome proportions is a fact of American higher education and a demanding pressure on undergraduate institutions.

Given such pressure and given circumstances which erode undergraduate education, the private college has three choices: it can throw in the towel, it can pray for a miracle, or it can seek new forms for its own salvation and the good of the Republic. Hampshire College will opt, as later sections indicate, for demonstrating that the third choice is not only most honorable, but best.

### b.  *The Consequences of Social-Cultural Disjunction*

Here discussion must shift from changes within higher education to changes of critical importance in the general society of which higher education is a part. The nature and consequences of these larger societal changes will be ignored by higher education only at its own peril and that of the society it serves.

As suggested early in this section, in an optimum theoretical state of things social structure and culture would be generally congruent. This is simply to say that in such a state the formal and informal social structure has a significant degree of *match* with the culture: the ways people feel, think, and act in the totality of daily life are reasonably in line with the expected roles, relationships, and institutional patterns that we call social structure. In their explicit character, colleges and universities are part of the general social structure and exhibit a social structure of their own. They are also part of the culture.

Whether a state of social and cultural congruence can exist outside of theory or outside of a society static to the point of tediousness is not the point. The hard fact is that social structure and culture in *our* society are increasingly out of phase with each other. There is a radical and growing disjunction of culture and social structure in contemporary society. Much of the way people feel, think, and act; their symbolic expression of ideas, art, and experience; their culture—is in conflict with a social structure which is changing less rapidly and often in directions which heighten conflict. This disjunction is seen nowhere more clearly than in the college and university. Nowhere else are its consequences more troubling or more demanding of intelligent attention.

Professor Bell remarks on four revolutionary "modes of experience" which mediate between social structure and culture, and which play a part in the contemporary disjunction between the two. One mode of experience is *number:* "the number of encounters each of us has, and the range of names, events, and knowledge we have to master—this is the most obvious fact about the world which today confronts us as a 'given'." [5] A second is complex *interaction:* what is distinctive about present society is not simply size and numbers but the vastly increased physical and psychic interaction which ties us directly and indirectly to so many other persons. A third mode of experience is *self-consciousness:*

> To the classic question of identity, "who are you," a "traditional" person would say: "I am the son of my father." A person today says, "I am I, I come out of myself, and in choice and action I make myself. . . ." For us experience—rather than tradition, authority, revealed utterance or even reason—has become the source of understanding and of identity. . . . The sociological problem of reality in our time . . . arises because individuals have left old anchorages, no longer follow inherited ways, are constantly faced with problems of choice . . . and find no longer authoritative standards or critics to guide them. [6]

A fourth dominant mode of current experience is *time-orientation:* our society is incessantly future-directed, mobilizing for specific ends:

> The greater pressures today devolve upon the young person. At an early age he is under pressure to make firm choices; to get good grades

in school, to enter a good college, to choose a vocation. At all stages
he is rated, and the performance ratings now become a card of identity
that he carries throughout his life.[7]

The consequences of these four modes of experience are essential
for the college and university to consider. Number and interaction as
constant modes of contemporary experience combine to shape human
sensibility in the direction of expecting and expressing *immediacy, impact, novelty, sensation,* and *simultaneity.* They indeed produce a world
*à go-go.* Self-consciousness (the modern "I") and the pressures of a
mobilized society on the other hand, are modes of experience which tend
to meet in direct conflict. The self-validating ego and a performance-
driven social order represent the essential disjunction of culture and
social structure. This disjunction of a demanding social order and a
subjectivized culture leads to more and more open and conscious responses of rebellion, alienation, retreatism, apathy, or conformity among
the young, *"particularly where . . . social mechanisms have been inadequate to handle the problems of innovation and adaptation."* [8]

Colleges and universities are having experience with such responses.
Kenneth Keniston deals with comparable phenomena from a somewhat
different approach. He finds substantial alienation among young men
and women who come from relatively advantaged homes, and who at
one level of their existence meet well enough the performance demands
of the society. Professor Keniston describes young people who are not
open rebels, deviants, or delinquents, but are nonetheless deeply disaf-
fected. They are caught up in modernism's definition of self as realized
only through experience; they reject (at least privately, where life is
"real") the highly organized society of adults as a costly and empty rat
race; and their inner conflict comes through in a yearning for fusion
with others, for absolute values, for the pure vision.[9] On the surface,
they are growing up; i.e., giving society the competent performance expected of them. Underneath, they hate the whole thing, resist adulthood
as they see it defined, and seek something better.

What is occurring with young people in colleges and universities is
only part of a much larger disjunction in modern life.

The nature of an advanced technological society is among other
things order, organization, time-orientation, problem-solving, discipline

in terms of mind and fact. It honors, among other things less lofty, knowledge, competence, professionalism, rationality. Through these and similar characteristics a technological society is able to master nature, achieve abundance, command unlimited energy, and comprehend more and more of the universe. It is also able to create gigantic problems, a goodly few of which remain drastically unsolved. But without the social characteristics it possesses, it is clear we would not have an advanced technology at all, and without the technology we would have more hunger, disease, drudgery, dullness, and death than we care to contemplate. The new society we have is in many ways vital and rich, and every part of the world is reaching for the kinds of benefits it can confer. The technological society is shaped increasingly by scientists, engineers, economists, and other professionals—a large range of related elites open to anyone able and educated enough to qualify. This, in broadest outline, is one of the two main massive thrusts in the modern period, legitimized and adapted to by the structure of society. It has its own flaws and limitations.* But its vigor and virtues, real and potential, are not to be denied.

Opposed to and yet curiously fed by the great technological society is another force, running deep and wide in the culture as a whole. Alienation and anomic response in youth are only a partial expression of a much greater and more inclusive nihilism which:

> has begun to attack the very core of culture and to proclaim a way of life that is really a withdrawal from society, a retreat into the "interior distance," a new gnostic mode which beats against all the historic, psychological taboos of civilization.[10]

The antecedents of "post-modern" nihilism are to be found in the effort of earlier modernism to free the individual from convention, to permit a radical detachment, to establish the autonomy of the ego, to let there be an "I"—in art, in social relations, in morality. The success of the revolution of modernism is with us. As Lionel Trilling puts it, the "I" has become an "us." [11] With a society of "I's" the only con-

---

*An engineer who can share in the elegant exercise of close-up photography of the moon may turn out to be a dull and opinionated bore in the drawing room.

vention left is the lack of convention, and a radical subjectivity takes each in his own way.

The great freeing effect of such radical subjectivity is evident in much of the art, creative experience, and life of the present century; so, too, are its dangers. If technology untempered by a wisdom in its uses can damage or destroy us, so perhaps can radical subjectivity.

Post-modern nihilism in the arts is no longer the cult of the few, expressed by men like Genet and Burroughs moving beyond the anesthesia of feeling into hallucination and degradation. The abolition of constraint by substituting experience for art and sensation for judgment is being extended rapidly into mass culture itself, justified as freedom, promoted by such diverse spirits as Susan Sontag [12] and Andy Warhol, and hastened by the media supplied by the magic wand of technology.

Professor Bell remarks that three new dimensions of cultural transmission contribute to the present extension of post-modern nihilism, or what he calls the apocalyptic mode:

> One is the heavy anti-institutional and even antinomian bias of the dominant literary culture. Few novels speak up for society or equate a social order with a moral order—even as a utopian possibility. Second, the receptive cultural media, eager for sensation, feed these ideas, albeit in vulgarized form, to a new and widening middle class market for "culture." Third, the radical ideas, though recurrent, trace a "widening gyre" so that at each successive turn more and more restraints crumble, all areas of the imagination are brought into explorable, sensible reality, and, in the hunger for experience, *anything* is possible.[13]

Whatever analysis one applies to cause and ultimate direction, it is clear in the present that the thrust of a technological social order and the thrust of a radically subjective or nihilistic culture are incompatible. As things now stand, and are likely to, this incompatibility comes into sharp focus in the college and university. Higher education is increasingly an instrument of the specialized, professionalized, technological social order. Even its operations, to say nothing of its curriculum, increasingly require the apparatus (computer scheduling, scientific management, cost accounting, etc.) of organizations in a technological society. Higher education is an instrument of the humanities, too. But given the student's consciousness of self as experience-validated and autonomous, and given the growing thrust of nihilism in both high and mass culture, the humanities do not provide the balance they once did. Many students, particularly those still mobile upward from modest circumstances and attending institutions of modest quality, will settle for the technocratic life without asking questions. Many others, like Professor Keniston's *Uncommitted,* will settle for competent professionalism in their public lives but be alienated and radically subjective in their private worlds. Others, and some of them the best, will disaffiliate altogether or as far as they can from any norms at all, having come to feel that not only is the given social order absurd, but that, indeed, all social orders are.

To the degree that the game falls out this way, all the players may be losers. The specific challenge to higher education in this context is to invent ways of playing the game that are not at the mercy of the social-cultural disjunction here reviewed. The social order can be technologically oriented *and* human, too. The culture can provide individual freedom *and* a sense of virtue in order, as well. Neither, while possible, is easy to demonstrate, now or any time. It is a crucial task of college and university to accomplish such demonstration, even against present odds. Hampshire College will undertake this task as a central matter of business.

## 2. ISSUES OF UNLIMITED DEMAND AND LIMITED RESOURCES

A second set of circumstances, interwoven in many ways with the first, raises questions about the proper nature, effectiveness, and continuation of the American four-year college pattern. These questions turn out to be especially thorny for the independent private liberal arts institution. They have principally to do with what can be expected of the liberal arts college in educational terms and whether the college is likely to have the academic and other resources to do its job.

There are important and responsible critics of "the idea of the college" in the liberal arts tradition who view it as moribund. It is argued on the one hand that the college is rapidly losing any really relevant function in liberal or general education because of widespread reform in the curriculum of secondary schools. This argument holds that a continuance of general education in the college merely repeats, in a sense, what most able students will have studied in high school. It is argued on the other hand, as the preceding section suggested, that the liberal arts college, particularly if independent, no longer can expect to have the resources in faculty and facilities to present students with the quality and depth of preparation required by the graduate school. This argument holds that the requirements of early specialization are not only alien to the liberal arts idea but are such, especially in the sciences, that the liberal arts college is not likely to be able to meet them adequately even if it wants to.

On the first count, it is undeniable that present student preparation in the secondary school is altering the relationship of school and college. For a decade, curriculum reforms on a scale never before undertaken have been directed at the high school. These (e.g., in physics, chemistry, mathematics, biology, geography, anthropology, history, economics, social science) have involved leading scholars, many teachers and students, and expenditures of a magnitude unheard of in curriculum development prior to 1956.[14] In addition to national projects for curriculum reform, the past decade has witnessed a variety of other efforts to improve secondary school education. These have included the John Hay Fellows program for high school teachers, the improvement of laboratories and audio-visual facilities under the National Defense Education Act, the Advanced Placement program, the many provisions for aid and development in the Elementary and Secondary Education Act of 1965, and a host of other undertakings, many gotten under way by foundations and not a few generated at the local level by teachers themselves.[15] Collectively, these reforms and changes add up to substantial alteration in the high school offering, especially for those students going on to college.[16] This alteration is uneven; it is centered, as Professor Goodlad points out, on individual subjects revised "from the top down";[17] and it is not often the result of current, across-the-board educational planning. Nonetheless, it is consequential in the relationship of school to college.

This is particularly true in terms of the first two years of college, the so-called lower division. Many high school graduates enter colleges where little real change in lower division curriculum has occurred for a decade or more. As they do, they may well encounter a "Gov. I" (introductory political science) or other course or courses that are repetitious of material they studied in high school. Or, where reformed secondary courses introduced them actively to genuine hypothetico-deductive inquiry (as in the PSSC physics), they may find themselves up against a didactic kind of collegiate instruction which is intellectually disappointing by comparison. To the degree that college studies now repeat earlier material or do not advance the student's sophistication in methods of inquiry, it is essential that they be criticized.

At the same time, it is important to assess changes in the high school accurately in order to be intelligent about their implications for the college. In several ways, school reforms leave much to be desired. First, the emphasis on upgrading single subjects has tended to undercut any inclination the high school might have had toward providing an integrative or synthetic general education for its students. In this sense, most of the secondary school reforms have not contributed to liberal education understood as seeing the relatedness of things.[18] Second, most of the "national' curriculum projects have not yet been nearly as national in their effect as observers may assume, nor have they been much related to each other in reshaping a whole, coherent high school program. The result is that many high schools remain relatively untouched by curriculum reform of any kind, and in many others the degree of change varies greatly from subject to subject.[19] Third, in spite of the intention of the majority of curriculum reformers to encourage inquiry in the inductive and hypothetico-deductive mode, what actually is happening in high school preparation for college is intensely dominated by two quite different things: the drive to "cover" greater and greater quantities of information and the drive to upgrade college entrance examination scores. Two results of this are (a) that today's abler high school graduates have a remarkable command of information in certain specialized fields, and (b) that they are intellectually provincial, lacking insight into such things as the centrality of method in inquiry, the way values affect inquiry, the way ideas relate to social conditions, and the way history is constantly with us.

Even the best high schools tend to propose narrow intellectual tasks for their students. Their graduates in consequence come to college as young men and women who are still intellectually narrow. Liberal education, it would seem, should yet have much to offer such students. This is not at all to say that the liberal arts college can do this effectively while staying just what it now is as far as program, stance, and style are concerned.

On the second count, the revolutionary development of research and knowledge in the best graduate schools, and the growing power and influence of those schools, indeed pose serious questions for undergraduate education. These problems arise in critical form in the natural sciences and mathematics and to some extent in the social sciences and humanities. In terms particularly of the natural sciences, these questions ask in one way or another whether it is any longer realistic for most undergraduate colleges, especially those which are independent and without great endowments, to continue to try to prepare students with "majors" in such fields as physics, chemistry, and biology.

Physics provides an example. A recent study prepared by the Committee on Physics Faculties in Colleges comments that a:

> student at a college typically has very little contact with contemporary physics, and little awareness of the excitement and competition found in it. His college professors are out of the main-stream of physics. Having fewer contacts, they are, for instance, less able to aid him in obtaining meaningful scientific summer positions and in counseling him realistically on graduate schools. His lack of experience and lack of strong undergraduate preparation—the advanced undergraduate courses are often weaker at the colleges than at the universities—make it more difficult for him to enter a graduate school which matches his potential ability. If he is admitted, he often finds remedial work necessary and he finds it harder to complete graduate school successfully.[20]

As the Committee sees it, the possible inadequacies of the small college center around such deficits as low faculty strength and quality, low endowment per student, lack of competitive faculty salaries, lack of secretarial services and research facilities for faculty, unduly heavy teaching loads, and a college emphasis on faculty as pedagogues, not teacher-researchers. The Committee concludes that there *"are* a few undergraduate colleges which are outstanding in their ability to prepare their students for careers in physics. There is no reason why the number of such schools cannot increase appreciably,"[21] if colleges can remedy the defects noted above. The Committee presents profiles of good physics programs at five private colleges to suggest what such quality would require. Among other things, the profiles show colleges which:

are close (10-90 miles) to major physics centers

have faculties preponderantly at the Ph.D. level

have low student-faculty ratios

have book value endowments of $5,000 to $40,000 per student

have high average faculty salaries

have appreciably smaller teaching loads than in most other colleges

have an average of five physics professors at each institution

have research grants (NSF, etc.) for faculty running as high as $30,000/year/faculty member

have active participation by physics faculty in publishing and other activities of their discipline

have bright physics students, three out of four of whom go on to study in leading graduate schools in physics or related fields

have available computers, secretarial assistance, regular sabbatical leave, adequate room for instruction and research and a separate physics or science library

The demands which must be satisfied in order to achieve adequate or good quality in undergraduate physics instruction in the private college are obviously stiff. When one looks at instruction and research at a major technical university, however, even these demands seem small. A single case may illustrate the point. One young physicist at M. I. T. teaches undergraduates the equivalent of one and a half hours per week. In addition he and his associates together instruct and supervise approximately twelve graduate students. This young man's research requires the use of very powerful nuclear accelerators. Although the Harvard-M. I. T. accelerator is new and powerful (six billion electron volts) he needs something better, and as a consequence commutes frequently to Stanford to use the twenty billion electron volt linear accelerator at Palo Alto. M. I. T. formally recognizes the value of continuing high energy physics research, the need of faculty for access to very powerful accelerators, and the necessity for the teacher-researcher to spend time at the accelerator facility. This young man does not see how even a major teaching and research institution can expect to have first-rate scientists without providing for very light teaching loads and time to travel to and use expensive research facilities elsewhere.[22] He sees the major problem of the small private college involved in undergraduate physics instruction as one of having enough faculty who are able to keep up with and incorporate into their courses the changes in scientific knowledge which result from the galloping pace of current research.

One bit of cold comfort in the case of this young scientist is that, confronted by the unlimited demands of modern research, even the research facility resources of the Harvard-M. I. T. complex turn out to be limited! The only way the researcher-teacher in this instance can proceed undeterred in his pursuit of knowledge is by being able to take his need for a more powerful accelerator to another institution. In effect, this young scholar's experience reflects a collaboration of available resources which is becoming increasingly characteristic of work at the frontiers of scientific knowledge. If collaboration and the development and mutual use of complementary resources is the economic answer in such cases, independent undergraduate institutions should be able to find some moral in the fact.

Dean Jerome Wiesner, Provost of M. I. T., in discussion with Hampshire leadership concerning the future of the independent college, expresses a formulation of the situation as follows. First, neither in its general education nor in its provision for students who wish to go on in a science specialization after graduation, can the college "really be a college without doing an adequate job in the science fields." Second, it is reasonable to expect that a good private college should be able to find the resources and faculty to handle the sciences competently on its own in the first two years of its undergraduate program. Third, only if it can develop resources and faculty at least comparable to those revealed in the five-college physics study, can the college do an adequate job on its own for science majors, and this does not appear to be a likely prospect for most independent colleges. Fourth, it is sensible, therefore, to expect that independent colleges should work out *collaborative arrangements with each other and particularly with universities and technical institutes for helping meet the needs that science majors have for advanced instruction.*[23]

This discussion, with its principal emphasis on the natural sciences, may obscure the basic point that in all fields the expansion of inquiry and study is of such magnitude that pressing logistical problems are raised across-the-board for the independent liberal arts college. This point is complicated by the increasing pressure of all graduate and professional education to demand what in effect is specialized career or vocational preparation of undergraduates. The college must assess the meaning of both developments in terms of what it wants to do, what it ought to do, and what it can do best.

That it is not an entirely free agent in making such an assessment is clear. The private college, even more than institutions in the rapidly growing public sector, faces severe, chronic problems of finance which constrain it to choices it might not otherwise make.[24] Algo D. Henderson comments that:

> it may be that the private colleges and universities will have to turn more and more to emphasizing distinctive purposes, exceptional quality, and experimentation. While doing a lesser share of the total job (due to growth in the number, size, and variety of public institutions), they can nevertheless continue to be highly influential in the evolving pattern of higher education.[25]

Professor Henderson might have added, and perhaps intended so to imply in his reference to "distinctive purposes," that in the face of unlimited educational demands and all-too-limited resources, the private institution may have to choose not to do a sizable number of things.

It might advisedly choose not to abandon a commitment to general education. Neither changes in secondary education nor the specialization pressures of the graduate schools are persuasive that the potential function of liberal education is obsolete. Present content and procedures of general education may be obsolete or uneconomic or both. But the function remains needed, and it is engaging to consider how it may be fulfilled in new, hopefully more relevant and productive ways.

The independent undergraduate institution may wisely not choose to try to go it alone in presenting advanced work in all the basic fields. Certainly *some* it should choose to do, where it is clear that resources are adequate for high quality. Others, as in the case of science, it should consider providing through the cooperation and assistance of other institutions.

The latter choice should be seen not simply as an expedient to save the liberal arts institution from deserved or undeserved extinction. Instead, it emphasizes as a concrete illustration *the urgent need to see all of education, certainly secondary and higher education in this instance, as a coherent, mutually interacting system.* A biological analogy that Julius Stratton used in another context is to the point here: ". . . we must advance from the anatomy of components to the physiology of the organic whole. . . ." [26] At present, higher education is largely an assortment of discrete and varying components. Each is isolated from the other for the most part. In isolation, each pursues its own program with whatever resources it has. In the process, wasteful duplication of effort is common; so too are shortages of resources in all the common fields.

What appears needed instead is not the absorption of all component institutions into a closed system or monolithic organic whole. *The greatest actual need, for the welfare of the whole educational enterprise, is to establish and radically strengthen the cooperative association of diverse institutions in regions or localities, or in special areas of interest.* This is beginning to happen in public higher education in new developments of the University of California, for example. It has notable precedent in the cluster of private colleges and university resources at Claremont. In England, to judge by the Franks *Report,* Oxford is moving in this direction: the "disjunction between the University and the colleges is dangerous to both. . . . The remedy, as Edmund Burke knew, is 'association'." [27]

For the years ahead in America, one perceptive observer has predicted that:

> A growing number of colleges and universities, both public and private, both the strong and the less strong, will enter into cooperative programs with neighboring institutions. In this way it will be economically possible for them to offer their students a wider range of special studies and facilities than any one institution could provide alone. In an era in which there will be far more than enough students to go around, the traditional competition among institutions of higher learning will give way to cooperation.[28]

In the Connecticut River Valley, four institutions (Amherst, Mount

Holyoke, Smith and the University of Massachusetts) have a history of unique association and cooperation between private and public institutions. This association has led to the organization of Hampshire College and other ventures. It remains, however, a nascent and hesitant association, rather than a bold effort to demonstrate and exploit fully the advantages of collaboration. As Hampshire College begins—adding a fifth institution to this group—a significant possible takeoff point has been arrived at in the Connecticut Valley. As later sections indicate, Hampshire College's establishment can provide the moment for rapid evolution of a rich, collaborative higher education complex which would demonstrate the viability of the Burkeian concept of association, would benefit each institution and its students, and yet would enable each institution to maintain its individual nature and quality.

### 3. ISSUES OF KNOWLEDGE: IMPLICATIONS FOR LANGUAGE AND INFORMATION TRANSFER

A third group of circumstances affects the college, higher education as a whole, and the society generally. Involved are the growth, organization, and exchange of knowledge, and the languages or symbolic systems we use in the process. Nothing is less separable from education than these considerations. Significant changes in them in turn change the conditions of intellectual life, including such conditions in school and college.

#### a. *The Exponential Growth and Differentiation of Knowledge*

The prodigious, accelerating accumulation of knowledge in our time has become a stock cliché of present social commentary. That it has should not obscure the fact that the accumulation of information is actual, and that it presents us with practical problems of prime relevance to education.

The expansion of knowledge is seen vividly in the field of science; the scientific journal, for example, provides a ready indicator of this growth.[29] The scientific revolution of the seventeenth century led to the appearance of journals intended to circulate new findings and theories. Scientists took advantage of the printed magazine as a device for the reasonably speedy transfer of information from one interested person to a number of others. By 1750 there were perhaps ten scientific journals in the world. By 1800 there were a hundred; by 1850 there were a thousand; by 1900 there were roughly ten thousand scientific journals being published in the world. The number has increased by a factor of ten every fifty years since 1750.

In 1830, a mutation occurred: the first *abstract* journal made its appearance. There were then some three hundred scientific journals being published, and it had become clear that the man of science could not possibly keep up with them without some new aid. The abstract journal gave the reader a summary of many articles in many journals; he could then select for a full reading those articles which seemed most pertinent to his own work But from then on, the number of abstract journals also increased at an exponential rate. In 1950 there were approximately three hundred abstract journals being published in the scientific world. And each journal itself tended to grow in size. One journal of abstracts in chemistry now publishes some thirteen thousand pages annually, not counting indexes and cross-references. A decade ago it was half this length.

Other figures are equally high. In medicine, approximately two hundred thousand articles in journals and some ten thousand monographs appear yearly. In the natural sciences as a whole there are currently sixty thousand books, one hundred thousand research reports, and 1.2 million articles being published each year.

Beyond the business of a sheer prodigious accumulation of scientific data in modern times, the situation of knowledge is made more complex by the fact that constant change occurs because new discoveries breed new differentiations of knowledge in new subdivisions and new specialties. Gerald Holton convincingly demonstrates this process of differentiation or branching by tracing the many and diverse studies which followed the 1929 brilliant work of I. I. Rabi in sending molecular beams through a magnetic field. These studies, taking off from Professor Rabi's breakthrough in pure physics, went in such directions as optics, masers, nuclear magnetic resonance, and atomic structure.[30]

Again, science is simply a most dramatic example of what is happening in the intellectual world generally. Illustrations of the expansion and differentiation of knowledge in the humanities, in the social sciences, in engineering, in social technology and government, and other fields could be added. But the point, while emphasized, would stay the same: modern civilization rides a rising torrent of knowledge and information. How it does so has a great deal to do with education.

Two of the main lines of reciprocal relationship between the revolution in knowledge and the process of education are those of developments in information transfer and developments in languages. The two are tightly related themselves, and in a sense are two sides of the same coin. For convenience, they are dealt with separately here, as though developments in language were principally conceptual and intellectual, and as though developments and prospects in information transfer were principally technical. In fact, conceptualization and technique are a part of both developments.

b.  *Language and the New Intellectual Technology*

Ideas are the great and classical instrumentality for controlling and using information. Science treated as essentially an accumulation or even as a classified inventory of factual information would be as wrong as the notion that history is principally a chronology of dates. Ideas (or call them theories, generalizations, propositions, etc.) are ways of stating succinctly and usefully the *meaning* of data. They, rather than information, are the language of the intellect. They enable us to use information without being engulfed by it. P. B. Medawar, Nobel laureate in medicine, argues indeed that:

> The ballast of factual information, so far from being just about to sink us, is growing daily less. The factual burden of a science varies inversely with its degree of maturity. As a science advances, particular facts are comprehended within, and therefore in a sense annihilated by, general statements of steadily increasing explanatory power and compass—whereupon the facts may be forgotten, for they have no further right to independent existence. Biology before Darwin was almost all facts. . . . Certainly there is an epoch in the growth of a science during which facts accumulate faster than theories can accommodate them, but biology is over the hump, though biological learned journals still outnumber learned journals of . . . other kinds by about three to one. . . .[31]

The point is well taken and underlines the necessity for education to be profoundly concerned with the use of ideas in structuring knowledge.

Even so, things are not quite so simple as that. The present tempo of information accumulation is too great to be handled just by the epochal evolution from facts to big ideas that Dr. Medawar relies upon.

Simultaneous with the radical expansion of information there have been, therefore, revolutionary developments in what might be called the linguistics of information. That is to say, there have been efforts to develop new intellectual tools with which to grapple with information and wrestle with it toward meaning and conceptualization. These developments, as yet, are more commonly encountered in the social sciences and in operations than in the natural sciences. In recent years these developments have included game theory, decision theory, simulation, linear programming, cybernetics, and operations research. They have, in a sense, grown up with the computer. They rely heavily on mathematics in developing new intellectual techniques that will, hopefully, lead to the emergence of comprehensive new theories of rational choice. This carries with it a clear "corollary that all future work in the social sciences will require a high degree of mathematical training and sophistication." [32]

For now:

> Paradoxically, though this new intellectual revolution seeks "perfect" information, it starts out in vast linguistic disorder. Any eruptive change makes for great confusion, the more so in the new intellectual technology, since its innovators and practitioners are a motley pack of mathematicians, physicists, engineers (of all varieties), statisticians, biologists, neurophysiologists, economists, management consultants, sociologists, and each man brings to the new field his own perspectives, terminology, and concepts. . . . Whatever the final clarification of terminology will be, it is clear that the computer and these techniques open up vast new possibilities. . . .[33]

The view of language expressed in this discussion is not confined to the problem of bringing linguistic order out of the newer intellectual technologies. In itself, this problem is one of the most exciting, exasperating, and potentially productive ventures of our time. But one must add to it other developments in language to get the full measure of possibilities.

Language as the comprehension and exchange of meaning in information is being approached in many other ways. Among these, one of the most promising is the new field of psycholinguistics. The name of the field, only ten or so years old, suggests the focus. Psycholinguistics examines the human use of linguistic symbols, the intersection of psychosocial factors with the machinery of grammar and lexicon.

Its purview of course includes the study of language in the common-sense meaning of the term. That is, it is occupied with investigating psychological and social aspects of language as a vital part of day-to-day life in whatever vernacular. One of its leading students says, with deceptive simplicity, "the central task of this new science is to describe the psychological processes that go on when people use sentences." [34]

But its possibilities of application go far beyond this pure search. They relate to the whole range of information-handling and meaning-production problems touched upon earlier:

> One thinks . . . of pedagogical applications, of potential improvements in our methods for teaching reading and writing, or for teaching second languages. If psycholinguistic principles were made sufficiently explicit, they could be imparted to those technological miracles of the twentieth century, the computing machines, which would bring into view a whole spectrum of cybernetics possibilities. We could exploit our electrical channels for voice communications more efficiently. We might improve and automate our dictionaries, using them for mechanical translation from one language to another. Perhaps computers could print what we say, or even say what we print. . . . We might, in short, learn to adapt computers to dozens of our human purposes if only we could interpret our languages. . . .[35]

George A. Miller, whose thoughts these are, is too good a scholar to let such possibilities carry him away from the first task, which is to get on with psycholinguistics itself. But Professor Miller's projections suggest, in the case of psycholinguistics, once again what a rich and moving field language now is and how central it is to the problem of knowledge. If we add to it developments in symbolic logic, in semantic analysis, in cultural linguistics and literatures, the emerging field of language may seem an amorphous and unmanageable behemoth. On the other hand, it may well be a most crucial and productive dimension of the new higher learning.

Hampshire College represents the latter view, as discussion in later sections will explain. A major consideration in setting forth a new definition of the content and function of liberal education at Hampshire College will be the need to bring language consciously into a principal position in curriculum.

c.  *The Technical Possibilities for Information Transfer*

The radical increase in available information and the experimental development of language and new intellectual technologies are paralleled on the "hardware" side by the rapid evolution of new machinery for information transfer. The connection between developments in language and new intellectual technologies on one hand and communications hardware on the other is intimate and reciprocal. Both are—and are likely to remain—in a state of continuous evolution. Both give promise— already remarkably demonstrated—that man will be able to keep up with the explosive expansion of knowledge.

The technologists of communication are rightly not modest about technical capabilities of their field. In the current year, the Carnegie Commission on Educational Television has been told the same thing repeatedly by America's leading telecommunications scientists and engineers. The net message, in reply to queries about what education can expect to have from communications technology in the next decade or so, is: "Anything you want." What such technologists say is that in terms of technical facilities for information transfer, the present state of the art is such that the only real limits are those that may result from timidity, lack of imagination, or lack of funds on the part of education. Even if a specific technical device does not now exist, if needed and demanded it is likely to be devised and produced.

This aside, there now already exists a far greater technology for information transfer than schools, colleges, and universities have begun to think how to use. Among these are or soon will be:

the capability for open and closed circuit radio and television, received in classrooms or elsewhere.

the capability for educational broadcasting from synchronous satellites to ground stations for rebroadcast. (The recent proposal of the Ford Foundation to the Federal Communications Commission in this regard illustrates the kind of relevant, audacious ingenuity that technology now permits.)

the capability for inexpensive electronic storage of audio-visual information for inexpensive playback. (CBS Laboratories have developed a 30-minute video disc which should sell for less than five dollars and be playable on a standard but inexpensive modified home TV set.)

the capability for multiple-access computer service by telephone connection.

the capability for facsimile reproduction of material via TWX or other wire service with delivery in one's study, office, or elsewhere.

the capability for inexpensive facsimile reproduction of books stored on microfilm and transferred to "book" pages by xerography. (Any of the 500,000 volumes, many rare, stored in the vaults of University Microfilms, Inc., of Ann Arbor can now be printed out by xerographic process, bound, and sold today at a standard price of 4½ cents per page softbound or 5 cents per page hardbound.)

the capability for programmed instruction via a wide range of devices from the simplest programmed textbook to the McGraw-Edison responsive environment device designed by Professor O. K. Moore as an outgrowth of his research at Yale.

These and other examples vary in their present value and potential usefulness. All, if used, ultimately depend for their value upon the quality of "software" (educational material, information, and ideas) with which they deal, and upon their being used not as disparate pieces of gadgetry but as integrated, functional parts of a coherent system.

If this is assumed, and if it is assumed that software commensurate in quality with the hardware *could* be produced, one is back to the question of demand. Should colleges and universities *want* the kinds of information transfer facilities and systems that modern technology can make available? And if they should, can obstacles of finance and lingering Luddite sentiment among faculty be overcome?

The answers to both questions, with some qualification, are likely in the long run to be affirmative. The reasons seem evident.

Higher education in every way deals with information and ideas. The astronomical growth and diversification of knowledge are making older ways of pooling and sharing information as unfeasible as they are economically indefensible. This is a hard fact of contemporary life and is basically not unique at all to higher education.* The expansion of knowledge, the new approaches to language and the new intellectual technologies, the increasing number of students and teacher-researchers, and the absolute importance of accessibility combine to make new techniques of information transfer essential in higher education.

A move toward adopting such techniques is on in many institutions. Harvard has established coaxial interconnection for video purposes on a campus-wide basis. The Irvine campus of the University of California is concentrating on computer-aided instruction in its initial planning. M. I. T. is engaged in a large-scale series of information transfer experiments in order to project a basic system for the institution in 1975. The M. I. T. information transfer system by that date will effectively replace one-half of what would ordinarily have to be library operations by information storage and retrieval via computer, serving the "on-line intellectual community" (students and professors) of the Institute. It is estimated that this system, "vastly different from the library of today in the scope of the services it seeks to provide," will account for $15 million in M. I. T.'s annual operating budget for 1975.[36]

All of this is not to say that such developments will subvert the book. Nor that they should. A uniform feature of the evolution of communications technology indeed seems to be that each innovation tends to reinforce the use of earlier techniques, even while supplementing them radically. Thus there is now far wider use of the phonograph than in pre-radio times, and far more use of books than in the pre-television era. Libraries, as they are now known and loved, will still be needed and actively used in the age of electronic information transfer.[37]

But there will be immense change. The two-year study for the Council on Library Resources reported by J. C. R. Licklider in his *Libraries of the Future,* provides a sophisticated view of possibilities in the electronic age. Dr. Licklider's discussion emphasizes the point that language inno-

---

*An automated direct-dialing telephone system, for example, presents the user with new and sometimes exasperating experiences. But it allows him to call a person three thousand miles away as swiftly as someone in the next block. And besides, without an automated switching system, the present volume of telephoning in the United States would require the services of the entire female work force of the nation as operators.

vation and computer evolution must go hand in hand. His conception of what will be involved in developments in the next twenty-five years argues for a major redefinition of the scope and capability that libraries heretofore have had:

> The systems in which we are interested are broader than present-day libraries; the systems will extend farther into the process of generating, organizing, and using knowledge. . . . Since the systems are intended to promote the advancement and application of knowledge, they are "for knowledge," and thus *procognitive systems*.[38]

Dr. Licklider indicates, in addition to the question of economic feasibility, twenty-five rigorous criteria (including eight "appreciated more by . . . librarians than by users of libraries"!) that computer-served procognitive systems of the future will have to satisfy. All, within the technical plan he projects, can realistically be met in the next quarter century. Meeting these criteria effectively would increase man's ability to interact with recorded knowledge by orders of magnitude far beyond the possibilities of present library techniques.

In addition to higher education's scholarly stake in the evolution of a procognitive systems approach to rapidly expanding knowledge, college and university have other reasons to be interested in the development of improved information transfer. Not the least of these is pedagogical.

Improved systems of information transfer by electronic means (including access to digital, pictorial, typed, aural, print facsimile, and other media) may reasonably be expected to serve two related pedagogical purposes. One would be to give the student increased direct experience *on call* with a far greater range of knowledge and service than he now can command. This is already the case in certain institutions. A student at Radcliffe, for example, can now be "on line" by telephone to a computer in Philadelphia, securing high-speed assistance in dealing with complex mathematical problems.

A second purpose, discussed by Jerome B. Wiesner in consultation about Hampshire College, would be to provide an electronic alternative to the tutorial system. Steps in this direction have been taken, for example, by Oklahoma Christian College in the design of its new library-learning center. The trouble at present, as Dean Wiesner sees it, is that adequately rich and flexible technology has not yet been produced to give us a suitably good substitute for the tutorial situation. But such production can occur if there is an educational demand for it; the McGraw-Edison individualized responsive environment suggests what could be done. It is not unreasonable to proceed on the assumption that many of the virtues of the tutorial's give-and-take ultimately could be displayed by a sophisticated electronic system. Nor is it unreasonable to believe that such a system could be created and operated much less expensively than tutorials on the Oxford basis.*

Such possibilities clearly exist for higher education today. Just as language, boldly conceived, offers a new frontier to the collegiate curriculum, improved information transfer offers a new frontier to the exploration of knowledge and the uses of pedagogy. A fresh and strongly innovative approach to language and information transfer would put new vitality into undergraduate education. It would confirm an essential commitment to teach the learner how to teach himself. And it could do so with significant, needed economies over time. These challenges are evident to Hampshire College.

### 4.  *Issues of the College in the Community*

The variety and uses of off-campus work-study and other experience in the community, variously defined, are described ably by Royce Pitkin and George Beecher in a recent study.[39] A remarkable number of colleges and universities provide a remarkable range of patterns for enabling students to enter and learn from "the community" as part of their higher education. The communities mentioned by Dr. Pitkin and Professor Beecher are as various as the Argonne National Laboratories, entered by science majors of the Associated Colleges of the Midwest in the capacity of research assistants for periods of ten to sixteen weeks, and metropolitan Chicago, entered by Antioch students in an optional field seminar on "The City."

Any reconsideration of undergraduate education today is likely to examine the possibilities and values of connecting academic life with educative experience beyond the college gates. In this examination, one is not apt to find a universal orthodoxy of pattern among institutions.

*These, as the Report of Lord Franks' Commission of Inquiry found, are even higher than had been supposed by Oxford itself.

Nor is there much in the way of research to validate the educational utility of community study, service, and experience. On the other hand, there is an undeniable morale about such programs clearly evident among students and faculty associated with them, and a good deal of common-sense evidence that they are useful. A new college is urged on many sides to make it possible for students to spend time in non-academic experience before entering college;[40] or to take leaves at specific intervals; or to take leaves for work, travel, or study whenever the time seems right.[41]

Hampshire College, as later sections explain, is committed to its own program of enabling students to have an active and educative experience in the non-campus world. But the College has a larger concern about community out of which its views with regard to the pedagogical uses of extra-campus programs arise. The present discussion deals with the background of that concern.

Historically and not always for academic or intellectual reasons, many American institutions of higher learning have tended toward separation in relation to their communities. Some goodly number have been happy in the Sainte-Beuve *tour d' ivoire* role, as scholarly enclaves surrounded by barbarian territory. Others have eschewed contact with non-academic society in order to preserve the youth in their charge from the sullying influence of worldly association. Frederick Rudolph reminds us that:

> The antipathy to towns as college sites was so strong in North Carolina that the charter for the University of North Carolina in 1789 provided that it could not be located within five miles of any seat of government or any place where law or equity courts met.[42]

Such extremes in the cause of purity are no longer common, but they are a part of the record of American higher education's stance toward community.

All institutions have professed a desire that their toil in the educational vineyard should contribute to the public good. Community colleges, state colleges and universities, extension programs, and private institutions have worked hard to serve the public interest. The motto of one great urban institution, confirmed by much of what it accomplishes, is: "A private university in the public service." Indeed, public service as a field for which it prepares students is one of the most often emphasized purposes of higher education.

But this is something different from the active civic involvement of an institution with the affairs of the community in which it lives. "Town and gown" relationships characteristically have been expected by institutions to be more a source of headaches than anything else. In moments of crisis in the institution or community such relationships may become close, even painfully so. The best one could ask for, perhaps, was that such relationships be smooth and at least superficially cordial.

In the present, however, there are growing signs that institutions may become more fully engaged members of the communities around them. The opportunity increasingly exists, in part because their generally enlarged role tends to free them from earlier isolation, for colleges and universities to act in concert with other institutions of community life. A tradition in this regard has long been set by such colleges as Berea, Antioch, Earlham, West Georgia, and Goddard.[43] Other institutions, in diverse projects, have moved toward more active roles in community life. Most of these, however, still confine themselves to ways of "serving the community educationally," "integrating educational values with community life," and providing field experience for students.

The really new dimension of opportunity is for institutions now to play a vital part in helping shape public policy in important community affairs. This opportunity exists least, perhaps, for the urban university engulfed in the complexities of the metropolitan community. It exists to a greater degree in areas which are not completely rural, but are beginning to become more densely populated. It appears to exist most in areas where there are still open-ended problems (e.g., those of land development and use), where urbanization is only setting in, and where there are institutions of higher education that stand in a cooperative relationship to each other.

In the latter instance, there is a major challenge for institutions in such areas to revise the traditional stance of higher education *vis-à-vis* community. The institution's controlling board, its administrative leadership, and to some extent its entire constituency would need to view the institution as an *active, corporate citizen* in community development. Most institutions might argue that this state of affairs is already true. In some interesting cases it actually is, but, in the terms meant here, the present civic involvement of institutions in their surrounding communities is more nominal than anything else. It is suggested here that, in areas of incipient urbanization, colleges and universities can become a genuinely moving force in the development of the community.

Some of the practical reasons why this is possible in such areas are these:

*Areas of incipient urbanization present a relatively open and fluid field of action.* Things are happening, often at a rapid rate and in a meta-static way (witness, e.g., the San Gabriel Valley in Los Angeles County, 1950-1960), but there are usually neither strong centralized controlling agencies nor overpowering cast-iron circumstances to contend with, as there tend to be in already urban places.

*Established, growing, and new institutions in areas of incipient urbanization possess potential power.* This is crucial, since the likelihood of having a real voice in important community decisions depends on it. The potential power of such institutions arises out of their character as significant employers and purchasers, as organized entities in the midst of disorganized community growth, and as owners and controllers of land which is a pivotal factor in urbanization.

*Such institutions in such areas have resources of technical, scientific and aesthetic capability which are potentially of great use to the developing community.* Most often the community does not think of these resources as applicable directly to it, nor do institutions go out of their way to create such awareness. The resources are there, nonetheless, and institutions can bring them into play if they so decide. Institutions in such areas may well have the most important concentrations of expertise about planning, public health, cultural services, engineering, and the like that are reasonably available.

Some of the practical reasons why it is desirable for institutions to adopt a vigorous role in the community development areas in the process of incipient urbanization include the following:

*Such a role can have an important constructive influence on decisions about the utilization of land.* Optimum land use is of extraordinary importance both to institutions and their communities. The chief characteristics of land-use development in areas of incipient urbanization are its planlessness, its motivation by short-term gain considerations, its abuse of the natural aesthetic qualities of the countryside, its lack of taste, and its installation of persistent problems (e.g., air and water pollution, water table damage, inadequate sewerage, inefficient traffic capability, etc.). Institutions playing a vigorous community role can enter into the matter of land-use development in many ways. Extensive land holdings themselves, if they can be afforded, put the institution in a unique position to affect urbanization, as Stanford University is demonstrating. Active participation in the formal and informal apparatus of local government likewise may give the institution a voice in land-use decisions.

Least tried, but perhaps most promising in terms of new ways for institutions to exercise constructive influence on land-use development in such areas would be their participation in new land corporations or cooperatives. Institutions could, without facing insurmountable legal problems, assist in the formation of new land development organizations (including private and other land-holders) which would make it possible by non-governmental initiative to coordinate and control the urbanization process in substantial sections of the area's available land.

*Such a role, exercised as noted above, can materially benefit the institutions involved.* A most direct corollary of successful participation in community land-use development is that colleges and universities stand to net long-term material gains themselves. These revolve principally around affecting the general community ecology in ways that produce a better life for the institution. In specifics, this could mean: having a more attractive and rich environment shifting toward urbanization in something better than a state of chaotic growth; having a sensibly planned pattern of traffic and transportation flow; having something like the "polycentered net" of surroundings described by Kevin Lynch,[44] with varying densities of population, centers of business and activity, and open spaces; having available land resources for future educational expansion to serve a growing population.

*Such a role, as its ideal aim, can contribute strongly toward shaping urbanization in the direction of "the educative city."* The term is John Dyckman's, who has used it principally in speculating about the future of major urban centers like New York. But his point is as well taken in the case of an area only now entering the stage of urbanization. The city always has been an "educative" place. In the future, "whatever is done, the city will be an instructional milieu";[45] that is, it will continue to be an incessant teacher. Willy-nilly and in a million directions, good and bad, this will be true. The question of "the educative city" is *what kind,* not whether. It is reasonable to suppose that the vigorous entry of institutions into the urban development of their communities could materially affect the educative quality of life in the area. Certainly, such entry could carry students more deeply into the nature of community life as an object of experience and study. More important, sustained entry of this kind would influence the emerging cultural character of the general community.

These possibilities and ends support the proposition that consideration of community should be taken into account in imaginative new ways in redefining the nature of undergraduate education. It seems clear that the function of the college in the context of community can be enlarged to the advantage of students and citizens alike.

*Summary*

Hampshire College enters the American system of higher education in a change-laden time. The form that Hampshire College takes, while grounded on the best experience of the past, will be resonant with major contemporary changes that call for a redefinition of undergraduate education in general and of the private liberal arts college in particular.

This discussion to this point has examined four sets of changing circumstance which affect higher education. Each of these, if responded to ineffectively or not at all, bids to cause serious trouble for American colleges and universities, especially for the *private* liberal arts college. Conversely, each can be aproached as a challenge. The four challenges interlock with each other in numerous ways. They are these, stated in terms of the independent college:

*Challenge One: To reconstruct the human purposes of education, so that young men and women can find acceptable meaning in a technological social order and acceptable order in subjective cultural freedom.* Professor Bell concludes his study of Columbia, Harvard, and Chicago by reference to this "great and troubling double task . . . to humanize technocracy and to 'tame' the apocalypse."

Among other things, this double task will require a new look at the uses of philosophy in the curriculum, at how faculty and students can meet on constructive ground, at arrangements for living and studying, and at off-campus experience.

*Challenge Two: To put the private college in a strong cooperative relationship with other institutions, so that instruction available to undergraduates will be adequate in quality and variety.* In all fields, but especially in the sciences, most independent colleges will find it less and less possible alone to provide instruction adequate by the standards of preparation for graduate study. Through pooling resources and avoiding duplication, groups of institutions should be able to do so.

*Challenge Three: To recompose the intellectual content and procedures of liberal education, so that it will include substantial attention to the linguistics of intellect and the use of new technologies for information transfer.* This challenge cuts across all fields. Meeting it in the fashion suggested would introduce *language* as a major new cross-disciplinary field at the undergraduate level. The intensive introduction of newer means of information transfer would be closely related to this substantive innovation. Of great importance, meeting this challenge would make more possible the establishment of a new coherence in liberal education around a central concern for achieving understanding through the competent grasp of the processes and structures of inquiry and conceptual innovation.

*Challenge Four: To reorient the college in relation to community, so that it and associated institutions will play a vigorous, constructive part in shaping community development.* This does not mean an intensified "public relations" or "community relations" effort in customary image-building terms. It means the active civic involvement of the institution as a corporate citizen sharing in policy decisions and actual commitments to affect the nature of the community environment. It appears especially feasible—and needed—in an area marked by incipient urbanization and inter-college cooperation.

These challenges form a major agenda for Hampshire College in present planning. The College intends to meet each as directly, boldly, and sensibly as possible. The next section briefly sketches the broad outlines of the position Hampshire College takes with great regard to these four matters. Subsequent sections detail more specifically the nature of the Hampshire program within these outlines.

# 2

## HAMPSHIRE COLLEGE AS
## AN INSTRUMENT OF CHANGE

*Because we are, inevitably, creatures of the past, our ten-
dency is to use each additional year of schooling as a mere
quantitative extension of previous years, and to fit our
schools into existing and familiar patterns. That habit was
not unjustified in the nineteenth century, but the justification for it has disappeared. We are confronted, in planning
for the next generation, with a demand for more radical
reforms. We are required to reconsider the functioning of
our whole educational enterprise, . . . to look at it not so
much in historical context as in the context of present and
future requirements.*

HENRY STEELE COMMAGER
*Universal Higher Education*

ALBERT SLOMAN has commented that "a university in the making
lacks the dispensation of the armchair critic. . . . [It] has to transform its ideas into reality." [46] In *A University in the Making*, Vice-
Chancellor Sloman gives eloquent testimony to the amount of planning
and building required to transform the idea of the new University of
Essex into a reality, almost overnight. What is true of a new English
university turns out to be true as well for a new American college
in the making. Planning and building are detailed and difficult acts.
But even more difficult, and not really to be left to armchair critics either,
is the prior articulation of ideas worth transforming into reality. In
America today, if this need is taken seriously, it means articulating ideas

33

which will produce what Professor Commager calls for, radical reforms arising out of a reconsideration of the whole educational enterprise.

The ideas that Hampshire College will transform into reality are in part implicit in what has been said so far. Institutions, like people, define themselves by their acts. Hampshire will define itself by responding to the challenges discussed in the preceding section, by articulating ideas relevant to these challenges, and by acting upon them.

In doing so, the central character of the College will be clear: Hampshire proposes to be both an undergraduate institution of excellence and an innovative force in higher education generally.

To have any meaning, these two generalities must be spelled out in terms of specific ideas, and these must be transformed into reality. Only through this process will it be possible to see what the College's intentions and character really are.

The dual proposition from which Hampshire moves forward has immediate meaning, however. Proposing to be "an undergraduate institution of excellence" means, above all, that the College regards its students, their intellectual, moral, and aesthetic education, as its over-riding commitment. The College exists first for them. Proposing to be "an innovative force in higher education generally" means that Hampshire College will be bold enough to make no small plans. The College intends to be an "experimenting" one, not tied to a narrow or doctrinaire "experimental" orthodoxy. It intends to innovate and experiment, in every dimension of collegiate education where it appears promising to do so. It plans to sustain an experimental mood as far forward in time as it can. It will regard no cows, academic or of other breed, as sacred. And it intends to have an impact on all of education. Hampshire College may be new and far from abounding in means, but it intends to make a difference.

These two general commitments of Hampshire College are expressed through four interconnected vectors. The College is seen as:

*A laboratory for experimenting with economically feasible ways the private liberal arts college can be a more effective intellectual and moral force in a changing culture.*

*A catalyst and innovator of increased interinstitutional cooperation in order to maximize the variety and quality of education available.*

*A pioneer in making language a substantive, vigorous component of liberal education, and in using advances in information transfer for increased effectiveness and economy in the process of education.*

*A corporate citizen actively involved in community development, joining the life and welfare of the academic community with that of the world around it.*

In Hampshire College, these vectors are not separable from each other. They make up a unified field of force. Improving liberal education for its own students *and* for the good of the whole educational enterprise is the unifying agent. Experimentation in academic program and campus life, pressing interinstitutional cooperation forward, pioneering in language and information transfer, and civic involvement are bound together in the central thrust of the College toward excellence and innovative impact.

### 1. THE NEED FOR HAMPSHIRE COLLEGE: 1958

Nearly a decade ago, four distinguished institutions of higher education in the Connecticut Valley outlined, as a part of their collaboration with each other, plans for a new private liberal arts college. A four-college committee, representing Amherst, Mount Holyoke, Smith, and the University of Massachusetts, worked for a number of months on this project, under sponsorship of the Ford Foundation. The results of their deliberations were published as *The New College Plan: A Proposal for a Major Departure in Higher Education* in 1958.[47]

The study had been requested by the presidents of the four institutions. They had "been aware for some time of the imminent demands upon American colleges to provide space and opportunity for a vastly enlarged body of students." In view of these demands, the presidents wished to consider "the possibility of creating a fifth institution in their general area, to which they might contribute and with which they might develop new departures in educational methods and techniques." Their "hope was to plan a new college which would provide education of the highest quality at a minimum cost per student." [48]

The need for a new institution was underlined by the 1958 faculty committee in approximately the same terms:

It is acknowledged on all sides that American higher education is facing a crisis and that if we are to continue "the pursuit of excellence"

on which our society's growth, health, and safety depend, we shall have
to bring to bear both great resources and great imagination. Many
things will need to be done to meet the rapidly mounting demand
which is the result not only of a drastic increase in the college age
population, but also of the steadily rising proportion of our young
people who are seeking a college education. Amherst, Mount Holyoke,
Smith, and the University of Massachusetts are already engaged in
exploring and carrying out measures which each can take individually
to meet the coming challenge. This report proposes that the four
institutions also make a contribution cooperatively by sponsoring a
new departure in liberal education of the highest quality.

The college which we propose would embody marked economies—in
staff and in other resources—but it is designed to provide an education comparable to that of the "prestige" colleges. There will be a
pressing need for more room at the top in an epoch when there will
not be room enough in our exceptional colleges for many of our exceptional students. But still more important will be the need to
demonstrate more efficient use of teaching resources, inevitably
limited in the coming period. . . .

To sponsor such a pilot plant should be a particularly appropriate
role for privately endowed colleges, since as they are presently con-
stituted they cannot, for economic reasons, expand rapidly and still
maintain the high standards which are their distinctive contribution.
Added significance and range will be given to the project by the happy
circumstance that three rather diverse private institutions are associated with a publicly supported university. Unless a drastic increase
in efficiency can be achieved, it may be that privately endowed institutions will not be able to sustain their role as leaders in the educational world. A restructuring of liberal education to meet this challenge is what is proposed in the plan for a cooperatively sponsored
institution which we are calling "New College." [49]

The need seen in 1958, therefore, was to restructure liberal education,
in order (a) to provide for increasing numbers of students, (b) to do so
at a level of high academic quality, (c) to do so on an economical basis,
and (d) to show that these things could be accomplished in a private
institution. The four-college committee proposed to demonstrate that
this need could be met by a new kind of undergraduate private college
in which curriculum and academic organization would be simplified;
students would take greater responsibility for their learning; increased

use would be made of mechanical and electronic learning aids; and the student-faculty ratio would be double that in colleges of comparable quality.

The model proposed by the 1958 committee struck a chord to which many in higher education responded. The New College Plan was intensively discussed in the Valley where it was born. In addition, it aroused wide interest elsewhere in the United States and England.

It came at a time when concern about rising numbers of students, about costs and quality, and about the viability of the liberal arts college was setting in sharply. It came at a time when many professors and administrators were becoming restive about a traditional curriculum which seemed at once regimented and wastefully proliferated. And the 1958 report came in the first flush of enthusiasm about the new auto-instructional machines. In consequence the New College model became a reference point in the planning and development of a number of new institutions, private and public. It was nowhere adopted *in toto,* but in many places its ideas and suggestions were drawn upon.

In a word, in 1958 there was a need for the kind of fresh, optimistic thinking the New College represented.

## 2. THE NEED FOR HAMPSHIRE COLLEGE RECONSIDERED: 1966

The chartering of Hampshire College in 1965 resulted from a conviction on the part of several men that the need identified in 1958 remained real and that the idea of a new, innovating college remained sound. Mr. Harold F. Johnson, Amherst alumnus, committed a gift of six million dollars to the new college and accepted responsibility as Chairman of its Board of Trustees. Dr. Charles W. Cole, President-Emeritus of Amherst, became Vice-Chairman of Hampshire's Board. The other founding trustees were Mr. Winthrop S. Dakin, Chairman of the Massachusetts State Board of Higher Education; Dr. Richard G. Gettell, President of Mount Holyoke College; Dr. John W. Lederle, President of the University of Massachusetts; Dr. Thomas C. Mendenhall, President of Smith College; and Dr. Calvin H. Plimpton, President of Amherst College.*

*The complement of the Board of Trustees remains to be completed. It is hoped to attract to trusteeship other distinguished scholars and cultural leaders with a

These leaders did not assume that the need of 1965 and after would be absolutely identical with the need perceived in 1958. Nor did they assume that the New College model of 1958 would constitute a precise prescription for the 1970's. They understood that a new diagnosis of need and a new projection of the institutional model were required.

As a step in the latter direction, on October 15, 1965 the trustees invited a new four-college committee of faculty to advise Hampshire College on the design of its educational program. The advice sought was to be within the general lines of ". . . an undergraduate program, experimental in nature, fashioned to encourage and take strength from the present and potential cooperative arrangements, which will make possible high quality education with the least possible expenditure." [50] This directive echoed 1958 in principle, but left the new Educational Advisory Committee relatively free to make a fresh approach to institutional model building.

The committee used the 1958 report as its "starting point and touchstone," and on April 13, 1966 submitted its own views. A number of its suggestions were new or at variance with the 1958 study, but all of its conclusions were felt to be "clearly within both the tone and the spirit of the New College Plan." [51] Many are incorporated in the present plan of Hampshire College. So, too, are many of the recommendations first made by the 1958 committee.

While much of the 1958 need and proposal therefore still stands reflected in the current design of Hampshire College, there are also changes. The need has changed in some critical ways; now and for the somewhat visible future it has dimensions which were not there to see in 1958. The College, in consequence, has features and functions which were not part of the 1958 planning.

The need for Hampshire College in the present period is heightened by a wide range of developments in the society and in higher education. These were treated from one angle of vision in the first chapter. The major problems—and opportunities—that these developments present to colleges and universities can be catalogued in other ways. No matter

strong interest in the future of liberal education in America. In this direction, the Board recently elected M. I. T. Professor Elting E. Morison, historian, biographer, and social critic.

how it is done, the need seen in 1958 is enlarged, made more complex and more acute. There is an even greater need in 1966 than in 1958 for "a major departure in higher education."

This is evident in John W. Gardner's perceptive agenda of major problems facing colleges and universities. Shortly before joining the Cabinet, Secretary Gardner spoke of the following as the things the times demand of higher education:

> *Restoring the status of teaching.* Teaching, particularly of undergraduates, is being slighted today. "The reinstatement of teaching as an important function of the undergraduate college . . ." may be hastened by student discontent, but the decisions that move the college in that direction must be faculty decisions.
>
> *Reforming the undergraduate curriculum.* Such a movement is under way; it will reappraise aims and transform instruction in all the major fields. It must stress interdisciplinary approaches and "reintroduce into the undergraduate program the breadth so essential for young people who will reach the peak of their careers in the 21st century."
>
> *Improving institutional planning.* To be able to provide education of high quality for the radically increased number of college students in the 1970's and after will require "an attentiveness to the economics of education greater than any we have exhibited in the past." Secretary Gardner continued with emphasis that *"we're going to have to learn lessons about planned diversity among institutions and also some hard lessons about cooperation among institutions."* [52]
>
> *Reforming the college calendar and making the four-year pattern flexible.* Virtually all institutions are going to have to go into year-round operation on some form of revised calendar. The four-year pattern will have to be made flexible, both for speeding up or slowing down: "We are now ready to dispense with the tradition of a four-year uninterrupted college education." Some students benefit by acceleration. Others "benefit greatly by a break in the four years—for a year abroad, or a year at work, or a year of traveling, or just a year to figure out what it is they want to be or do."
>
> *Bringing the small independent liberal arts college back into the mainstream.* Such colleges presently "can no longer compete with the universities in attracting able and highly motivated faculty members *or* students. . . . The best chance of salvaging the small liberal arts college lies in devising new means of cooperation among institutions. . . .*[53]
> [The] need is for the small college to relate itself to *some* larger system

in such a way that it can retain its autonomy but still enjoy access to the richness and diversity of resource that professors and students demand."

*Developing leadership in continuing education.* Colleges and universities "should provide intellectual leadership with respect to such education"; if they do not, the movement will proceed anyway, but without needed guidance.

*Playing a responsible part in the urban community.* One of the greatest struggles of our time will be to try to solve the problems of urbanism. "Coping with these problems is going to be very near the top of the national agenda. . . . There are no institutions better equipped to serve as a base for that struggle than the colleges and universities, but they have played a negligible role to date."

*Reconstructing the academic institution as a healthy community.* On "every college or university campus in the nation the sense of community is diminishing." The neglect of teaching, the anonymity and impersonality of student life, the rise of the disciplines as powerful professional communities, the impact of urbanization, all contribute to the decline of community in the academic institution. It is crucial to offset these factors and provide youth with education in a face-to-face academic community which has internal coherence, shared membership, and morale.

Secretary Gardner's diagnosis of needs that higher education must meet, like the discussion of challenging circumstances in the previous chapter, suggests why a "major departure" in 1966 must go beyond what was specified in 1958.

In the intervening years it has become evident that the major questions include *much* more than increasing student self-instruction through student-led discussion groups, teaching machines, and other techniques. Questions of survival and effectiveness, especially in undergraduate education, have become acutely clear. These involve more than keeping costs within sensible limits. They include qualitative questions of the first order: e.g., whether undergraduate education will help students find any sense of meaning and worth in themselves and society; whether undergraduate education will occur in an intellectual and moral community which may have tensions but also has pride and morale; whether undergraduate education will contribute to the health of the general culture; and whether colleges will make a real difference in the swift development of urbanism.

John Gardner said further that he did not:

> believe that the colleges and universities will go under because they are carrying heavy burdens. If they deteriorate it will be because they lacked the morale, the internal coherence, and the adaptiveness to meet the requirements of the future; it will be because in the moment of their greatest success they could not pull themselves together to face new challenges.[54]

The New College of 1958 had relevance to needs as seen then. The decade since then has accented the earlier needs and added new ones. The justification for Hampshire College is that, like its antecedent model in 1958, it proposes major departures to meet major needs. As such, the College aims at realizing the full excitement of liberal education in new terms, suited to tomorrow's students and their society. As such, the College hopes to have a measure of constructive influence on the evolving character of higher education as a whole.

# 3

# UNDERGRADUATE EDUCATION AT HAMPSHIRE COLLEGE: AN ORGANIZED VISION

*It is difficult enough to know what a proper professional education ought to be in fields which are rapidly changing; it is even more difficult to determine how the undergraduate ought to be educated. When an increasing number of undergraduates are planning professional careers, there is a real hazard in making the college serve the purposes of the professional schools. If the college is simply a "corridor," the last one to be traversed before the really important room is entered, the nature of the undergraduate's experience is considerably affected. This is not simply a matter of raising questions about the adequacy of a particular curriculum. It extends to more basic matters such as how a college community ought to be organized, what services it must provide, and what demands it may legitimately make of young people. When the content of specific courses is at issue, that is a matter easily resolved. When, however, the utility of courses generally is brought into question, more fundamental issues are touched. The problem today is not simply to know how mechanical inventions may be used to bring popular lectures to audiences of a thousand, or even how to introduce new methods for language instruction, but what the significant educational experiences of young and intelligent men and women ought to be.*

STEPHEN R. GRAUBARD
*Daedalus,* Fall, 1964

N O MAJOR DEPARTURE, no new and consequential venture, is made without a context and a vision.

The general context of Hampshire College is an experimental society faced by great constraining tendencies which are in need of redress by new alternatives.[55] The particular context for Hampshire is a time of difficulty for undergraduate education when new possibilities are needed and being sought.

The question of vision is related to context. Part of the trouble with much of liberal education today is that it has lost a vision of itself. It has lost what Whitehead called "the atmosphere of excitement" that marks education capable of transforming knowledge from cold fact into "the poet of our dreams . . . the architect of our purposes." [56] Perhaps this is to say it has lost what it all too seldom had: a soaring imaginativeness in its consideration of learning, which connected knowledge with the zest of life. Cant and cliché disguise essential confusion or sterility as best they may, but liberal education often seems well organized in unimportant ways, in ways empty of vision.

Another kind of difficulty is common in those cases where energetic efforts are being made to reform education in the undergraduate college. Attention tends to focus on "experimental" as meaning changes in calendar, curriculum organization, grading and testing, and the like. All of these can be important. But their importance, if it is to exist, has an absolute prior condition. Innovation and reconstruction, to add up to something, must be more than impulses to do good deeds in a naughty world or new things for their newness alone. Too many present efforts, worthy as their intent may be, are uninformed by a coherent vision of what liberal education now should be and do.

We have said that Hampshire College is to be a laboratory for experimenting with ways the private liberal arts college can be a more effective intellectual and moral force in a changing culture. This role implies a redefinition of liberal education and depends upon an organized vision which can guide the process of redefinition.

The central task of liberal education at Hampshire College is to help young men and women learn to live their adult lives, fully and well, in a society of intense change, immense opportunity, and great hazards.

Stated so briefly and abstractly, Hampshire's chosen task sounds no

more real than most college catalogue rhetoric. Liberal education in
the West has never been unconcerned with helping the young learn
to live fully and well, although these abstract adverbs have had different
meanings in different times and places. Nor has society in the West of
the modern period ever been without change, opportunity, and hazards.
What makes the statement of Hampshire's task real and not rhetoric is
that in this age, more than any before it, living at all means encounter
with the damnifying and the redemptive on a scale we can scarcely assess.
As de Tocqueville put it, "care must be taken not to judge the state of
society, which is now coming into existence, by notions derived from a
state of society which no longer exists. . . ."

The first students of the College will live out a quarter or more of
their lives in the morning of the 21st century, whose dawn already trembles
in the sky. One cannot tell what living fully and well will come to mean
for them and the students who come after them. We can at least guess
that they may encounter more change, more options, more complex
dilemmas, more possible joys, more chance of surprise and wonder, more
dead-ends, more demands, more satisfactions, and more of a fighting
chance to be human than men have known before. We have simultaneously given them the unthinkable in destructiveness, the unlimited in
abundance, the chemistry to control reproduction and completely alter
the social conditions and consequences of mating, the technology that
will make work obsolete as man has known it, the transport and telecommunications that annihilate distance, and a flood of knowledge which
would make the position of the sorcerer's apprentice seem high and dry.
We have given them too much to begin to list. And they in their time
will create even more. Intense change, immense opportunity, great
hazards. Living fully and well. These abstractions, far from empty,
cover an incredibly various and largely yet-unknown reality. Living fully
and well will only be defined as our descendants, now living and yet to
come, wrestle with the reality they both encounter and create. The same
is true of the content of the society they will experience. It will be up to
them. The College cannot give them any handy new prescriptions that
will do the trick. Nor can it give them the liberal arts, "the same again as
before," with any conscience that this is the best we can do. The task of
the College in its own view is at once more complex and more simple than
either of these factitious alternatives. It is to give students, for whatever

worth they themselves can make of it, the best knowledge new and old that we have about ways man may know himself and his world. This means that the College must help them acquire the tools with which it looks as though men in the future may be most likely to be able to build lives and a society they consider worthy. The most continually experimental thing about Hampshire College will be its constant effort, in collaboration with its students, to discern what these tools are and how best they may come to fit one's hand.

To this end, the College will begin by seeking to help each student through every useful way:

> to gain a greater grasp of the range and nature of the human condition —past, present, and possible future.

> to gain a greater sense of himself in a society whose meaningfulness and quality *depend in significant degree on him.*

> to gain a greater command of the uses of his intellect in order to educate and renew himself throughout life.

> to gain a greater feeling for the joy and tragedy that are inherent in life and its mirror, art, when both are actively embraced.

The vision of liberal education at Hampshire is one of hospitality to contemporary life, tempered and given meaning by two ageless virtues which may seem archaic in the modern world: duty and reverence. The essence of education as a door to full engagement with life is that these virtues are its threshold. As Alfred North Whitehead said about education in his presidential address to the Mathematical Association of England in 1916:

> Duty arises from our potential control over the course of events. Where attainable knowledge could have changed the issue, ignorance has the guilt of vice. And the foundation of reverence is in this perception, that the present holds within itself the complete sum of existence, backwards and forwards, that whole amplitude of time, which is eternity.[57]

In such terms, Hampshire College is committed to a view of liberal education as a vehicle for the realization of self *in* society. The disjunction of social order and culture in today's society is a conflict deeply felt in college and university, and likely to be so for the future. It is the business of liberal education to reconceive itself, and to innovate in educational practice, in the hope that this deepening cleft in man's life may be closed.

In a very real sense, Hampshire's organized vision of liberal education is most certainly not new. The realization of self in society, and engagement with the life of society are hardly novel ends for education. Two things, however, make their restatement and renewed pursuit a major departure. One is that these ends are only nominal ones in most of liberal education today, and the ways institutions have sought to follow them have too often become worn, irrelevant, hollow, and lacking in coherence. Second, while these ends have atrophied into nominality and emptiness in many college programs, the world around the college has changed in directions that cry out for their reassertion.

## 1. The Intellectual Implications

The task of liberal education defined in terms Hampshire College has chosen implies certain distinctive intellectual objectives for the institution's program.

Hampshire aims at educating people to live successfully in the contemporary and future society. This aim directly involves the College, as it plans its program, in reexamining the store of available information and ideas, old and new, from which knowledge most appropriate to this task may be drawn. Customary selections and patterns of knowledge encountered in college programs are not automatically assumed as a given. The College instead assumes that it has a *continuing* obligation to identify, organize, and make available knowledge relevant to its educational purpose. And it must do so in ways that will make such knowledge usable by students in their education and lives.

In the process of review and selection of information and ideas most worth study, and in considering how such knowledge can best be made accessible to students, certain major guidelines are used. The substance of liberal education at Hampshire is shaped by the desire to develop as much understanding as possible of some very complex sets of things Among these are:

The nature of man
The nature of social order

The nature of culture
The nature of power
The nature of ideas
The nature of the interconnectedness of things
The nature of growth and change
The centrality of method
The question of value

The problem of intellectual substance in liberal education, as Hampshire College defines it, is *to determine as best can be done what experience with inquiry, materials, and ideas will contribute most to understanding such central and difficult matters.* The operating assumption is that, if students can get at ideas, principles of inquiry, and information of relevance to these things, they will have a better chance to comprehend life and live it well.

Hampshire's constant intellectual goal is to enlarge the capability of each student to conduct his own education. The 1958 *New College Plan* stressed this aim:

> It has long been the goal of liberal arts colleges to prepare students for a lifetime of self-education. The means of education, however, frequently come to obstruct its goals. What we want to create is independent initiative and intellectual enterprise. Yet too often, faculty complaints about "spoon feeding" go with a course program which minutely prescribes what the students shall do and gives them so much to do that they have little time left for independent work. . . . It will be a major goal of the College to develop and sustain a style of life which will make it habitual for students to work together in groups, and individually, without constant recourse to the faculty.[58]

Achieving this goal requires a program at Hampshire which from the beginning of a student's experience educates him in the use of the intellectual tools needed for adequate independent work. He will be introduced to procedures of empirical and experimental inquiry from the start. He will be expected to become increasingly skillful in processes of philosophical and logical analysis, with as much rigor as possible. He will learn to expect much more of his ability at such analysis than what Professor Morton White calls "undisciplined talk . . . on the problem of value, on the patterns of history, on the nature and destiny of man."[59] There will be a need for the acquisition of skills in the analysis of lan-

guage, a consideration to which later portions of this paper give attention. It will be essential for him to have some command of available
insights into the processes of cognition, if for nothing else than to arm
himself against the perils that perception is heir to. Skill in discourse
will be an important part of the intellectual equipment the College helps
the student gain, so that his thinking will come through to others.

The paradoxes and imperatives of the whole matter of intellect, its
tools, and education are matters we are only beginning to understand.
P. W. Bridgman once commented on present inadequacy and challenge
in this regard that he:

> would place as the most important mark of an adequately educated
> man a realization that the tools of human thinking are not yet under-
> stood, and that they impose limitations of which we are not yet fully
> aware. As a corollary it follows that the most important intellectual
> task for the future is to acquire an understanding of the tools. . . .[60]

Along with his caution and recommendation, Professor Bridgman added
that man's hand is "on the hem of the curtain that separates us from
an understanding of the nature of our minds." [61] Major breakthroughs
in our understanding and command of the tools of thinking—and awareness of their limitations—are in the offing. In the present it is imperative for education to give students as much understanding of such tools
as it can. As breakthroughs occur in Professor Bridgman's sense, it will
be imperative for education to translate these into the uses men make
of their minds.

## 2. THE ARTS AND LIBERAL EDUCATION

The manner in which Hampshire College defines liberal education
likewise implies distinctive objectives in the arts.*

The humanities as they now are in undergraduate and graduate
schools promise a good deal more than they usually deliver. In certain
disciplines and courses, the humanities open young minds and hearts
to a greater sense of history; to a recognition of beauty in language, line,

---

* As the term is used here it comprehends literature, the graphic and plastic
arts, music, drama, the dance as parts of the humanities along with history and
philosophy.

and sound; to an awareness of man's ideas, triumphs, and follies; to a touch of the comic spirit and the tragic; to the meaning of taste. But delivery on the humanities' promise is sorely handicapped in much of liberal and graduate schooling by an inanition of long standing.

The trouble lies in the fact that with notable exceptions a field— which if any should be as varied, robust, sanguine, and vital as life itself —has been emptied of liveliness. The field suffers from a surfeit of leeching, its blood drawn out by verbalism, explication of text, Alexandrian scholiasticism, and the exquisite preciosities and pretentiousness of contemporary literary criticism. In more measured language, William Arrowsmith has arraigned his own field on counts like these, with considerable discussion and argument the result.[62] The trouble lies, too, in the simple fact that the arts, in the performing and creative sense, are commonly not thought of as operational components of programs in the humanities. A good part of Professor Arrowsmith's criticism of present humanities programs is that they leave out the dimension of art as performance and aesthetic experience more often than not. The arts within the humanities are treated most frequently as objects of analytical and verbal study, not as experiences for one to enter into as a deeply engaged witness or as a human being striving to create or perform. The divorce of *study about the arts* from *engagement with their actuality* is as damaging to liberal education as it would be to conduct the study of science without introduction to its practice in the laboratory. Jerrold Zacharias once said that "the best way to learn science is to do science." A similar aphorism might to some degree be appropriate to the humanities.

The reconstruction of liberal education, as Hampshire College sees it, requires the breathing of new life into the humanities. The reason is clear in terms of the things the College hopes its students will gain. Professor Elting Morison, historian and no enemy of intellect, argues in a letter about Hampshire College that:

> both colleges and scholars overemphasize today the mind as the exclusive weapon to deal with contemporary conditions. There are other instruments in the human being that are equally important, and this is where the arts come in. . . . Just as I think everyone at the College should take courses which move and shape the intelligence, so should

they take courses which move and shape the feelings, and which provide exercises for the expression of feelings, which is a considerable part of what art is about. . . . Rather fewer people than is now believed are creative in the common meaning of that word—that is, that they can do something out of themselves more interestingly than it has been done before. But everybody is creative in the sense that they can give expression to themselves. . . . [The] objective of work in the arts should be to give people practice in as complete and accurate expression of themselves as they can manage.[63]

In the humanities, Hampshire plans no turning away from intellectual treatment of materials, men, and the artistic event or object. But the College sees a further pressing obligation to open the arts actively to as many students as possible.

Any extension of opportunity in the arts raises issues of taste and quality. The danger that "the new democratic amateur" and his well meant motives will produce "an artless art, and a use of past art that is also artless" is clear and present, as Jacques Barzun pointed out a decade ago.[64]

The vulgarization of art as an upshot of mass industrial society and social equality is scarcely something Hampshire intends to accelerate. Nor does the College mean to contribute to cultural nihilism, which may be more to worry about than Dean Barzun's dismay that the new amateurism in painting reached as far as the stolid precincts of the White House in the 1950's.

Hampshire does not see liberal education "substituting experience for art, sensation for judgment." [65] In opening the gates of feeling through the lively arts, freedom of experience and expression must be assumed, or the uses of art in liberal education are meaningless. But this liberating potential turns finally on being related to judgment and intellect, on far more than indiscriminateness and the idea that undifferentiated experience can amount to art. The view of this that Hampshire College takes is very close to that of Professor Bell:

... to show that order has virtue is more difficult when the appeals to instinct and irrationality, bound up in the coil of pleasure, begin to weave their lure. Yet . . . the thread of redemption may emerge from the reassertion of an older kind of pleasure—the pleasure of achievement and of making, of imposing a sense of self upon the

recalcitrant materials, physical and intellectual, of the world. For in
the process of making and achieving, one learns that it is not the
business of art to use chaos to express chaos, nor is it the character
of experience to be entirely unreflective.[66]

Hampshire's program assumes that the uses of art can give new life
and relevance to areas of the humanities now gone dry. It assumes that
they can do this only in an atmosphere which invites and frees artistic
expression. And it assumes equally that such freedom will thrive best
where sensibility is insistently informed with demands of judgment. Art
indeed is experience, not the other way around. In the new humanities,
it is experience to be explored with the resources of man's considered
heritage at hand.

### 3.  IMPLICATIONS FOR THE CULTURE OF THE COLLEGE

Hampshire's view of the task of liberal education also implies certain
things about the culture of the College.

To talk about culture at all is to deal with a term that has by far
less manageability than a handful of quicksilver. Earlier in this paper,
culture was defined simply as the patterned ways people feel, think, and
act. Perhaps this is as useful a way of handling such an elusive and
complex concept as the present discussion needs.

Edward B. Tylor in 1891 soberly articulated the classic definition
of culture as "that complex whole which includes knowledge, belief, art,
morals, law, custom, and any other capabilities and habits acquired by
man as a member of society." [67] (Lord Raglan once defined culture
more simply as "everything that people do and monkeys don't.") Sixty
years after Tylor two leading American anthropologists, A. L. Kroeber
and Clyde Kluckhohn, analyzed a total of 164 definitions of culture
then currently in scholarly use.[68] They could not come to a single brief
abstract statement which would, in their view, satisfactorily include all
of the elements of life then meant by "culture." They saw culture, however, as largely made up of "overt, patterned ways of behaving, feeling,
and reacting," underlaid by unstated premises or "implicit culture,"
learned for the most part early in life, varying greatly among societies
and sub-societies, including ideas and values, and inseparable from
symbols.[69]

However defined, we recognize that educational institutions not only exist within and express cultures, but have cultures (and internal sub-cultures) of their own. Call it climate, atmosphere, ethos, or culture, each college has its own ambient quality. David Riesman says wryly: "We all know that some institutions have a fairly monolithic atmosphere, whereas others are more pluralistic; some have a powerful scent, while others have an atmosphere like those gases one cannot detect until it is too late." [70]

In recent years, there has been a great deal of research about the nature and effects of the undergraduate college environment or culture.[71] These studies underline three sets of generalizations:

> A college does have its own unique culture or climate. This stays relatively constant over time, tends to attract the same types of students with remarkable consistency over the years, and has the same kind of effect upon them.

> The relations of students with each other and with faculty are very important features of college culture. These relations affect student attitudes and values more strongly and significantly than does instruction in the classroom. Academic achievement itself is affected by the characteristic total culture of the college.

> Activities *outside* the classroom can increase a student's desire to learn and his sense that learning is relevant. The most intellectually and educationally productive colleges are those where culture does not rigidly separate classroom and non-classroom into two unrelated worlds.

As James G. Rice has brightly put it, the professor is not all there is at the other end of the log.[72]

The direct implication for any institution, and certainly for Hampshire College, is that the campus culture needs to be considered instrumental to the ends of education. The distinctive objectives of the College involve conscious decisions which will affect its culture, and in doing so recognize that the student is a person, not simply a classroom fixture. The obligation seen by Hampshire College leadership is to spur the development of a strong institutional culture which will be distinctive not for the sake of distinctiveness, but in its relevance to the vision of liberal education described earlier.

That this can be done is evident. A vivid example is Reed College, whose strongly defined total climate has been clear from the beginning, attested to by students, old grads, and outside observers alike.

The Reed culture is no accident. From the day the college opened in 1911 it has left little doubt about what it stands for and what kind of atmosphere it has. The earliest bulletins of Reed asserted vigorously that this institution would be a no-nonsense, highly intellectual place. There would be none of the rah-rah about Reed; students who expected sports and "social" life were clearly not wanted. The first Reed catalog was unequivocal:

> Intercollegiate athletics, fraternities, sororities and most of the diversions that men are pleased to call "college life," as distinguished from college work, have no place in Reed College. Those whose dominant interests lie outside the courses of study should not apply for admission. Only those who want to work, and to work hard, and who are determined to gain the greatest possible benefits from their studies are welcomed.[73]

For at least ten years, pronouncements of comparable severity and militancy came from the Reed leadership. By the time Reed was in its second decade, the spirit of such views had long since taken hold in work and life on the campus. Reed's "difference" was something its students were proud of; they came to the college because of its announced tough-minded intellectualism; they found that intellectual life in classrooms with men like Aragon spilled over into late-night hours in residential halls; and, if students survived, they went on to the adult life of the intelligentsia identifying themselves as "Reed people." Burton R. Clark comments, in a study of entering students at four colleges, that:

> Reed has tried to be different and has succeeded. Its perceived difference has influenced who applies. . . . In addition, the image of the college held by its own staff and alumni has shaped the recruitment of faculty and students alike.[74]

The case of Reed illustrates the point that college leadership can affect what the college culture will be. This is not to say that the college culture will not be affected by many other factors; most certainly it will be affected by students in their successive cadres and by the faculty.

The Reed illustration emphasizes that college leadership has its main impact on the formation of a distinctive campus culture by a vigorous, demanding assertion of what the college will and will not be. The organized vision of Reed in 1911 was expressed with take-it-or-leave-it bluntness. These terms set the style of the college and from the outset established the selection of students on ground that would support that style.

The asserted vision is the critical variable from the first. Whether it is a fatuous cliché or a commanding statement, it will have effects on the culture of the college. If the former, the climate of the college will show it and be shaped instead by other forces for good or ill. If it is the latter, the assertion will have direct consequences of its own that may be likely to last. In view of this, the asserted vision needs wisdom at least as much as vigor.

The other ways that a college can affect its climate, culture, ethos, or what you will, follow from its stated vision. They involve, as Dr. Rice has pointed out, affecting the "quality of things present in the campus situation, the quality of persons present, and the kind and quality of *interactions* among them." [75] In connection with such means, Hampshire College planning and development exhibit a conscious design to use, as Professor Keniston has suggested, "every architectural, institutional, psychological, and educational strategy to create a climate in which students and faculty share a common excitement about the educational process." [76]

One aim is to provide ways and means for ample, friendly communication between faculty and students. This hardly means to make first-name palship the mode, or to obliterate the very real differences between faculty and students. Nor does it mean casting faculty in the role of intellectual and moral eunuchs. It does mean finding ways to overcome unnecessary barriers that commonly lie between students and faculty in arrangements for study and teaching, in living accommodations and dining, in lack of privacy and time for counseling, in lack of opportunity for informal contact and discussion, and the like.

Hampshire aims to make the out-of-classroom life of the College vitally related to what occurs in the classroom, rather than separated. "Such a separation," as Professor Keniston put it, "lends itself too easily to a translation into a social and personal life devoid of intellectual excitement, or a notion of intellectual activities as something one carries on only from nine to five and in a special setting." [77] The aim is not to make the College a dawn to midnight academic grind for all concerned. Hampshire's intention instead is to so kindle intellectual excitement in seminars, classes, and independent study that it cannot help carry over into informal discussion and the rest of the life of the College. There are implications here for curriculum, for the location and nature of places of study, for the view faculty take of themselves and their work, and for building the campus so that intellectual give-and-take can happen in classroom and out.

Another Hampshire aim is to expect students from the beginning to share in shaping decisions about the College, and to take principal responsibility for making decisions about themselves as individuals. To say that students should share in the shaping of decisions is not to say that they can share in *making* all decisions. Basic policy decisions, however, can benefit by the consideration and advice students give, if procedures exist for the purpose. As Philip Sherburne has pointed out, student evaluation of programs and alternatives can be considered in academic policy determination with value both for the college and the student.[78] In the area of rules and regulations governing life on the campus, it seems sensible for these to be kept to a minimum consonant with civilized living. Mr. Sherburne, president of the United States National Student Association, recommends that, where regulation is necessary, students be largely responsible for it. If the community of the College were seen as a college community classically is, something like a crown colony with an unfranchised native population living in isolation from the viceroy's compound and police headquarters, this recommendation would be persuasive. As further discussion will make clear, however, the crown colony metaphor will not fit Hampshire College's community. There will be membership in it, and participation in its affairs, by faculty and staff as well as students. It will be a mixed community in this sense, with a need for differing roles and responsibilities in its governance. But it will be shared in by students as fully as a healthy balance of varying interests in the welfare of the whole community will permit.

The culture of the Hampshire College campus, in any event, will be neither normless nor joyless. The College—and this has little to do with rules and regulations—will expect a high degree of what John Kennedy termed *civility* in every part of its life. The College's use of the term refers to the basic attitude and stance of people in their dealings with each other, not to superficial niceties for their own sake. Jerome Bruner's thinking about pedagogy is nowhere closer to the heart of things than when he stresses that real teaching must reflect *courtesy* in its approach to the student. That is, it should say to the learner, "I respect you and your mind—enough, indeed, to ask you to *think* and to think hard about something important." Bruner's *courtesy* is similar to what Hampshire means by *civility*. In the College, it translates into every relationship. It means attention to taste in day-to-day life as well as in events and undertakings of larger moment.

Freedom is alien neither to grace nor dignity. In a time when freedom is too often glossed as formlessness, Hampshire believes that freedom is not necessarily alien to form either. The College will admit students who see civility as freedom's normal dress, to be worn with a certain pride. Indeed, as Reed's first president might have said, others need not apply.

By the circumstances of its close relationship with nearby institutions, and by conscious intention, Hampshire's atmosphere will not be that of a rigid closed system or private academic enclave. It will have a sense of movement and interplay with the swiftly developing communities around it. Students will not find themselves locked into a procession in which the pace and program is the same in every major way for everyone. Students will find an important feature of their own campus culture is that it will be continually infused by what other cultures, even those distant in place and kind, have to offer.

It will be possible for a student to take one or two sanctioned years off for his own purposes—for study or travel abroad, for the same in this country, or for work in business, government, poverty programs, or the like. And the College will have a "guaranteed admission" policy by which a student admitted may defer his entrance as long as twenty-four months (or more in special cases) to work, travel, or take military service before he comes to college.

## 4. THE STATED VISION IN SUM

Many voices have been listened to in considering what the vision of undergraduate liberal education at Hampshire College should be. A great deal of what has been heard is reflected in the College's present position.

The general purposes stated by Byron Stookey in connection with the University of California at Santa Cruz seem representative of much current thinking elsewhere. Mr. Stookey suggests that an undergraduate education ought:

> to transmit knowledge, and with it understanding of the significance, methods, inadequacies, and interrelations of our various ways of looking at the universe;
>
> to cultivate the basic intellectual skills involved in perception, expression, inquiry, and the handling of ideas;
>
> to teach habits of intellectual honesty, accuracy, sensitivity, and independence;
>
> in part by enlarging his understanding of his heritance, to develop the student's ability to understand as a consequence his location and opportunities, and his capacity, perhaps partly in consequence, to think "creatively";
>
> to foster some sense of competence.[79]

Hampshire accepts a good part of these purposes. But they fall somewhat short for Hampshire on three counts. One is that they seem narrower than necessary in their intellectualism. Beyond intellectualistic ends (e.g., greater grasp of alternative ways of looking at the universe, increased intellectual skills, better intellectual habits, more detachment, more capacity to think "creatively," and more sense of competence), Mr. Stookey's purposes do not look at questions of *knowledge for what,* or *what knowledge.* A second reason is that their consideration of the student appears limited to a view of him as an unattached rational individual. Third, these purposes take no explicit account of the not-always rational society and culture. General education, it seems to Hampshire, should help the student learn to live a life that joins intellectuality and rational behavior with aesthetic sensibility and social commitment beyond self. Mr. Stookey's purposes fall short because they take too limited a view of the needs of the student and the problem of knowledge in general education, and no direct view of the character of society or culture.[80] They seem a nearly pure and well put statement of what Professor Bell calls the technocratic view of man and his education.

Professor Bell himself strikes nearer to what Hampshire regards as the mark:

> The university cannot remake the world (though in upholding standards it plays some part in such attempts). It cannot even remake men. *But it can liberate young people by making them aware of the forces that impel them from within and constrict them from without. It is in this sense, the creation of self-consciousness in relation to tradition,* that the task of education is metaphysics, metasociology, metapsychology, and, in exploring the nature of its own communications, metaphilosophy and metalanguage. This, in itself, is the enduring rationale of a liberal education and the function of the college years.[81]

The College expects its students to wrestle most with questions of the human condition. What does it mean to be human? How can men become more human? What are human beings for? Such questions are both global and personal. They can be illuminated by historical study, the social sciences, the natural sciences, literature, the lively arts, philosophy, and language. They need to be approached with the discipline of intellect, the drama of feeling, the demanding kinesthetic of action. They lead into far fields and abstract knowledge; equally they lead into the immediate surround of daily life, with its joys and terrors, its obligations and rewards, its emptiness and fullness. They require ultimately the paradoxical combination of detachment and commitment that only the educated can have.

To the same end, the College asks its students to examine the tension between universal and particular, the relation between society and self. It is, indeed, concerned with "the creation of self-consciousness in relation to tradition." But Hampshire goes further, saying that liberal education should give the student a greater sense of himself in a society *whose meaningfulness and quality depend in significant degree on him.* It is more than a matter of self-consciousness and tradition. It is a matter of discovering self, not only fully as a creature of one's time, as Charles Eames puts it, but to some degree its captain.

This is the hardest task of all for education, because it runs against the riptide of social-cultural disjunction discussed earlier. As Professor Kroeber wrote:

> [When the total culture is] varied and enriched, it also becomes more difficult for each member of the society really to participate in most of its activities. He begins to be an onlooker at most of it, then a bystander, and may end up with indifference to the welfare of his society and the values of his culture. He falls back upon the immediate problems of his livelihood and the narrowing range of enjoyments still open to him, because he senses that his society and his culture have become indifferent to him.[82]

Against this, the College pits itself to help students find acceptable meaning in both society and self. It will expect students to become strong enough to help shape the way society is to be, in politics, the arts, education, race relations, or any field. The academic program, the life of the College community, off-campus internships, work-service projects, sanctioned sabbatical leaves, and other parts of the program are planned to help them toward such will and strength. Students who feel that self can have little meaning or satisfaction in the acceptance of social responsibility are not likely to find Hampshire the right college. Hampshire believes that man has a fighting chance to shape his world. It believes that Norman Thomas was right when he said, "the joy of life is a fighting chance." It is committed, as John Gaus once said of Alexander Meiklejohn, "to the idea that intelligence must record itself in action."

The aim, too, is to increase the intellectual capacity of each student so that he can undertake a significant part of his undergraduate education himself and carry his own education forward through life. In practical terms, the College will open for study some of the most complex and persistent matters with which man has experience. It will do so neither obliquely, incidentally, nor through the astigmatic wide-angle lens of the "survey." It will do so head-on, with concrete studies that require and demonstrate disciplines of inquiry at work. Problems or phenomena studied may be deep in historical time or happening at the moment. But the intellectual exercise they require will strengthen a grasp of methodology and conceptualization indispensable in learning still to come. Students will find a high premium put on intellect at Hampshire, especially on the relating of intellect to the big questions—with respect for adequacy of data, thoroughness of analysis, and defensibility of concept. A new intellectual dimension of undergraduate liberal education at Hampshire will be its program in language, including linguistics from several points of view, semantics, philosophical analysis, and other topics, as well as new departures in the study of foreign languages.

Hampshire aims at a rekindling of the arts in the humanities. Hampshire hopes to increase the educative power of the humanities, which now serve too often as mere diversions or as objects for critical analysis. Professor Morison suggests that they "should be approached in such a way that a student may be stirred by them, in such a way that he recovers his power, now almost lost, to be moved. The surest way to discover the existence and then to examine the meaning of the affections is first to feel them." [83] At the College, this approach means that active and creative engagement *with feeling and expression through the arts* will be expected and available. The humanities will come to meaning through more than books and words. Using Jerome Bruner's formulation, *action* and *imagery,* and the feelings that go with them, will be the frequent preface to *notation* or verbalized meaning. For Hampshire students, this means a richer, far more active life in the arts than most secondary schools have led them to expect of college.

The culture of the College will be a principal educative element aiming to help students find a complementarity in self and society. The culture of Hampshire, as a community lived and worked in by younger and older people, by students and faculty, by people occupying different roles and statuses, will be distinctive in important ways. Neither crown colony nor Brook Farm in style, it will be a culture with room in it for meaningful participation in shaping what goes on. It will have room in it, too, for individual initiative and individual privacy. Its unity will not come from sameness, but from the diversity of ways the people of the College come at a common concern: the problem of man in our time. The quest for an identity of self and an identity of society, not at war with each other and not mutually defeating, will take all the sinew, mind, and feeling that students and faculty alike can bring to it.

In this quest, Hampshire will be an experimenting college, a laboratory in ways the private liberal arts college can be a more effective intellectual and moral force in a changing general culture.

# 4

## THE HAMPSHIRE ACADEMIC PROGRAM:

*Base Points, Structure, Requirements*

*Not only do professors get tenure, but courses, fields, disciplines, and, above all, departments get tenure. At least a professor is mortal: departments go on forever. Perpetuity, as someone observed, is a long time. The discipline as the primary organizing principle of academic life is of course essential to the maintenance of standards of both faculty appointments and educational rigor. But to permit it to be the be-all and end-all of academic strategy is inevitably to risk the exclusion of generalizing, synthesizing college education on one hand and the pursuit of transdepartmental intellectual excitement at the most advanced levels of research on the other. . . . There is no gimmick solution.*

KINGMAN BREWSTER, JR.
*Ventures,* Spring, 1966

As PRESIDENT BREWSTER says, there is indeed no gimmick solution for the college or university to deal with the rate of intellectual obsolescence in its own house. Lofty academic tradition and earthy academic politics, according to Yale's president, make it difficult even to approach the question of change. Further, and as it rightly should, the very nature of the educational enterprise tends to confound ahead-of-time devising of strategies or plans for change. The nature of every college or university, in its own way, is to try to develop people, ideas, and perceptions that will have a significant impact on thought, art, and action. To do that requires an element of creativity. And as President Brewster puts it, "the creative, by definition, will defy prediction's plan."

Professor C. L. Barber, one of the principal architects of the 1958 *New College Plan* and therefore no stranger to the devising of new academic strategies, has emphasized in discussion that the actual academic program of Hampshire cannot realistically be specified in advance. It must come from the able, exciting men and women who will form the faculty of the College. This *caveat* has been listened to at Hampshire; in its present stage of development, what is put forward concerning academic program is therefore provisional indeed.

## 1. THE OFFICIAL AND THE REAL IN CURRICULUM

But the ends of education are many, and a new institution must make the best choice among them that it can. A college pursues its ends in a variety of ways; the most manifest is its official curriculum of studies.

Curriculum is at once elusive in reality and inordinately changeproof once installed. No matter what the bulletin of studies says about "curriculum"—and it usually does so in a special labyrinthine prose—the *real* curriculum in fact turns out to be whatever a faculty member and his students do when they get together. The official curriculum, as contrasted to this, usually acquires a degree of infrangibility which makes it unbreakable for long periods of time. There is little originality but some truth in saying that it is as easy to change a curriculum as it is to move a graveyard.

Making a curriculum, then, seems superficially easier, but it is a rather presumptuous business. Once made, it conveys no necessary assurance that it really will serve the ends the college has chosen to pursue. Nor, given the happy independence and variability of human beings—a genus which includes faculty members—is there any assurance at all that its paper prescriptions will be followed dose by dose. On the other hand, once made, the written curriculum has such inertia that it can inhibit healthy institutional adaptation to change, even if it does not inform the day-to-day act of teaching with any very precise direction.

There are certain moral lessons to be drawn from this. One is that a formal curriculum of academic substance and sequence should not be expected to contain mirabilia which will bring all the educative ends of the college to pass. Another moral is that, since faculty and students in their dealings with each other construct the *real* curriculum, the official curriculum had best be a general framework. The third moral is that every formal curriculum should be born with a dated death warrant in its hand. If this figure of speech seems too inhuman the point can be put another way: any formal curriculum should contain a high frangibility factor—it should be made subject to termination or alteration from the beginning. You should be able, in the argot of this peculiar age, to "turn off." All of these moral lessons are in mind as Hampshire College's curriculum is planned.

The College expects that its formal academic program will be successful if it accomplishes *part* of the institution's aims in liberal education. Even so, the formal curriculum will need to be continually checked to determine whether in fact it is doing its part. The College expects that the real life of its academic program will be defined by its faculty and students, so only the most general and provisional structure is presented here. Finally, the moral of the dated death warrant is taken to heart; the framework discussed in this section should not be allowed to go without complete overhaul for longer than a period of five years.

To these lessons, Hampshire College adds a further proposition, which it proposes to test. This proposition is *that an academic program of good quality can be organized, in an independent college collaborating with nearby colleges and a large university, so that its costs can be met principally out of tuition income.*

## 2. BASE-POINTS OF HAMPSHIRE ACADEMIC PLANNING

The Hampshire College provisional academic program outlined in later discussion includes certain starting points which may be useful to note. The following are specific premises and features of Hampshire's present academic planning:

### a. *The Idea of Successive Approximations*

Hampshire College subscribes to the view that curriculum development is a continual process. The College does not believe it is possible to prescribe a fixed curriculum which will remain adequate to the demands liberal education must meet in a world of revolutionary change. Instead, Hampshire's basic principle of academic planning is one of development by successive approximations.

The academic program arises out of a continuous process of staged planning or approximations in which a variety of people play important parts. The first major approximation of the Hampshire academic program was developed by the four-college committee which prepared the *New College Plan* in 1958. The second major approximation of the College's academic program appeared in the 1966 Report of the Educational Advisory Committee, another interinstitutional committee of faculty in the four Connecticut Valley institutions.[84] The third approximation is presented in this paper. It is prepared by the College leadership as the academic year 1966-67 begins and is based heavily on the recommendations of the earlier documents and the advice of a number of consultants.[85] It is, as the introduction to this chapter pointed out, highly provisional. The current approximation will be revised as the result of critical examination by the College's academic consultants. As the academic leadership of the College is enlarged and faculty are engaged, the program will take further and perhaps different shape. Successive, frequent, and broadly considered approximations will be the rule in Hampshire's future.

b. *The Idea of Continuing Self-Study*

Along with academic program development by successive approximations, Hampshire subscribes to the view that continual evaluation of all of its work is essential. Institutional "self-studies" on an occasional basis are helpful. But for an "experimenting" college to be what it claims to be, there must be provision for steady observation, assessment, and interpretation of the consequences of the enterprise. This entails building into the College certain practical means for doing this kind of job. Kenneth Keniston sees three needs in this connection and suggests a solution which the College will thoroughly consider:

First, the College itself—particularly the faculty and the administration —must have rapid access to good information about what is happening . . . in order to evaluate the success or failure of experimental programs. Second, I think that students themselves should be encouraged to scrutinize and understand as well as possible the impact of the college on them, and their own contribution to college life. . . . Thirdly, the foundation of Hampshire College provides an invaluable opportunity for a really good study of undergraduate development. . . . One way to meet all three of these needs . . . might be to create a Council on Educational Development, which would consist of the President, elected members of the faculty, and elected members of the student body. Its size should be small—not more than seven. Such a Council might then act as an advisory body to a small number of researchers (some of whom might be teachers in the college, others of whom might be full-time staff researchers) who would be encharged with a comprehensive study of the College. Such a research group might . . . [provide] continual feedback to the Council on its findings. . . . The Council might then . . . make recommendations to the general faculty as to educational revision and reform.[86]

c. *The Idea of Maintaining an Innovative Climate*

Both a. and b. above are integrally related to a third view Hampshire represents: that what starts as an "experimenting" college should continue to be one. An initial innovative stance, however, can too easily soften into institutional stasis. Academic program development by successive approximations, backed up by a process of continuous evaluation, will help to maintain an innovative climate. But more will be required than this.

Professor Barber urges the notion of a regular "diagnostic summer session" as a vehicle both for evaluation *and* innovation. His suggestion is that members of the academic community of the College should be enabled to work together on curriculum for sustained periods in the summer as a matter of course.[87] Professor Samuel Baskin of Antioch suggests that Hampshire faculty be allowed time for developing academic innovations just as they might be allowed research time of the traditional sort within their instructional loads. Both suggestions are being considered at Hampshire as viable ways to keep innovation, experimentation, and intellectual vitality at the liveliest level.

These qualities come back always to the men and women who make up the faculty and its leadership. For this reason, Hampshire intends if possible to take a leaf from the Claremont book. There, faculty members are able to take a fully paid semester of sabbatical leave on a regular three-year basis. It is possible, as Professor Donald McNassor pointed out in consultation with Hampshire, for a Claremont faculty member to combine a summer and a sabbatical semester for a total leave of nearly seven months. Leaves of such frequency help to insure the kind of intellectual self-renewal out of which new and exciting teaching may come.

Many other ways and means to maintain an innovative liveliness for the College appear promising; one suggestion is to have "a vice-president in charge of revolution." [88]

### d. The Idea that Hampshire's Campus is the World

Without intended pretentiousness or melodrama, this view is that the curriculum of Hampshire aims at overcoming a dichotomy between "academic" and "real" life, which may seem irrelevant and unimportant to an older generation but is very much a reality for many undergraduates. The academic program of Hampshire College is intended to utilize field experience actively in connection with course work, to allow students time out either before or during college for extended leaves, and to use the "interim" midyear break for off-campus work and study projects, especially after the student's first year.

The College takes more than a passive position of permissiveness in this area, however, and intends to cultivate purposefulness more than opportunity for random drift. Where appropriate in terms of their individual needs and maturity, students will be *actively encouraged* by the College to take time off to work in ways that will enlarge their capacity for caring, for expressing concern through action, and for learning what it means to do a job. They will be given the sense that responsible experience in business or government, in poverty programs, Peace Corps work, community development, military service, and other endeavors is very much a part of Hampshire's idea of modern liberal education. Dr. Julius Stratton puts the basic rationale for such a position clearly:

> The classical idea of a liberal education is important. But it is also important for students to have a purpose, to know what they are seeking an education for, and to plan their course accordingly. There is a great deal to be said for learning to do something with your hands, learning to do the world's work. The liberal view is, in fact, an attitude, not a particular course of study. . . . The transformation that comes

with sensing that you have something to give is a worthy goal both for the student and for the educator.[89]

### e. *The Idea of Academic Coordination with Related Colleges*

In practice, Hampshire's academic program is planned to complement in useful ways the programs of the other Valley institutions, to offer their students certain distinctive opportunities at Hampshire to avoid wasteful duplication of offerings, and to enable Hampshire students to pursue certain advanced or special studies on the other campuses. A separate later section deals with concrete potentialities for further collaboration of the Valley institutions.

### f. *The Idea of Academic Program Flexibility*

The 1958 *New College Plan* in many ways helped break the lockstep features of undergraduate education. One of these ways was its "dethroning of the course as *the* unit of knowledge," whose steady accretion over four years would add up to a liberal education. Hampshire College's academic program will indeed offer students four years of study in a variety of basic, intermediate, and advanced work. But it will not consider an accumulation of any combination of courses as being either compulsory or equivalent to satisfactory completion of the collegiate phase of education.

While the Hampshire academic program will contain essential coherence and continuity, it will give students great freedom and equivalent responsibility in determining how they can make best use of what the College offers. The College will neither hold students to a rigid formula of required course sequences, nor will it allow flexibility to result in a random smattering or simply "the widest possible exposure to a variety of subjects." [90] Constraints of order will arise out of a field and integrative examination procedure, discussed later in this chapter, to which the student will determine his own response.

### g. *The Idea of the Student as Teacher*

The *New College Plan* stressed, as a principal concern of its academic program, the active and practical preparation of students to teach *themselves*. The 1958 Plan and the 1966 Report suggested also that students be engaged in teaching *others* through student-led discussion seminars, through acting as assistants to faculty in academic classes, and through serving as tutors and research associates. The Hampshire College academic program in its present approximation subscribes strongly to these recommendations. A great deal of faculty time will be devoted to teaching the student to teach himself. Time and care will be devoted also to training abler and more advanced students to act as teaching assistants. The principle which here affects the academic program of Hampshire was cogently put by the 1966 four-college advisory committee: "the best learning is that in which the student progressively acquires the ability to teach himself." [91] To this, the College would add that the best teaching tends to bring students into a colleague relationship with faculty, where students and faculty alike are learners, and alike share on occasion in the act of teaching others.

h. *The Idea of the Teacher as Teacher*

The view expressed above is complemented at Hampshire by a stress on the central role of the teacher. The faculty at Hampshire, as at any college worth the name, will be infinitely more important than the organized curriculum. In Hampshire's program, with its emphasis on enabling the student to teach himself, a strong faculty role will be indispensable. If students are in effect to become scholars, in the sense of having the will and ability to pursue learning on their own, they cannot do so in an atmosphere where the adult models available to them are neuter.

Such students need exposure to faculty who are obviously willing and able to pursue learning themselves, and who teach one how to learn as much by their own vigorous example as by anything else. The real teacher is never an intellectual or moral cipher in his stance toward students. Nor does he ignore the full complexity of his relationship to students who need to be helped toward independence. He must be an example of man thinking, man concerned, man acting. Despite a tendency in current American culture to suggest that adults are best seen and not heard, Hampshire considers the adult teacher necessarily an "intellectual leader of his time," as Alexander Meiklejohn put it at Amherst in 1912.

The leadership role of the faculty member dare not be narrow in

Hampshire's program. The Muscatine Report at Berkeley includes a "homily on the importance of teaching" which is much to the point for Hampshire:

> . . . some of the most lasting things that we also teach are qualities, abilities and attitudes exemplified in the way we have taught, in our stance toward the student himself. A class taught by an unprepared teacher teaches the student neglect of scholarship. A department which encourages professors to hide from students, teaches the neglect of human relations. If a scholarly attitude is—as it should be—part of what we teach, the teaching process must exemplify in all its details the scholarly attitude of the teacher. . . . [And] no defect of humane consideration is acceptable in our transactions with students. The image of the teacher will be no trivial part of what the world is or could be in the student's mind.[92]

### 3. THE CONTROLLING EDUCATIVE FACTOR

The ultimately controlling factor in Hampshire College's academic program is the view of liberal education which the College has chosen to take. This view is that the College exists not alone to prepare students for the high level technical competency demanded by preparation for graduate school, nor to prepare them in skills of inquiry, nor to give them an opportunity to explore the development of themselves through art and experience. All of these things are subsumed under Hampshire's view of liberal education, but the College has a larger and higher aim than any of these taken separately.

Earlier it was said that the central task of liberal education at Hampshire College is to help young men and women learn to live their adult lives, fully and well, in a society of intense change, immense opportunity, and great hazards. For the academic program of the College, this central task controls what it chooses to try to teach. Earlier discussion sought to stress the logical implications of such a view of liberal education in connection with the entire design of the College.

Hampshire College is deliberately designed to equip the student, as best we know how, to *learn how to make his own way* as a whole person in the emerging age. Recapitulating a point made at the beginning of the preceding chapter, no institution has a 20/20 crystal ball which reveals the future in which our young will live. But we can be relatively sure of its main features.  It will be increasingly technological in every aspect; it will be marked by accelerating change, increasing complexity, and simultaneous tendencies toward diversity and uniformity; its society will be increasingly large and urban; individual human relationships within it will continue to increase in number but not necessarily in depth, and the impersonality that marks much of our present day-to-day dealings with people outside our own immediate circle will continue; it will be a society in which there is an abundance or overabundance of continuous and chaotic stimulation.

On the assumption that it will help them learn how to live in a future whose dimensions may have these general features, the academic program in Hampshire's view should enable students to acquire:

*knowledge relevant to major sets of understandings about man's individual and social life and universe,*

*awareness of the ways of inquiry that have led to the present store of knowledge about these major considerations,*

*acquaintance with the ways man has of expressing the experience of living,*

*competence both in ways of inquiry and in ways of expressing the intellectual and emotional dimensions of their own encounter with reality.*

The curriculum needs an underlying structural coherence so that there is a chance such gains can be approached with a degree of order.  It needs equally to have enough explicit freedom so that students and faculty can come at such gains in ways which will engage them most fully and directly.

But beyond understandings, knowledge, and competence—hopefully arrived at through a mix of underlying coherence and explicit freedom in the process of education—students at Hampshire should confront *the question of what those things are for.* If the academic program fails to teach students to teach themselves how to face this question as their lives unfold, it has succeeded in too little, and the whole idea of "learning to learn" turns out to be shallow.  The College has a view of itself as more than either a complex teaching machine or an academy for the creation of young gentlemen and ladies.  In connection with James A. Perkins' *The University in Transition,* Professor Morton White commented that:

. . . I think that there is such a thing as knowledge of good, bad, right, and wrong, and that the university is as good a place in which to learn it and teach it as any in our society. Whatever one may think of some of the student demonstrations and teach-ins, many of them reveal a heartening concern with the moral problems created by an increasingly heartless world. More than ever, it is the responsibility of the university to help students transform their more admirable feelings into defensible beliefs and actions, for by doing so it may keep both students and professors from becoming mere technicians in the service of goals they never examine. The truth about prime numbers, electrons, DNA, the Civil War, and mass society is not enough for today's American university. . . . If it critically examines the ends it is asked to serve and serves only those that pass muster, it will go a long way toward convincing the American student that his teachers are still dedicated to liberal education, the civilized life, and the free society he is required to read about as a freshman but often advised to forget about when he becomes a graduate student seeking research grants.[93]

Professor White's remarks were addressed to the moral role of a large university in our time. They seem equally applicable to the moral role of the undergraduate college today.

Of all the things it might do in liberal education, Hampshire College has chosen to pursue its stated goal through a program intended to enlarge certain major understandings mentioned earlier. These have to do with such complex sets of things as the nature of man, social order, power, culture, ideas, creative and aesthetic experience, growth and change, the interconnectedness of things, and the problem of value. Such major understandings are dealt with through an academic program which is organized into four principal fields of related subjects of knowledge and disciplines of inquiry and expression. At Hampshire, these fields include the three traditional ones: the natural sciences, the social sciences, and the humanities and arts. In addition, the Hampshire program includes the field of language studies. Academic work within these four main channels is related to the central task of liberal education as Hampshire sees it, to the major sets of understandings identified above, and to the ultimate moral questions men must face for themselves.

## 4. THE FOUR SCHOOLS

At Hampshire College, the four fields noted above are called Schools.

Each field or School is a group of many related subjects; each School uses a common discipline or group of related disciplines in approaching the subjects and major understandings with which it is concerned.

In some cases a high-order problem or major set of understandings may be of concern to one School alone, but it is more likely that such a concern will be held by another School as well, or by all of the Schools. The disciplines with which the Schools deal are in each case a group of analytical concepts ordered into a body of theory and applied to subject matter. Thus Economics would be a discipline, while International Trade would be a subject. A subject is a specific matter, phenomenon, or group of many related specific matters or phenomena (Elizabethan drama, genetic codes, molecular structure, etc.) which can be studied via one or more disciplines.

A high-order problem or major set of understandings may be seen as a question likely to affect man perennially, likely to involve a variety of subjects, and capable of being understood—in the sense of successive approximations—by applying concepts from different disciplines. Thus such a perennial and pervasive matter of the human condition as the nature of power is a general high-order question involving a wide range of subjects and rationally approachable through many disciplines, such as those of political science, sociology, psychology, literature, and others.

The College and its four Schools are organized to enable students to get at major understandings through increased competence in disciplines of inquiry and experience without a departmental organization of disciplines.

One of the principal departures recommended by the 1958 *New College Plan* was the avoidance of departmental organization according to disciplines. The four-college committee of 1958 argued that:

> It is the pressure generated by departmental organization, in combination with the course system, which is chiefly responsible for the proliferation of courses. The department as a whole seeks to produce thoroughly trained majors by offering many courses; individual teachers add courses to make a place for themselves and their interests in the department. The New College Plan eliminates departments while preserving the three customary academic divisions. But at the same time it recognizes that the intellectual life of a college must be structured to a large extent by the specialized disciplines. The training of faculty

members should be exploited rather than ignored. Individually, most of them approach learning from the viewpoint of a single discipline. It is the tool which they know best and can most effectively share. Further, students who are just beginning to learn the difference between facts and the analysis of facts can progress more rapidly if several approaches to understanding are not presented simultaneously in the same course. This is not to deny that the various disciplines have much in common; but what is common should emerge as the liberal arts student moves forward in his education.[94]

When the Educational Advisory Committee of 1966 reviewed this thinking, its members found themselves in agreement with its essential principle, preferring only to stress the positive features of divisional organization rather than the negative features of departmentalization. The 1966 Committee concluded that the "departmental system is nurtured by the graduate school without regard to whether or not it is appropriate at the college level." [95] They agreed that a divisional organization of the College would not neglect specialization but would fit it into a broader background more suited to the exploratory and synoptic functions of undergraduate liberal education, and would thus make for a better college.

The 1966 Committee regarded the question of divisional organization from many points of view. They noted that:

> possible combinations are numerous, convictions about them strong, and any choice among them so intimate a part of an educational philosophy that the ultimate decision about divisions at Hampshire College has to be made by the new administration. No divisional organization would be successful that did not represent the profound convictions of an administration and of the faculty which it appoints.[96]

Out of their consideration of the question of divisional organization, the Committee produced a recommendation which has unusual originality and significance. The 1966 Committee recommended a structure of four rather than three divisions. To the humanities, the natural sciences, and the social sciences, the Committee added a strong recommendation for a division of languages which would deal with human communication in its varying forms. The leadership of Hampshire College is convinced that, as the first chapter of the present paper indicated, the study of languages as a major field, in the sense meant by the 1966 Committee, would open up a new and promising dimension for liberal education.

The Committee stated its four-field recommendation as follows:

The *New College Plan* proposed three divisions: humanities, natural sciences, and social sciences. In this three-fold set-up, however, there is no appropriate place for such semantical and syntactical studies as language, logic, mathematics and epistemology. We therefore suggest four divisions, as follows:

1. *The Humanities.* This division would concern itself with man as revealed in his art, his literature, his music, his history, his religion, and his philosophy. What are his values, his aspirations, his inspirations?

2. *The Natural Sciences.* This group would involve primarily a study of the inorganic and organic environment of man and a study of man himself as an organism. It would deal with such concepts as natural law and scientific method.

3. *The Social Sciences.* This group would bring together the studies of man and society: historical, economic, sociological, psychological and philosophical. It would examine the manners in which societies operate, the concept of social law, and methodology in the social sciences.

4. *The Languages* (including mathematics and logic). The central focus here would be communication. This would involve a study of language in its three uses: the analytic development of calculi and their syntaxes, the synthetical development of empirical statements and their semantical functions, and the creative employment of language in literature. The history of language would also necessarily be involved. The foreign language program would be the responsibility of this division.

Philosophically, these four divisions seem sounder than the earlier three.[97]

Hampshire College agrees with the thinking of the Educational Advisory Committee about this general structure. In details and application, in each case there are points where the College will differ from the Committee; but the four-fold structure appears in broad outline both sound and intriguing enough to warrant serious trial. In consequence, the organization of the College begins, as noted earlier, with its studies grouped in four Schools, each with a basic faculty and a dean. These principal academic fields of the College are designated as:

The School of Humanities and Arts
The School of Natural Sciences
The School of Social Sciences
The School of Language Studies

Students will distribute their studies among these four Schools, and usually will undertake a concentration of intermediate and advanced study in one School only. Field examinations, as explained later, will be given in a three-stage sequence. Integrative courses, examinations and advanced seminars will give students opportunity to test the linkages among fields and among disciplines.

The offerings in the School of Humanities and Arts will feature educational experience of a creative and aesthetic nature more strongly than the 1966 Committee proposed, as might be expected from what was said in the third chapter of this paper. Where the 1966 Committee proposed, for example, that the Humanities staff include a musicologist, the College is much more likely to invite a modern composer to join its faculty. The difference in this illustration is between an emphasis on *knowledge about* music which a musicologist might well provide, and an emphasis on what Whitehead called "the art of the utilization of knowledge."

Ulysses Kay, a contemporary composer and teacher, has suggested modest ways in which the College may offer students not only an introduction to theory, but opportunities as well to express themselves in music, through composition, reading of music, and performance, as well as listening.

It is this spirit which will be fostered in much of the program of the School of Humanities and Arts. But this is not to say that studies in history, literature, and the academic side of art will be neglected. In all studies of this School, however, a major emphasis will be on art as experience, as discipline, as something to be *done* as well as to be read about. The exact substance of offerings in the School will depend for determination on the interests of its faculty, who will be selected with an eye to their involvement in the aesthetic and creative, as much as in scholarship.

The School of Social Sciences will, in line with the recommendations of the 1966 Committee, focus on studies of *man in society* in ways that often cut across and link disciplines that are usually taught in almost complete isolation from each other. Again, the precise formulation of curriculum in this School will rest on the faculty who come to comprise it.

But for the present, the 1966 Committee offers a striking set of proposals to consider. These will be the starting point for specific curriculum development in the School. In abridged but still rather full form, some of the Committee's recommendations are the following:

> We have chosen to begin with the assertion that we wish to offer a coherent program focused on the study of man in society. Here we assume that the current state of knowledge permits us to define the major dimensions of such a study. Thus the initial grouping under *origins, organization, ideology, behavior, systems and methodology.* Assigned to each of these major topics is a set of courses. They draw from a variety of disciplines.

*Suggested Areas for Division of Social Science*

Origins
    Pre-literate cultures—cultural anthropology
    Early literate cultures—Egypt, Greece, Rome
                        Indian, Chinese

Study of Social Organization
    Introductory sociology
    Comparative governments
    The family
    Economic structure

Ideology
    Comparative religions
    Social ethics
    Social values
    Political philosophies—political theory
    Constitutional law

Methodology
    Sampling statistics—probability
    Non-parametric statistics
    Research design
    Metatheory—computer

Social Behavior
    Social development
    Behavior change
    Behavior analysis

Social Systems
    Trade and commerce
    Comparative economic systems
    Political organization—parties
    Social class–class structure
    International—economy
            —law
            —politics
            —conflict

The area titles can be seen to be a sampling of topics currently honored by several disciplines. We argue that instead of studying a discipline explicitly, and the subject of social science implicitly, we wish to reverse the process. The student is studying man in society explicitly in the programs offered, and implicitly encountering the disciplinary techniques and languages which have produced this knowledge. . . .

The subjects listed are offered as examples, and not as our best judgment of what should be taught. The area choices, however, require justification. The social sciences take as their common focus the social intercourse that men have with one another. Such intercourse may concern a wide variety of objects, functions and effects. These range from two-person systems for purposes of socialization, persuasion and personal gratification through multi-person systems for economic, protective and educative purposes to such impersonal systems as governments, international arrangements and major instruments of planning and policy. Traditionally, a variety of disciplines has contributed to our understanding of these processes, but there has been no responsibility for a unified approach. As a result there exist large gaps in our knowledge; e.g., of behavior modification and control, as well as gaps in our understanding of the relationships between existing bodies of knowledge; e.g., anthropology of pre-literate cultures and philosophies of social ethics. But at least the outlines of social science are coming clear.

. . . Several of the disciplines have felt the impact of "systems analysis" as a technique of study. This serves to remind us of the role that new methods frequently play. Methods have a way of creating their own intrinsic disciplines, of forcing new ways of looking at familiar observations, and of sharpening our understanding of older methods.

Hence the recognition of the study of method in its own right. It is expected that the choice of methods to study will follow from those being used in the division as a whole. It is argued the methods courses must be cast as ways of creating techniques of analysis whose study leads to an appreciation of how to create such ways as well as how to use them.

It must be admitted that the creation of this division as suggested runs counter to the traditional set of attitudes characterizing the relationships between disciplines. The social science disciplines have tended to discount and deride the methods of one another, and hence their contributions. In asking that faculty trained to such loyalties work together, we require a willingness to place the problem before the discipline, an unfamiliar requirement.

The student whose interests lead him to a particular academic discipline will find that the present offerings provide not more than one-half the normal topical coverage found in the undergraduate major. Hence we must be prepared to create opportunities for tutorial and independent study to carry him well beyond the formal offerings. Here we estimate that again at least half of the normal coverage can be achieved at Hampshire. Once this has been accomplished, the student is faced with filling in his remaining interests through four-college elections. These will concentrate in those topics requiring particular facilities or teachers.[98]

It must not be assumed, from the length of this excerpt, that the School of Social Sciences at Hampshire will necessarily follow this program. But the program suggested by the 1966 Committee will assuredly be discussed as Hampshire faculty in the social sciences organize their curriculum.

The School of Language Studies is treated in a later chapter of the present paper.

## 5. The Question of Distribution, Concentration, and Integration

Curriculum in American higher education has in a sense been almost as much affected by fads as the curriculum in the much-criticized lower schools has been. Trivium and quadrivium gave way under the pressures of a changing society for preparation in the so-called new subjects, the modern languages and the sciences, as the pressures of an industrialized democratic society made themselves felt on American colleges and universities in the 19th century. The triumph of the elective principle by the beginning of the 20th century brought with it substantial benefits and debits as well, as Frederick Rudolph has noted:

> Election permitted the professor to indulge his interests and the students to follow theirs; it encouraged the accumulation of knowledge and welcomed into the world of learning subjects that had been forbidden through an ill-considered belief that the ancients knew everything worth knowing. . . . The elective principle moved the individual to the center of the educational universe and boldly asserted that all educated men need not know the same things. The elective system, by giving free play to the great motive power of interest, freed the curriculum from the deadening influence of latent or open disinterest and hostility. . . . The elective principle was the instrument by which the departments of knowledge were built, by which areas of scholarly interest were enlarged, and therefore it was the instrument that enabled colleges to become universities. . . . Of course the ledger had its debits. The elective principle, enemy of one kind of superficiality though it was, could spawn a limitless number of short courses that might not add up to anything very substantial. On occasion it could make for a system that was (as Samuel Eliot Morrison wrote) "haphazard, illogical, postulated on too high an expectation of a young man's will to learn and too low an estimate of the many attractive side shows outside the main tent."
>
> It surely underwrote a good deal of the motivation problem in the American college and university by encouraging the notion that one subject was no more important than another and by making it possible for the non-serious student to find an easy berth.[99]

By 1931 at the University of Nebraska the elective principle had succeeded so far that a student could take courses in Early Irish, Creative Thinking, American English, First Aid, Advanced Clothing, Ice Cream and Ices, Third-Year Czechoslovakian, Football, Sewerage, and A Man's Problem in the Modern Home.[100]

As a kind of Thermidorian reaction to the revolution of the elective system, the general education movement began at Columbia University in 1919, continued through the famous Harvard Report which was prepared between 1943 and 1945, and on into the 1950's. As Bell has said about general education at Columbia, the movement came about as the result of a curious mixture of parochial, sociopolitical, and philosophical motives. The radical growth and changing composition of the

American college student population in the years of World War I and
after contributed to an increased sense of need for higher education
to provide the educated leadership of a heterogeneous nation with an
understanding of the principles of a free society and a consistent image
of American experience and our heritage of Western culture. Certainly,
too, the movement was affected by the New Humanists, such as Irving
Babbitt, who found that under the elective system "the wisdom of all
ages is to be naught, compared with the inclination of a sophomore." [101]
The position of the New Humanists was that the full, free, unexpressed,
undisciplined chaos of the elective curriculum needed to be countered
by an assertion of the validity of intelligent control, an interest in what
is human about a student rather than what is merely individual about
him.[102] Whatever the background and causes, as Professor Rudolph has
pointed out:

> Where the general education or core-course program received its most
> dramatic treatment, there the forces of chaos had earlier made their
> most dramatic impact. Columbia, Chicago, Amherst, Wesleyan, and
> Harvard were especially vulnerable to the charge that they had lost
> touch with the ideal of learning as a body of thought and values by
> which an educated man was identified, for in all these institutions the
> elective principle had substituted an era of almost uncontrolled in-
> dividualism for the older humanistic tradition.[103]

Colleges moved toward varying schemes of general education which
diminished the electives available to students and strengthened the demand for students to take certain common, core, or basic courses. One
example was the new curriculum that Amherst College established in
1947, which required all freshmen and sophomores to take a two-year
sequence in science, history, and the humanities within the framework
of a four-course program.[104] Of special interest in connection with later
developments, the Amherst curriculum of 1947 also moved toward the
institution of *laboratory or seminar* courses in history, the humanities,
and the fine arts as well as in the sciences.

The ferment of American higher education has been such that wherever schemes of general education were installed they very soon came
under further faculty study and scrutiny; in some cases they became
the object of academically cosmic conflict. *General Education in a Free
Society,* the Harvard Redbook of 1945, tried to formulate a complete

educational philosophy for American society in the course of dealing with curriculum and other matters. The Redbook became the bible of general education, particularly in smaller colleges and state universities, but, like the Bible itself, was often either unread or sometimes read too literally.[105] At Harvard, the Redbook was followed by the Bruner Report of 1949 (known as such because of the committee chairman, Professor Jerome Bruner) on the problem of science in general education, and the 1964 Doty Committee Report (named for its chairman, Professor Paul M. Doty) reviewing the status and problems of Harvard's general education program. Elsewhere, in varying degree and with differing results, faculties assessed the consequences of general education.

Five major approaches to general education were common; distribution requirements; comprehensive survey courses; "functional" courses; the Great Books curriculum; and individual guidance. The first of these approaches involved a simple limitation on complete elective choice, so that the student was required to distribute a flexible portion of his course work among different fields. The second approach involved comprehensive survey courses organized most often in the humanities, social sciences, and natural sciences. The "functional" course approach to general education was intended to prepare students for immediate problems of life such as those of personal and community health, social adjustment, marriage and family life, and vocational guidance. The Great Books approach was identified with St. John's College, and required four prescribed years in the study of approximately 100 important books of the Western heritage, along with the study of ancient and modern languages, mathematics, and laboratory science. The fifth approach, that of individual guidance, was found in such colleges as Black Mountain, Sarah Lawrence, and Bennington; after a student had explored various fields for two years he or she would pursue a reading and tutorial program planned around a central individual interest. No matter what the approach, general education represented an effort to give a degree of coherence and some commonality to the first years of college for all students. The approaches also characteristically involved a move toward specialization or a "major" in the last two years or "upper division." There were exceptions to this, as at Chicago, where the original intention was for a common four-year education.

The general education movement persisted in various forms, but it was subject to increasing tension as the 1960's approached. Stress came from at least three sources.

One of these sources was a strong feeling that the values of an elective system must be expressed in a curriculum which would indeed be liberalizing for the student. This feeling was reinforced by improvements in secondary education which introduced pre-college students to "basic" subject matter more adequately than before. And it was expressed by faculty and students who disliked the apparent regimentation of uniform requirements.

A second source of stress was the pressure for specialization, reflected in the interests and demands of departments and a sense of urgency students increasingly felt about being able to enter graduate specialization as well prepared as possible. Pressure of this kind underlined a view that general education courses, even if intrinsically well handled, meant time lost in getting on with a special line of study of greater importance than "shallow breadth" could claim.

Finally, stress came from the knowledge that somehow liberal education should provide for all students an awareness of the indivisibility of knowledge, of the connectedness of events, of the wholeness of things. This was the stress which in various manifestations had helped to produce the general education movement in the first place. Caught on the horns of this trilemma, higher education began looking for a new mode or style.

The emerging modishness, in America but not in England, turns sharply away from a pattern of required general education "core" courses. In some instances, as at Harvard, the dominant note is set by the press for specialization, reflecting a strong impulse in the society toward insisting upon and rewarding the highest possible professional competence among the well-educated young. In other instances, the mode is the reverse of this, accenting virtually complete freedom of individual choice of what to study and how to study it. Some experimental colleges, such as Goddard in Vermont, provide pure examples of this mode. But they are not alone.

"Experimentalism" in the late 60's generally tends to mean adventures in making the curriculum flexible, sometimes to a point which conservatives regard as formless. Flexibility is interpreted most often in current experimentation as the "individualization of academic programs," the principal canon of orthodoxy in this new mode. Such experimentalism, in a sense, is part of the general cultural impulse toward radical subjectivism discussed earlier. In some few other instances, strenuous efforts are being made to reconcile the impulses toward focused specialization and subjective individualization of curriculum within programs that retain a degree of common intellectual experience for all.

This is principally being attempted by two means. One involves reliance upon "distribution" and "concentration" requirements, with the first intended to assure that, even with electives, students will have some exposure to studies in several fields, and with the concentration requirement intended to assure that he will also focus on a special field, discipline, or subject. The distribution-concentration formula alone provides no inherent solution to the need for liberal education to perform an integrative function. Current efforts to add a dimension to the formula which would satisfy this need try to do so not through common courses of study, but through centering attention on *inquiry*. The new mode in liberal education, in other words, accents process rather than substance as the unifying element in general education.

The latter solution was foreshadowed in a 1954 reexamination of the Amherst "new curriculum" of 1947. Among many other things, this reexamination commented that:

> If integration is to occur at all, then, it must occur in the student's mind. No mere juggling of courses and scrambling of course contents will achieve it. . . . It is mere *knowledge about* that produces what Whitehead calls "inert ideas," and it is inert ideas which cause mental dry rot. The only possible way, therefore, of obtaining an education is through active participation in some type of project. It is this participation which brings us into real contact with things and makes us genuinely acquainted with them. And it is for this reason that Whitehead defines education as "the acquisition of the art of the utilization of knowledge." . . . This is the part of Amherst's "new" curriculum which, wherever you find it in the new curriculum, is, for a college course, really new. . . . [When] one attempts to reach the art of utilizing knowledge, one deliberately gives up the attempt to teach subjects and instead more modestly tries to initiate the student into the kind of work that is done by the professors of those subjects. . . .

For the truth of the matter is that one cannot integrate by using the encylopaedic approach. Such omnibus survey courses must progressively include less and less about more and more.[106]

The reasons for moving to the establishment of *conceptual inquiry as the central organizing principle in the college curriculum* are stronger and deeper than this relatively informal Amherst commentary of 1954 might suggest. These reasons may be summarized as follows:

Conceptual inquiry (*i.e., seeing the uses of mind as involving learning, using, and revising propositions, theoretical constructs, concepts, and methodological principles in inquiry, not inquiry simply as gathering and classifying or categorizing data*) has become an intellectual necessity in general background or basic courses as well as in advanced courses of a specialized nature: it cuts across all fields and all levels.

A grounding in methods of conceptual inquiry is the only practical way to become educationally equipped for the kind of intellectual mobility and continuing self-renewal the rapidly changing world of knowledge and work requires; it is no longer sensible to educate a person for a static "job," when all specializations are swiftly modifying (or becoming obsolescent) and new ones are constantly appearing.

Conceptual inquiry has been made central to the advanced sections of all fields of knowledge since the conceptual revolution in physics in the 1920's and the subsequent overturn of the structure of scientific thought. In physics, new discoveries in radioactivity, the principle of relativity, the nature of the atom, and the like, made obsolete the older view (held by men like Karl Pearson and Lord Kelvin) that inquiry in science was involved only in laying bare the facts of nature and reporting on the observable and measurable. Physicists were forced to treat space, time, place, magnitude, and other matters in a new way, not as objects of self-evident truth or mere empirical verification. New conditions of knowledge made it necessary to rely heavily on *science as conceptual structures or principles of inquiry,* which could be revised as developing complexes of theory, bodies of data, and criteria of scientific progress dictated. A shift of emphasis from Whitehead's *knowledge about* to an emphasis on conceptual structures and principles of inquiry has tended to occur in all the sciences (e.g., biology) and in the social sciences. The latter still retain some of their earlier flavor of positivism (seeking to discover "regularities" in social phenomena comparable to the laws of Newtonian physics), and still are heavily involved with traditional descriptive history.* But it is increasingly clear that the problems the social sciences now face require a reliance on conceptual and analytical structures and their constant reexamination.[107] And in the humanities, too, there is evidence of some shift in this direction, as the work of Professor E. H. Gombrich on perception in art suggests.[108]

Conceptual inquiry is at the heart of the apparently permanent revolution in knowledge in which we now live. Currently the rate of *revision* of theoretical knowledge in the sciences may be twenty to a hundred times higher than it was less than 100 years ago. In such a state of flux in all the fields of knowledge, the centrality of method becomes clear. Inquiry; ways of discovering and knowing; of analyzing; of going from hunch to hypothesis to test to reconsideration, with conceptual tools to help you;—these make up a reasonable keystone for general education now.[109]

Hampshire College finds these reasons persuasive, and in consequence variety and depth of experience with conceptual *inquiry* is a principal element depended upon to give a sense of coherence to liberal education in the College.

The *New College Plan* in 1958 developed a curriculum for a college with a relatively large enrollment compared to the number of its teachers. The Plan disavowed a return to some new version of the old system of required courses for all, even as a means of economy. Instead, it proposed to preserve "the vital freedom of choice among courses and teachers" and include a requirement of distribution and concentration. The New College model aimed to devote faculty time principally to teaching students to teach themselves, fitting students to master subjects chiefly on their own initiative "by providing them with the necessary skills, resources, and intellectual stimulation." [110] Training for self-conducted inquiry was a central emphasis of the *New College Plan*. This would occur in a variety of courses in the regular curriculum and was to:

> be complemented by the common experience all students will share in taking two college-wide courses during a month-long mid-winter term, to be held each year after the Christmas vacation, between the fall and spring terms. This will be an occasion for projects integrating different disciplines.[111]

*Witness the fairly acrimonious conflict between traditional descriptivism and behavioralism in political science.

The *New College Plan* foresaw that the two mid-winter courses would include subjects or problems of general importance. One course would deal with some aspect of the Western cultural heritage; the other would deal with one or another of the great non-Western cultures. In a four-year cycle of mid-winter terms students would have studied four different aspects of their own culture and a central feature of each of four other great cultures. Thus, in addition to variety and elective specialization, students would have shared in common, broad studies.

Since 1958 many colleges here and in England have tried or are trying other solutions to the problem of distribution, concentration, and integration. At Harvard in 1965, Dean Franklin Ford proposed a scheme which sought to maintain a commitment to general education along with accommodating the impulse toward specialization. In the new Harvard plan each student would be required to take at least four year-long courses outside of his own field of concentration. Three of these would be in general education in the fields of the social sciences, the humanities, and the natural sciences. But the student would *not be required* to do so by taking any of the broad introductory lower-level courses; instead, he could satisfy the general education requirements by taking upper-level courses in the three main fields if he could meet departmental prerequisites. Under Dean Ford's proposal the student in the natural sciences could forego any general education courses in that field.

At the University of Chicago the question of general education is being met beginning in the fall of 1966 by a plan put forward by University Provost Edward Levi. The Levi system divides the college into five "area colleges," each with its own Master and its own comprehensive program. Chicago's five "area colleges" are in physical science, biology, social science, humanities, and "civilizational" studies. The "area colleges" will not be residential in nature, but will be "intellectual unities." While patterns remain to be worked out by faculty, students will take two courses in common in the first year, one in the second, and an integrating seminar in the final year. The relationship between concentrations and the general courses will be established by the faculties in each "area college." The basic principle is that in each field of specialization the emphasis would be on the *structure of inquiry* as it becomes manifest through subject matter. The underlying proposition is that by developing experience in the processes of inquiry in a special field, students would understand the principles of description, exposition, and argument that are applicable in other subjects as well.[112]

At a time when common requirements in general education are being de-emphasized in the United States, it is interesting to note that in England a somewhat different line is being followed. This is especially true at the new universities formed in England during the early 1960's.

The University of Sussex provides an illustration relevant to plans for Hampshire College. At Sussex, as at Chicago, the faculties are not organized in department, but in "schools." The Schools at Sussex are in such fields as Physical Science, the Social Studies, European Studies, Educational Studies, England and American Studies. The Schools of the University of Sussex are designed to bring students and faculty together in a common field, instead of in specific disciplines. Courses in each discipline are given, but the principal effort is to (a) provide students with interdisciplinary work within fields and (b) *provide them with common course work which links the fields of the several schools.* Degrees at Sussex are given in Science, the Arts, and the Social Sciences. There are certain required first-year courses which all students must take. Before a student is permitted to concentrate either in the Arts or Social Studies, he must, for example, take a common course in "Language and Values" and a common course in "An Introduction to History." [113] Students taking degrees in Science are required to take two common courses in "Structure and Properties of Matter" and "Mathematics with Physics," plus electing either "Further Mathematics" or "Chemistry."

In the Sussex program, as at Hampshire, there is an emphasis on educating individuals for contemporary life and problems. The Sussex design for accomplishing such education is to emphasize early in the college program analytical and methodological questions and procedures, to progress through common or linked subjects, and finally to specialize in particular subjects or disciplines. One American observer concludes that:

> *It is clear that general education in this British conception does not mean survey courses, or simply a distribution requirement of work*

*in diverse fields, but a genuine effort to "find links between subjects."*
*It is an experiment well worth watching.*[114]

In his reconsideration of general education at Columbia, Professor Bell has made recommendations which are distinctive in themselves but have an interesting resonance with the new developments at Chicago and at Sussex. The Bell proposals have two objectives: first, to reorganize the two years of Contemporary Civilization courses and relate them to the Humanities courses in order to accomplish a more unified early college experience; second, to try to integrate the lower and upper college courses to provide for a coherent development of analytical skills and ideas.

The Columbia recommendations emphasize the first year of college as the time for acquisition of necessary historical and background knowledge, the second and third years as the proper time for training in a discipline and the application of the discipline to diverse subject matters within a field, and the fourth year as the proper time for advanced seminar work in a specific discipline along with participation in integrative courses in the major areas of the sciences, the humanities, and the social sciences.[115] Daniel Bell summarizes his own position by saying:

> The nature of college education can now be envisaged as a series of logical steps in which first comes the acquisition of a general background, second the training in a discipline, third the application of this discipline to a number of relevant subjects, and fourth the effort to link disciplines in dealing with common problems. It is this progression, involving at each step of the way an awareness of conceptual innovation and method, that is the heart of the ordering of a curriculum.[116]

Professor Bell sees necessity for the restoration of history as a central subject in his triadic design for liberal education and as the first logical step in the ordering of a curriculum. He argues this position because history can:

> redress the passion for the abstract by emphasizing the concrete, thus demonstrating a social situation in its manifold complexity and actuality;
>
> provide a "vocabulary of reference" for the historical imagination, both to stretch the imagination and to forestall the limited (and sometimes false) analogies that can be invoked to justify or explain events;

emphasize the role of contexts in establishing the meaning of ideas;

identify the relevant antecedents that have shaped the present;

be a source for comparative analysis.[117]

In arguing for the teaching of history as a basic part of general education, Professor Bell is far from advocating historical survey courses. Instead, he feels it necessary for students to study historical problems and periods with some intensity and depth in order to (a) "see history as the efforts of peoples and societies to deal with some recurrent problems of social order" and (b) to grasp principles of historical explanation and the nature of evidence as ways of understanding basic complex social processes. In urging this view, Bell suggests examples of studies which are not dissimilar from those being developed by the Social Studies Program of Educational Services Incorporated, under the leadership of Professor Elting E. Morison.[118]

For Hampshire College, examination of past trends and recent developments in general and liberal education has led to certain conclusions about the questions of distribution, concentration, and integration in the academic program. These will become evident in the broad framework of the Hampshire academic program. Hopefully, the discussion of Hampshire's academic program that follows will make clear that curriculum at the College:

is not committed to a totally elective or individualized approach to studies, while allowing great room for choice;

is determined not to allow narrow specialization to dominate its character;

regards its central task and major understandings as requiring certain common studies for all students;

accepts *conceptual inquiry* as its pervasive pedagogical style, and training in it for continued self-use as a principal obligation of the College.

The academic program will give students from the beginning an idea of what the College means by "liberal education." Students will have direct experience in inquiry in each of four fields, will learn the principles of a discipline and its uses in inquiry and expression. They will have the experience of applying the resources of a discipline to an advanced special project, and will have opportunities from the beginning of college until graduation to deepen their understanding of some very complex sets of things.

## 6. THE DIVISIONAL SEQUENCE

The academic program for the College as a whole and for each of its Schools is organized in a three-phase divisional sequence. Each Division constitutes a stage in the academic program with its own purposes, related studies, and field examinations.* Each divisional stage has an expected usual duration within the usual four years of the College. But individual students may in some cases take a longer or shorter time than is the usual pattern for any one or more of the Divisions. In a sense, the three Divisions as a sequence take the place of the traditional Freshman, Sophomore, Junior, Senior class sequence according to which colleges are most frequently organized. Just as Hampshire College, in the words of the 1958 Plan "dethrones the course as *the* unit of knowledge," so it also departs from the class-year sequence as *the* mode of progression through the College.

The nature of Divisions in relation to their purposes, course work, field examinations, and integrative examinations will be dealt with more fully in later discussion. They are noted briefly here:

a. *The Division of Basic Studies*

Ordinarily this divisional sequence would require approximately one academic year for a student to complete. Its major purpose is to introduce the student to the intentions and process of liberal education at Hampshire, giving him limited but direct experience with the use of disciplines of the four broad School fields for inquiry and expression, and certain common elements of background, method, and skill necessary in undertaking one's education within Hampshire's terms. A student will have completed this sequence when he has passed Division I field and integrative examinations which assess his development in the College's four

---

*"Division" in the present Hampshire terminology is not to be confused with its earlier use in 1958 and 1966 documents. The term does not here mean a *field,* but a *stage.*

areas and his development in background and methods which link these fields.

### b. *The Division of Disciplinary Studies*

This divisional sequence would usually occupy two academic years out of a student's usual four in the College. The principal objects of Division II are to enable a student to explore the disciplines of the four School fields further, to become accepted as a major student in one of the Schools, to become initially trained in the concepts and methods of a single discipline through inquiry and experience applied to real subjects and projects, and to broaden his knowledge of the linkages among disciplines and fields. Completion of this phase will be reached when a student has passed a School examination directly involving the application of his selected discipline to subjects, field examinations dealing with the treatment of subjects in areas and disciplines other than his own, and an integrative examination requiring the application of all the disciplinary resources at his command to a high-order problem which cuts across fields. The student's work in this sequence will increasingly be independent, with time for individual projects and studies, the pursuit of reading programs, and study at other institutions.

### c. *The Division of Advanced Studies*

Usually this final sequence would require the last academic year for completion. In at least one-half of the sequence, a student will independently pursue an intensive study or project related to one limited subject within his discipline. The study or project will have been outlined by the student during the latter part of his Division II studies; it will have to have been approved by his School as a suitable advanced undertaking prior to the completion of the Division II sequence. The completion of a student's study or project will take a form appropriate to his discipline or field. In many cases, perhaps particularly in the Schools of Natural Sciences, Social Sciences and Language Studies, completion of an advanced study will result in a thesis submitted to a faculty advisor or committee. In the School of the Humanities and Arts, an advanced project might instead result in an artistic creation (as, for example, a sculpture, a musical composition, a painting, a novel, etc.) executed at a level of competence considered by the School to demonstrate advanced performance.

A further element of Division III is participation in an advanced integrative one-term seminar, in which the student will encounter a broad topic requiring the application of various disciplines, including his own. Such a seminar might deal, for example, with the Development of New Nations, or with Science and Government, or with other complex topics which cannot be handled alone by a single discipline, and which involve value and judgment as well as data and method. The student would have time available for other studies of an elective variety. His work in Division III and his College studies would be completed when his intensive study or project was accepted by his School, when he had passed an advanced School examination in his discpline and ones related to it, and when he had passed an advanced integrative examination involving problems that require a relating of fields and disciplines to major sets of understandings with which the College is principally concerned.

## 7.  REQUIREMENTS FOR GRADUATION

Undergraduate education in America, as the 1958 *New College Plan* and other critiques have pointed out, has been dominated by a view of knowledge as being acquired in units called courses. Most commonly, courses are given "unit" values in terms of the amount of "class time" they require students to "put in" during a given semester. Thus a course meeting in classes three hours per week for a sixteen-week semester may be a "three-unit" course. If a student "passes" four or five courses of two to five unit values each during each of eight semesters, in what a college regards as a suitable combination of studies, he will have "accumulated enough units" to graduate.

Other requirements, such as a comprehensive examination, a language examination, or a senior thesis, may have to be met as well. But the basic thing is to accumulate enough units of knowledge, measured in hours of course work with passing grades, to justify the baccalaureate degree.

The accompanying features of this system are familiar. A student registers each semester for a series of courses, some of which may be "required," and some of which may be elective. In every practical sense, *all of his course work is required,* since he must accumulate a prescribed number of course units in order to graduate.

Once enrolled in his courses, the student is expected to attend them. Indeed, attendance with minimum absence is usually compulsory if the student plans to pass the course. His physical presence is regarded as essential in order for him to acquire the units of knowledge which the course is intended to impart to him. The good sense of this is self-evident if one accepts the initial premise that education occurs through the accretion of units of knowledge measurable in hours of class time.

To insure physical presence, it is not uncommon for attendance at each class meeting to be verified in one fashion or another. Sanctions are applied to a student if his attendance becomes irregular or spotty, or if he is not prompt in appearing for class.

The course in any given instance is likely to require the completion of considerable outside reading and problem-solving; to present the student with frequent short tests, periodic larger tests, and a final examination; and to require him to prepare one or more papers on topics related to the subject of the course. All of these, like his attendance, are evaluated.

Evaluation takes the form of scaled grading, usually by numerical values from 0-100, by letter-categories of value from F-A, or by some complex variation or combination of these. The mysteries and subjectivities of this process are at least as painfully evident to the professor as they are to the student.

Somehow at last, the student finds himself at the end of a course with a grade, which is presumed to symbolize the degree of adequacy he demonstrated in acquiring the units of knowledge in the course. Hopefully, the symbol indicates he has "passed"—that the intricate evaluational bookkeeping and his record of attendance warrant his being regarded as successfully educated in the content of the course.

This simplified description of the dominant process in undergraduate education leaves out variations and exceptions which can be found in most institutions. To this extent it is exaggerated and not altogether fair, but not enough so to diminish it significantly as a reasonably accurate depiction of the largely prevailing system.

Hampshire College, in its academic program, provides a sharper break with this system than the 1958 Plan suggested. The present system is regarded as having so many disabilities and undesirable consequences

—both in terms of "academic" education and the larger development of the student as a person—that a departure from it is warranted.

Essentially, the present system is one of frequent extrinsic rewards and punishments which tend to produce short-term high performance behavior in connection with discrete and limited objectives. The system in the long term produces diffuse behavior in terms of its educational results, and by its mechanical authoritarianism tends to contribute to self-hate and generalized hostility. Short-term learning, unreinforced by its further use in a structured context of larger understandings, fades fast.

For these and other reasons, the Hampshire academic program does not view education as an evaluated accretion of course-units of knowledge, nor does it assess a student's education in customary terms. Instead, the College has a very limited set of absolute academic requirements which all students must meet in order to graduate. These are:

(1. The Division I basic field and integrative examinations noted in the preceding section.

(2. The Division II intermediate School examination, other field examinations, and the integrative examination noted in the preceding section.

(3. The Division III advanced School examination, and advanced integrative examination.

(4. The completion and School acceptance of a Division III intensive independent study or project.

(5. The Foreign Language Examination, an individual demonstration of oral-aural competence in understanding and speaking a language other than English. This examination may be taken at any time prior to two months before graduation, suitable to the readiness of the student and the convenience of examiners.

*No* courses in the Hampshire College academic program are in the ordinary sense required for graduation. Outside accreditation and other demands aside, it would be possible in academic principle for an admitted Hampshire student to receive his baccalaureate degree without attending any seminars or courses, if (a) he and his advisors considered him realistically able to attempt all of the five requirements noted above, and (b) he could satisfactorily demonstrate this ability.

Such a case would be rare, to say the least. The point that this extreme example illustrates, however, is that the academic program of courses and studies can be abridged or modified. It is not rigid and inviolate, either in its common courses or its elective ones. On the other hand, abridgment or modification is not a matter of absolute free choice by the student. He may propose abridgments or modifications, but appropriate faculty will determine whether his proposals are realistic in connection with his preparation to meet the fundamental academic requirements at his highest potential level of performance.

With the five fundamental requirements noted above as the only central *academic* criteria of student progress through the College, it is likely that some students may receive their degrees in less than the usual four years. Others may take a longer time, either because of a need for further learning or because of off-campus leaves.

The eventual nature of the required examinations, intensive advanced studies, and individual advanced projects will be determined by faculty in consultation with outside examiners. All examinations and advanced studies will be either School (field) or inter-School in character, in the sense that they will examine in disciplines as related to a context of other disciplines. They will not be departmental "comprehensives" or narrow course subject finals. As the 1958 Plan suggested, "breadth of factual knowledge will be required, some of it acquired independently; and the ability to apply analytical skills to large areas of subject matter will be tested" (1958, p. 22). Outside examiners will assist in evaluating the fundamental examinations, studies, and projects, thus helping to assure that students will be held to recognized standards, and that faculty will benefit from detached judgment of their students' work.

While Hampshire's academic program does not compel a sequenced fulfillment of courses, and rejects the concept of course-unit accumulation as the criterion of educational progress, it does present each student with a coherent academic offering in each Division. Some of these are specified in provisional form in the next chapter.

The College recommends that each student take the fullest advantage of such offerings, including common courses intended for all students and optional courses intended for special interests and needs. This recommendation is based on the premise that the divisional offerings will enable students to gain background, analytical and methodological skills, synoptic views, and powers of synthesis which they will need in meeting the College's fundamental requirements. The College considers that a four-year program of basic seminars, lecture-student seminars, lecture-demonstrations, independent study, and advanced seminars provides an essential framework for the academic program.

Students, as noted, may on occasion find it desirable and possible to abridge or lengthen this sequence. The policy of the College to allow sanctioned leaves or student sabbaticals in any case will require the four-year framework to be subject to amendment for individual students.

Examinations may be given in courses where faculty find them useful. Only three categories of grades, as suggested by the 1958 Plan, will be used: fail, pass, and distinction. No grades, however, will be more than advisory to the student and helpful to his faculty counselors, except the grades on the fundamental Division examinations, studies and projects. Grades in the latter instances will be determinant.

The usual program for a student in any semester will be the equivalent of three full courses. Division I courses will vary in size of enrollment but in general will emphasize the use of tutorials and small groups in order to give entering students direct experience with scholars actively exploring limited subject matter, and to allow students maximum immediate involvement in inquiry and discourse. Division II courses will have some small faculty-led seminar work, but will emphasize larger lectures combined with student-led seminars, and independent studies under faculty supervision. Division III courses, or equivalents, will be as noted earlier.

Degrees will be awarded *rite, cum laude, magna cum laude,* and *summa cum laude.*

## 8.  THE FOREIGN LANGUAGE PROGRAM

The College requirement for every student to pass a proficiency examination in speaking and listening comprehension in a language other than English was noted in the preceding section.\* The required level of

---

\*This requirement runs counter to the 1958 Plan which eliminated any language requirement for graduation "in the conviction that students who take a language on compulsion and without aptitude gain too little from the experience to justify what it costs them and the College." See pp. 26-27 of the 1958 Plan. The 1966 Educational Advisory Committee Report made a similar recommendation, but with somewhat less certainty. See pp. 38-41 of the 1966 Report.

specific performance in this examination will be determined by faculty, but it is intended to insure that each Hampshire graduate will be capable of a reasonable even if limited fluency in conversation in another modern tongue.* There is no College requirement for foreign language course study, but the College program contains many opportunities for students to increase their proficiency in other languages. These are touched upon in subsequent discussion.

For admission to Hampshire College, students ordinarily will have completed no less than three years of high school study in one of the modern foreign languages, most often French, German, Spanish, Russian, or Italian. At entrance, a student ordinarily should have already scored satisfactorily in the College Entrance Examination Board Achievement Test in the language of his high school program.

In those cases where, because of special conditions of his background, a student has not had such high school preparation, it will be possible for him to take an intensive summer course in elementary language, complemented by scheduled special training in the Foreign Language Laboratory.

Course experimentation in elementary language instruction during the academic year will likewise provide such students with opportunities. An example of such an experiment is described in Appendix IV of the 1966 Report:

> . . . a recent innovation at MIT for Italian merits the attention of the planning committee. There a two-semester course in Dante is given, in the original, for students who have *never* had any Italian before. A first unit is devoted to an intensive presentation of the most irreducible essentials. Then the students, with the help of several dictionaries, reference books, and even translations, start in reading *The Divine Comedy*. By the end of the year, they have learned a tremendous lot of Italian, and have made a commitment to one of the greatest masterpieces of literature. . . .

---

*An exception to this general requirement may be made with students whose secondary school preparation has been in ancient languages, and who desire to continue in these languages at the college level. Students desiring Latin and/or Greek in the College, either as electives or as concentrations, may be enabled to do so by arrangement with other institutions.

Such elementary course experimentation in the regular academic year will be limited at Hampshire, however, because extensive course offerings in foreign languages are not part of the Hampshire plan.

In seeming paradox, the Hampshire College academic program gives intense attention to foreign language learning, but in special ways.

a. *The Foreign Language Laboratory*

A subsequent chapter on the College community and its campus design details the installation and operation of a high-capability language laboratory in Hampshire's School of Language Studies. The College intends to have the most modern and well-equipped laboratory it can develop. The laboratory will provide electronic systems and instructional programs for group and self-instruction in elementary and intermediate foreign language according to need during the academic year. Its resources will be managed by the Director of Foreign Language Studies with the assistance of a staff which will be small in the fall and spring terms and substantially larger in the summer. The permanent staff will include part-time or joint-appointment faculty, technical assistants for laboratory operation (some of whom will be student associates or interns from Hampshire and the other institutions), and native-speaking part-time assistants to act as tutors. Students may elect group or independent foreign language study as part of their regular three-course programs after completion of Division I. It will be possible, of course, for them to make voluntary use of the laboratory for individual reviews, brush-ups, and other purposes.

b. *The Intensive Summer Language Institutes*

One of the most prominent features of the Hampshire academic program is its intention to serve its own students, those who may be interested from the other four institutions, and students from elsewhere (ranging in age from their early teens or younger to late adulthood, and including independent students as well as those who may be enrolled in regular institutions)* in special summer programs.

*One model for such a range is the summer program of the University of Poitiers at Tours, where a class group has been known to include a ten-year-old English boy, a fifteen-year-old American boy, a twenty-four-year-old Australian girl, and a sixty-six-year-old Turkish businessman—as well as a number of others— all taking elementary French by the "direct method."

It is likely that, at least in the beginning, the Hampshire Foreign Language Institutes will be a small experimental program.* In time, the intention of the College is to build a highly active, large-scale summer program. One purpose will be to give Hampshire and other students who desire it intensive experience in elementary, intermediate, and advanced study *and use* of foreign languages. A second purpose will be to create, among the five institutions of the Valley, a unique and strong instructional service which will contribute to the educational resources of the five-college complex in a significant way. A third purpose will be, for a period of eight weeks, to make use of facilities at Hampshire which would otherwise stand vacant and idle. It is economically essential for the College to make as nearly full year-round use of its plant (residential as well as academic facilities) as possible.

The Hampshire Foreign Language Institutes will *not* be of the nature of usual "summer schools." They will instead be *total-culture simulations,* somewhat in the sense the 1966 Committee Report suggested:

> . . . taught exclusively by native speakers in a simulated foreign atmosphere in which students pledge themselves to hear and speak nothing but the language of their choice. . . . (The 1966 Report, p. 42)

If Spanish, for example, were the focus of an Institute, the simulation would perhaps take the following form, including elementary, intermediate, and advanced programs. One of the Houses (see the chapter on the College community and campus design) would be, in effect and as far as possible, converted into an Hispanic environment. All students of the Spanish Institute would live in the House cluster, as would their faculty. The dining hall would, to the degree feasible, serve food characteristic of Spanish and Latin American cuisine, *paella* instead of pork chops. Students and faculty would take all meals in the House. *Decor* would be altered in inexpensive but striking ways to increase the sense of being in a Spanish setting. All bulletin boards, announcements, directions, and the like would be solely in Spanish. Music available would be Latin; recreation activities, sports, and social customs would reflect Spanish culture; a modest House library of Spanish materials would re-

---

*In initial summers, it is planned to concentrate on only one Western European language and with a relatively small enrollment.

place any other House library collection; a news store would sell only Spanish-language newspapers, periodicals, and paperbacks. All conversation and all instruction would be in Spanish. Teaching would be done exclusively by faculty native to the tongue. This would mean assembling a temporary faculty from Spain, Latin America, or other parts of the United States.

A higher faculty-student ratio than that in the regular academic year would be needed. Tutorials and small-group instruction would be the predominant pedagogical mode. On frequent occasions, students would attend lectures, motion pictures, and other presentations in larger groups. All formal and informal instruction not requiring the laboratory would occur in the academic and lounge facilities of the House. The laboratory would, of course, be used daily.

Tests in the ordinary sense would be minimized. A Hampshire student desiring to complete his required language examination, however, might well do so through the Institute. Tuition charges for the Institute would at minimum equal those for one-half of a regular semester; room and board fees would approximate those for a similar period.

This description of a Spanish Institute as a total-culture simulation is abbreviated and oversimplified; it serves only as an illustration of the College's intent. Actual Institutes would be a matter for careful planning by the permanent foreign language staff of Hampshire during the regular academic year and for detailed management during the summer term. After the College's initial experimentation with an intensive summer program of this kind, it would be desirable and possible to mount several Institutes in different languages in each summer. Adjustment of certain of the Institutes to serve the teacher training purposes of the National Defense Education Act could be a useful service. The dual aim is to achieve as comprehensive summer offerings in language as the College can provide at a level of high quality, and to achieve as full summer use of campus plant as possible.

c. *The Opportunity for Language Study Abroad*

Hampshire students, because of the College's encouragement of sanctioned leaves and student sabbaticals, may find it convenient and useful to incorporate any further language proficiency development they need in residence abroad. At this stage, the College has no plans for establishing its own centers overseas as many other institutions have done. But Hampshire students financially able to do so will have opportunity to arrange academic and residence programs in other countries with the assistance of the College.

# 5

## THE ACADEMIC PROGRAM:
### Curriculum Models for a Divisional Sequence

*Self-education means two things—connected but not identical—first a desire on the part of the pupil to learn, and second a self-directed attention, a personal endeavor to acquire. . . . The second meaning of self-education—that of self-directed attention, a voluntary use of the mind for a conscious purpose—increases in importance with the maturity of the student. . . .*

*To create artificially a voluntary effort on the part of students seems a contradiction in terms, and there has been a tendency in American education to avoid the paradox by making the effort as effortless as possible . . . [or] to assume that since the effort should be voluntary it must be exerted in some subject in which the student has a natural interest, with the result that he often proves to have a more natural interest in play, or in doing nothing, than in study. The fact is that in most people interest in serious things is not inborn. They do not do things because they are interested in them (although they think so) so much as they are interested in things because they do them.*

ABBOTT LAWRENCE LOWELL
In Henry Aaron Yeoman's
*Abbott Lawrence Lowell
1856–1943*

THE EDUCATIONAL REFORMS that Abbot Lawrence Lowell introduced during his tenure as president of Harvard remain on the record in some reproof of what was said earlier about the difficulty of changing the academic program of an institution, and the nominal limits such change

usually has if made.  If President Lowell's reforms represent an exception
to the rule of academic inertia, it is because he was an exceptional man,
who knew what he wanted and did not equivocate in going about getting
it.  His overhaul of the elective system, installation of the general examination, establishment of the tutorial system, setting up the "house" plan,
arranging the reading period, all were acts of decisive leadership.
Harvard's new chief after 1909 was no less monarchical in his own style
than President Eliot had been in his.

More to the point for Hampshire College than would be a discursive
comparison of presidential styles at Harvard, is to note the conditions of
self-education that President Lowell articulated.  His leadership at
Harvard was exercised in many ways with the deliberate intention of
resolving the apparent paradox mentioned in this chapter's epigraph.
He believed an institution could and should do things to teach its students
to teach themselves.  His reforms aimed "to create artificially a voluntary
effort," to set up the conditions which would lead to a "voluntary use
of the mind for a conscious purpose" as a habit of maturity.

But he had little patience with the notion that this could happen either
through conditions that were simply easy and pleasant or that relied
altogether on "natural interest."  The function of the institution in
educating for self-education required, in Lowell's view, a good deal more
than this.  It meant establishing at least two conditions:  expecting the
student to do some tangible, identifiable things, the *doing* of which would
be likely to kindle interest; and setting up mechanisms (e.g., tutorials,
houses, reading periods, etc.) which would *support the conversion of
interest into sustained voluntary effort.*

It is this view, in its own way, that Hampshire College takes in its
emphasis on self-education as a principal outcome for its students.  The
academic program at Hampshire avoids either a system of forced spoon-
feeding or a non-system in which the only direction given to studies is by
what President Lowell described as natural interest.  This course of action
is likely to please neither those who feel education should follow a strictly
prescribed set of lines and "cover everything important" within such
lines, nor those who feel education is good only when its lines are wholly
set by the student according to his "felt needs" and present interests.
Considering this, Hampshire may take comfort from a wise comment

Mendès-France once made when he was premier: that you can be fairly sure an international treaty is a good one if both sides are somewhat dissatisfied with it. On the other hand, it needs to be remembered that, for all his Gallic wisdom, Mendès-France had an even shorter tenure than most who have held that high office in his land! In any case, the broad outlines of Hampshire's *provisional* program of Divisional Studies are put in evidence.

## TABLE 1

### Main Outline of Divisional Sequence

*A Summary of Programs of Study Provisionally Presented in Chapter V*

1. THE PROGRAM OF STUDIES IN DIVISION I

   (Ordinarily a period of one academic year)

   a. The Fall Colloquy
   b. The Sequences A, B, C in Science as Inquiry
   c. The Division I Seminars and Tutorials in Humanities and the Social Sciences
   d. The Fall Term Case Study of Man
   e. The Fall Term Seminars in Logic, Language, and Value
   f. The Spring Term Lecture-Student Seminars in the Language of History
   g. The Midwinter Term
   h. The Reading Period

2. THE PROGRAM OF STUDIES IN DIVISION II

   (Ordinarily a period of two academic years)

   a. Sequences A, B in Science as Inquiry
   b. The Division II Seminars
   c. The Division II Lecture-Student Seminars
   d. The Division II Program of Independent Study
   e. The Midwinter Term
   f. The Reading Period

3. THE PROGRAM OF STUDIES IN DIVISION III

   (Ordinarily a period of one academic year)

   a. The Division III Advanced Study or Project
   b. The Division III Integrative Seminar

    c. Electives

    d. The Midwinter Term

    e. The Reading Period

### 1. The Program of Studies in Division I

It was suggested earlier that the purposes of Division I are to introduce students to the life and basic concerns of liberal education at Hampshire College. Such an introduction means first of all clarifying the concern of the College with the realization of self in society, and opening up an awareness of the complex sets of understandings which the College regards as relevant to this concern.

In addition, Division I proposes to give students direct experience in conceptual inquiry in the company of faculty scholars who have a command of disciplines with which to approach subjects and problems they are really interested in. Through such experience, students will be exposed from the beginning to the centrality of method and structured inquiry in the application of disciplines to subjects within fields, which in turn provide channels into the consideration of the larger questions of life.

Students in Division I will exercise and develop intellectual skills and attitudes which are basic to carrying on one's own education oneself. They will have, in addition to intellectual experience with inquiry, the experience of creative expression. The individual student will face challenges to work on his own, and he will need to work cooperatively with others on group tasks. Division I seeks to give the student experience in *relating himself both to a demanding academic program and a college microcosm of society, without alienation.*

Certain courses in Division I are planned to be useful for all students and are considered common courses. Other courses are intended to let students explore fields which they think might interest them, or to pursue studies in which they are already strongly interested, and are considered electives. No courses are compulsory, as noted in earlier discussion. In view of the field and integrative examinations, however, it is advisable for students to plan balanced programs which will give them an introduction to the four-field scope of the College as well as some initial depth in a single field.*

*For a provisional version of a balanced Division I program see the chart on the following page.

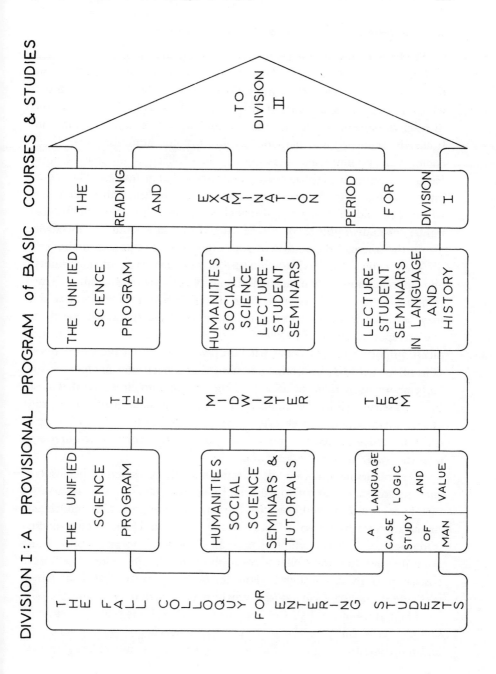

DIVISION I : A PROVISIONAL PROGRAM of BASIC COURSES & STUDIES

TO DIVISION II

THE READING AND EXAMINATION PERIOD FOR DIVISION I

THE UNIFIED SCIENCE PROGRAM

HUMANITIES SOCIAL SCIENCE LECTURE - STUDENT SEMINARS

LECTURE - STUDENT SEMINARS IN LANGUAGE AND HISTORY

THE MID-WINTER TERM

THE UNIFIED SCIENCE PROGRAM

HUMANITIES SOCIAL SCIENCE SEMINARS & TUTORIALS

A LANGUAGE
A CASE STUDY OF MAN — LOGIC AND VALUE

THE FALL COLLOQUY FOR ENTERING STUDENTS

### a.  *The Entering Student and the Fall Colloquy*

Students come to college today in far greater number and variety than in times not long past. They come because they cannot afford not to if they have middle-class aspirations. They come to an institution which is usually as authoritarian as the high school. In it, they find themselves dependent on the interests and moods of teachers and controlled in residence and activities by institutional administrators. They come with oversimplified ideas about what college is and means, most frequently seeing it as the necessary door to job opportunities. They come into a setting where there is usually less choice than they wish for, where they find that, as in high school, students do not have inalienable rights, nor many rights at all. As Martin Meyerson has put it: "Students are on the fringe of the adult world, but not in it. They are in limbo." [119]

They enter college with a mixture of high expectation, uncertainty, and apprehension. Their naiveté about college can be poignant. They come from the forced spoon-feeding of high school into a world which may bewilder them with its ambiguity or frustrate them because there is more spoon-feeding than ever, a high school with knobs on. Of immense importance, they come with unspoken and often unformed questions about self and the world, questions that schools and parents assiduously never asked them to ask. And they come with little knowledge of the ways liberal education could help them to ask such questions as men and women. College more often than not does little to listen to their questions unless forced to, and less to link and transform their questions into the stuff of exciting education.

The academic program of Hampshire College therefore begins for entering students with a two-week Fall Colloquy which is a sharp departure from ordinary freshman first-semester experience. The model assumes an entering group of 360, divided into four House groups of 90 students each. The intention of the Fall Colloquy is to give students an accurate sense that the College sees them as people, that education is not abstracted from life, but when right, is absolutely engaged with knowing and understanding life and the universe in which it occurs.

The nature of the Fall Colloquy in general terms is that of an intensive two-week full program or workshop in which all entering students and representative faculty of the Schools take part. It introduces students to the College, its Schools, and its disciplines in the context of a concentrated exercise with problems of the nature of man. These problems are approached in the Fall Colloquy at two levels: the level of the entering student as a person in society, and the level of the trained scholar of the College. The Fall Colloquy precedes and pre-empts all other college work for the entering student.

Two highly specific purposes of the Colloquy are: (a) to open up problems of life as seen by students and by mature scholars, and (b) to expose some of the means that the educated intellect can use to get at such problems and gain understanding of them. In sum, the Colloquy will demonstrate the asking of questions at the commonsense level and the use of analytical tools (disciplines applied to subjects in fields) in dealing with specific phenomena, the reality in which "problems" reside or take form.

## (1. *A Provisional Model of the Fall Colloquy*

The following discussion presents a tentative model for illustrative purposes. In College operation, the Fall Colloquy will be given specific form by the leaders of the Schools and faculty members who conduct the Colloquy. The following, then, is not at all a blueprint, but one rough sketch among many possibilities. The schematic drawing of a provisional schedule to be followed for two weeks (see following page) should be considered in this light.

It should be emphasized that the morning and afternoon schedule of the Fall Colloquy is *not* intended to resemble the usual "freshman orientation" programs found in many colleges. Mornings and afternoons in the Colloquy are occupied principally with an introduction to the educational concerns, intellectual organization, and disciplines of inquiry and expression of the College. Introduction to the College as a community— and "orientation" in the traditional sense—will occur mainly in small and large House meetings in the evening.

The present illustrative model of the Fall Colloquy deliberately has a global topic as its point of focus: the human condition. Three questions which Jerome Bruner has used in pedagogical experimentation are raised in connection with the topic:

What is human about human beings?

# THE FALL COLLOQUY

PROVISIONAL SCHEDULE—MODEL OF A TWO-WEEK INSTITUTE FOR ENTERING STUDENTS

| MONDAY | TUESDAY | WEDNESDAY | THURSDAY | FRIDAY |
|---|---|---|---|---|
| LECTURE | LECTURE | LECTURE | LECTURE | LECTURE |
| STUDENT-LED GROUPS OF SIX | STUDENT-LED GROUPS OF SIX | STUDENT-LED GROUPS OF SIX | STUDENT-LED GROUPS OF SIX | STUDENT-LED GROUPS OF SIX |
| GENERAL SESSION: QUESTIONS | GENERAL SESSION: QUESTIONS | GENERAL SESSION: QUESTIONS | GENERAL SESSION: QUESTIONS | GENERAL SESSION: QUESTIONS |

LUNCHEONS .... FREE TIME .... INDIVIDUAL CONFERENCES

| | | | | |
|---|---|---|---|---|
| FREE AFTERNOON | ORIENTATION TO A SCHOOL FIELD — LECTURE-DISCUSSION ON A SELECTED SUBJECT AND MATERIALS — GROUPS OF 45 | SEMINAR EXERCISE ON SUBJECT AND MATERIALS — GROUPS OF 15 | ORIENTATION TO A SCHOOL FIELD — LECTURE-DISCUSSION ON A SELECTED SUBJECT AND MATERIALS — GROUPS OF 45 | SEMINAR EXERCISE ON SUBJECT AND MATERIALS — GROUPS OF 15 |

| HOUSE MEETINGS EVENING | HOUSE MEETINGS EVENING | HOUSE MEETINGS EVENING | HOUSE MEETINGS EVENING | HOUSE MEETINGS EVENING |

How did man become human?
How can man become more human?[120]

The Colloquy approaches these questions *indirectly and directly* as an exercise which gives students an immediate chance to enter the intellectual-moral life of the College. The Colloquy pursues two general levels of discourse, seeking to involve all entering students and the full range of academic fields in the College.

In morning lecture sessions involving the whole entering group of 360, the level of discourse is what some might call Pop-intellectual—in the most honorable and non-condescending sense. Talk is about conditions of being human in the lives we lead now. It is the kind of talk, in a direct and often affect-laden fashion, that adults are used to in some degree. And it is the kind of talk from which adults usually exclude youth. Discourse is about things that people feel deeply and which affect their lives profoundly. To the extent possible, the actual subjects or questions for morning lecture-discussion sessions in the Colloquy should be suggested by the students themselves.

Lectures might begin things for forty minutes or so each morning. They may take any form that is honest and effective, using whatever means—a man talking, a film, a demonstration, a telelecture from a distant place, or whatever. The basic requirements are that such presentations—no matter in what style—be intellectually and morally provocative on solid ground, and be cast in terms of contemporary conditions. They should be neither preachy, glib, facetious, condescending, nor too technical. Their themes should tap into the lives students have led, into where they are presently, into what they wonder about, want, enjoy, and fear.

Stating examples of themes that might do this is hazardous; they may seem more banal than relevant or provocative. Some quickly free-associated examples, which may make the whole idea seem an effort to revive Chautauqua, include: "Education, or What to Do Until Big Brother Comes"; "Science: The Glorious Entertainment" (*vide* Jacques Barzun); "Woman: Inventing a Future"; "The American Family: What Its Chances Are"; "Man and Work, or How to Succeed in Life Without Really Dying"; "Sex: Myth, Reality, and Meaning"; "Art: What Its Radar Tells Us of Ourselves"; Death: Its Uses in Life"; "Self:

The Quest for Identity"; "Fun, or Listening for the Last Laugh"; "Joy: Looking for the Bluebird."

After the lecture session, there would be a short break. Then, continuing in the same room, students would be asked to form themselves into small circles of six, with one student in each circle asked at random to take over the leading of discussion. Such small discussion groups are easily and quickly formed without any elaborate procedure, and can be organized effectively within assemblies of very large size. Most of today's American youth take to flexible groupings for discussion with ease and a certain amount of genuine competence.*

Each day's groupings are likely to vary in composition by chance if not by plan; such variation is something to encourage. Each day as a circle meets it has two jobs. One is to make its members acquainted with each other; this is well worth the time it takes. The second task is to formulate what the group agrees is the most important question or point to raise for further discussion—if possible—by the lecturer. Once formulated, the question or point is put in writing by a member of the group and given to the leader of the general session; the whole process of student discussion will have taken thirty minutes or so. Everyone has a chance to be heard and seen; everyone has been asked to think.

After another short break, the larger group reassembles. The lecturer then takes on a selected variety of points or questions that were generated in the student discussions. He does so alone, or with a panel of faculty and/or students, or in a variety of ways. Many combinations of large group-small group interplay and many methods of presentation may be used. At the close of the general session, a faculty member or dean gives a concise review of discussion, emphasizing questions that remain—as most of the important ones will—unresolved.

At noon and in the early afternoon, the Colloquy leaves time open for luncheon at a civilized pace, for individual conferences, for casual games or walks or just plain loafing.

In the afternoon session of approximately two hours, there is a marked change in the character and organization of discourse, hopefully without

*It is likely that, in connection with the Fall Colloquy and with many other phases of instruction at Hampshire, professional faculty and student teaching associates would need some simple but essential training in the uses of variable group methods of discussion.

losing touch with whatever sparks were struck in the morning. Afternoon discourse also is about being human, about the sources and processes of man's becoming human, and about future possibilities. But these matters —the very edge of them only, of course—are touched *through the disciplines in the four fields of the Schools.*

Each School has two afternoon sessions of two hours' duration on two consecutive days, with all entering students participating. Unlike the morning discourse, the afternoon draws upon materials of times long past or of great cultural distance from America today.

In the first of its two-hour sessions, a School meets with students in eight lecture-student discussion groups of forty-five. The first session of two hours focuses on a selected subject approachable by one or more disciplines in the field; e.g., the School of the Social Sciences faculty might raise and discuss the apparently simple question of what a tool is. Here again the pedagogical techniques used would include small-group student-led discussion to supplement faculty presentations and introduce in simple form the experience of the student-led seminar.

In the second two-hour session the next day, the School meets with twenty-four seminar groups of fifteen, with selected materials having been read by students overnight. These materials should contain data, rather than interpretation, arising out of an event or a specific case and related to the more general discussion of the preceding afternoon. In this seminar session, School faculty lead students directly into the data; e.g., the second session of the School of Social Sciences sequence might examine the apparent inferable consequences for man of a single tool, such as the stern-post rudder or the horse collar.* The door could open on some beginning consideration of the proposition that while man maketh the tool, the tool maketh man.

---

*To one unacquainted with the history of technology in ancient and medieval times, the horse collar may sound like an hilariously bucolic topic for discussion. In fact, of course, the invention of the horse collar and the extension of its use during the course of the Middle Ages are felt by some scholars to have had a profound effect on the social and economic features of agrarian life and to have contributed to the long-term shift of European society out of quasi-slavery as a principal source of power for production. The Romans, for all their engineering brilliance, had not developed a collar against which a horse could draw, applying pressure at the strong skeletal structure of his shoulders. Instead, they used what amounted to a noose around the horse's neck. Horses, being notoriously wise, in

(2. *Some Possible Results*

By the close of the Fall Colloquy students have had a view of the College and some of its larger concerns. They will have had a taste of active student participation in discussion of matters education usually treats as too big or vague to take time for. They will have been briefly in large lectures, in very small groups, in lecture-student discussion sessions, and in discipline-centered seminars. They will have gotten acquainted with each other to some degree, and will have talked with faculty and staff in a situation without grades or tests; they will have been treated as intelligent human beings. They will have seen the Schools in action and the College alive.

b. *The Sequences in Science as Inquiry*

The rationale for the centrality of method and conceptual inquiry in liberal education is nowhere clearer than in the natural and social sciences. The notion of education as conceptual inquiry has moved a number of leading scholars to attempt curriculum reform in the secondary schools; Jerrold Zacharias and his associates in physics provide a principal example. Examples in other fields are numerous.

The older idea of science as a bounded area of knowledge to be filled in by further research and experimentation assumed there were fixed principles that guided scientific work. *But the principles were not viewed as problems themselves.*[121] Professor Joseph Schwab argues that:

> . . . it is precisely here that our system of rewards and of education has been remiss. We have maximized the social, financial, and psychological rewards for technical and stable contributions—new fuels, new missile designs, new vaccines. . . . Where we have at all designed our school and science programs to attract young people to the sciences, the designs have been shaped to attract the potentially competent technician and the avid, able, but docile learner. Our teaching

consequence did not push forward with full strength; doing so would have strangled them. When the horse collar came on the scene in Europe in the early medieval period, available horse-power was dramatically increased simply because a horse could push forward with full strength in drawing a load and still not choke to death. Why didn't the Romans develop or apply this fantastically simple device? Why did it begin to appear in the early medieval period? What consequences did it have?

laboratories invite students to discover the satisfaction of techniques mastered. They emphasize the desirability of patience, accuracy, and precision. They testify to the soundness of existing knowledge. But rarely indeed do they invite students to discover the limitations of present knowledge or to identify unsolved problems and areas of ignorance. Much less do they invite students to invent, devise and explore possibilities alternative to current formulations. Our classroom work is imbued with the same dye of established law and accepted knowledge.[122]

Professor Schwab's criticisms appear to underestimate the achievements of those like Zacharias in secondary school reform and to undervalue the exciting work of such master teachers as Professor Arnold Arons in physics at Amherst. But despite such exceptions, his argument applies to much of science teaching in school and college today.

There is a simple need to approach science teaching in a spirit consonant with what actually happens in the best of science. This requires *putting a critical—and perhaps creative—examination of the organizing principles of each science discipline directly into the process of teaching the discipline itself.* One leading physicist, Professor Leon Lederman, has reacted to this proposition as the best teachers would: "But, but . . . this *is* the way we teach it!! How else?" [123]

The point in emphasizing inquiry is *not* simply to teach the tools for acquiring knowledge. In the sense of learning essential principles, methods, and techniques for carrying on one's own education and work, this is obviously a valid end. It is a large part of the justification for advocating the centrality of method in the modern collegiate curriculum. But a higher justification lies in seeing methodology itself as a proper object for scrutiny and reconceptualization *in the process* of education. The centrality of method could be interpreted simply as meaning the acquisition of static knowledge, in this case *knowledge about* (as Whitehead would have said) conceptual and analytical tools. So interpreted, we are left again with inert ideas, and emphasis on inquiry could be just one more dead-end in the search for a viable modern curriculum. The full interpretation of centrality of method—*not in science alone*—should make clear that *method* is as much (or more) important to think about critically and imaginatively as any *object* of study or research. Indeed, it is inseparable from the research problem and its object.

Education which encourages such thinking occurs when the direct use of tools of inquiry with real problems of knowledge is accompanied by inquiry into the tools themselves and the structure of ideas behind them. This is the route to the highest skill: the innovation of more adequate concepts, the creative formulation of change.

In this full view of the centrality of method, Daniel Bell sees:

> . . . a positive new role for the college as an institution standing between the secondary school and graduate research work. One of its fundamental purposes must be to deal with the modes of conceptualization, the principles of explanation, and the nature of verification. . . . The emphasis in the college must be less on what one knows and more on the self-conscious ground of knowledge; how one knows what one knows, and the principle of the relevant selection of facts.[124]

The rationale reviewed above implies that certainly in the natural sciences (including mathematics), and in other fields as well, the best curriculum will involve the student in concrete experience with a discipline at work on actual problems. The student needs to see firsthand how the discipline goes about its business, what its techniques and principles are as applied in real cases. Hypothesis, experiment, observation, conceptualization, and ordered interpretation need to be gotten at—without blind acceptance—with one's hands on substance which would be intractable without such tools. Abstract treatment of the elements of discipline will not do the job.

Beyond this principle, two other main factors affect the provisional design of the science sequences in the Hampshire College academic program.

One of these factors, emphasized in the *Report* of the 1966 Educational Advisory Committee, is the growing interdependence of the science disciplines. The need seemed clear, in the judgment of the Committee, for Hampshire College to establish from the beginning a two-year unified mathematics-science program for prospective scientists. Development of such programs at the University of Michigan,[125] at the University of California,[126] and elsewhere, is taking place; the Committee judged that even the relatively limited experimentation with unified programs in other institutions is sufficiently promising to warrant a full effort in this direction at Hampshire. The Committee was especially concerned that prospective scientists entering Hampshire should receive a flexible, well integrated, basic mathematics-science offering of high quality. The Committee concluded that the College should be fully able both to do this in the first two years of student work, and to provide adequate course work for non-science students.

A second factor affecting curriculum in science at Hampshire was touched upon in the earliest section of the present document. This is the difficulty the small independent college now faces in providing sufficient faculty strength and quality, and sufficient research facilities and opportunities, to insure advanced undergraduate preparation in science, commensurate with the requirements for entrance into the better graduate schools. *It is manifest that Hampshire cannot expect to provide such advanced preparation on its own.*

The current approximation of Hampshire's science program shows a realistic recognition of this limitation. The science program of the College is based on the assumption that adequate strength in advanced science preparation for Hampshire students can be assured *only through interinstitutional collaboration in the Valley.* In the foreseeable future, the latter assumption is very likely to be true for science students of *all* of the Valley institutions, considered singly. The 1966 Committee commented that:

> It is in the area of upper-level science that Hampshire College might make significant use of five-college cooperation. Many existing science departments among the four colleges would welcome more students at this level. Hence it would not be necessary to offer the full range of advanced courses at Hampshire.[127]

Hampshire College is grateful for this opinion and trusts that it represents an actual and generous readiness of the other four institutions to help supply Hampshire science majors with the advanced specialized work they need. On the other hand, Hampshire believes in mutuality as the essence of cooperation and would have no intention of being an uncontributing partner. Advanced offerings at Hampshire will be strong in certain limited areas. Hopefully, these will complement offerings at the other institutions and give their students special opportunities that would otherwise be unavailable.

The science sequences for Division I (and in part of Division II) outlined briefly here must be viewed as the very tentative models they are.

Again, in the process of developing Hampshire in the next several years, the *operational* models will be planned by faculty of the College, in consultation with faculty at the other institutions of the Valley, and with other expert advice.

### (1. *Science as Inquiry: Sequence A*

This two-year sequence would begin in Division I and carry forward into Division II. It would be offered to entering students of very high proficiency and interest in mathematics and science, demonstrated in their secondary school work, on test scores, and in interviews before or during the Fall Colloquy. Enrollment in Sequence A would be a matter upon which such students would then decide for themselves. Projection of enrollment is virtually impossible at this stage of the College's development, but for purposes of this model, it is assumed that twenty per cent or 72 students in an entering class of 360 would elect Sequence A.

Sequence A students would go at once into a highly flexible program conducted by a team of faculty which would include a mathematician, a physicist, a biologist, and a chemist. The faculty team, within only such limits as those imposed by other commitments of their own and of their students, would work out matters of scheduling, selection of subjects for study and their sequential arrangement, the relationship between mathematics instruction and work in the science disciplines, desired variations in seminar-lecture-laboratory-tutorial patterns, adjustments of program to the individual abilities of students, and the like. The faculty team would not be engaged in offering a survey course. Their work with students would focus on specific problems of interest to themselves as mature scholars. Specific problems would be ordered in such a way as to enable the separate and common strategies of inquiry of the several disciplines to come into play and be examined. Faculty would seek, as it seemed right to do so, to bring students into a colleague status, as research associates, scientists engaged in individual studies, tutors of other students, and in other ways.

It seems likely that mathematics would be the spine of Sequence A, with the science disciplines hooking in to exploit the tools of mathematics in the exercise of their own methodologies. In the two-year sequence, students would deal with such features of mathematics as calculus, linear algebra, differential equations, probability, and matrix analysis. Elements of the science disciplines would be selected by the faculty team in terms of maximum utility in revealing basic structures of inquiry. The course would be a heavy one in the degree to which it involved student time, occupying between eight and nine hours a week of organized participation or independent work during the two years.

Students who found Sequence A to be something they did not wish to continue with could move out of it into Sequences B or C before the Division I field examination in the Natural Sciences. In the second year of Sequence A, those who wished to could move to Sequence B, or to another program altogether. Contrariwise, unusually able students on occasion might move forward in Sequence A and beyond it on a timetable suited to their abilities. It is probable that Sequence A would require the equivalent of three full-time faculty for its staffing.

## (2. *Science as Inquiry: Sequence B*

This year and one-half sequence also would begin in Division I and continue into Division II. Sequence B would be available to all entering students. It should be considered especially by those who demonstrate a good degree of proficiency and preparation in secondary school mathematics and science, who are motivated by a degree of intrinsic interest these disciplines have for them, and who plan to go forward in a discipline (for example, in the Social Sciences, or Language Studies) where a fundamental command of mathematics through probability and statistics is now essential. Here again, any accurate projection of enrollment size is impossible at this stage. For purposes of the present model, an arbitrary projection of forty per cent, or 144 students, is made for Sequence B.

Students electing to enroll in Sequence B would have a choice between a three-semester mathematics-biology workshop or a three-semester workshop in mathematics-physics. In either case, the mathematics elements would be likely to include introduction to calculus, intermediate calculus and linear algebra, and an introduction to probability and statistics. Physics dealt with might include selected topics and problems from mechanics, kinematics, wave motion, relativity, optics, atomic and nuclear structure, and electricity. Biology would provide selected problems and topics relevant to such matters as biology's relation to chemistry, principles of cellular structure, hypotheses concerning genetic action in the control of cellular processes, and the ecology of living organisms and their environments.

Ecological studies will be given considerable emphasis in the Sequence B math-biology option. It is planned to offer Divisions II and III advanced study in problems of human ecology in the contemporary world, using cross-field resources of the School of Natural Sciences and the School of Social Sciences. Hampshire hopes that advanced study in contemporary human ecology will be particularly useful to women students who would find it helpful to them in later careers, community service, and leadership. Dr. Esther Raushenbush, in consultation with Hampshire leadership, has urged that the College make an especial effort to provide women students with opportunity for background in the biological sciences. Dr. Raushenbush's argument in this direction is not so much aimed at the preparation of young women for graduate work in biology, as it is at enabling them to have a greater range of realistic and challenging choices in later life. She is persuasive to Hampshire that young women will benefit from a grounding in the elements of biological science, and a grasp of the possibilities of applied biology in improving man's lot. Benefits would lie in their being better able to continue to learn in fields which are uniquely open to women for careers and social action.

In any case, students electing either option in Sequence B would enter workshop groups, each with an enrollment of approximately twenty-four. Again, purely for the use of this model as an illustration, an arbitrary assumption is made about enrollment. It is assumed that elections of math-biology and math-physics in Sequence B will be equal, with 72 students in each option. The groups are called "workshops," since they are something of a combination of lecture-class, faculty-led seminar, student-led seminar, and laboratory. They would be staffed in each case by a team of a mathematician and a natural scientist. Of the two, the natural scientist would give twice the time given by the mathematician, because of the former's involvement with laboratory work. For a mathematician, a workshop would constitute one-third of ordinary load; for a natural scientist, a workshop would account for two-thirds of his assigned load. The two-man team would not meet the workshop together in the usual course of things, but they would plan together in deciding what topics and problems interested them most and, at the same time, would be most productive as student exercises in inquiry. Each faculty team would determine for itself what the specific inquiry exercises and materials of the workshop would be.

The pedagogical style of the workshop would be participant, as well as demonstrational, with frequent student-led small group exercises in problem-solving, independent student work with inexpensive equipment, and other activities and projects. It would be preferable to schedule workshop sessions in substantial blocks of time to include both work with mathematics and work in biology or physics within the same block of several hours. This is in contrast with college patterns where "class" sessions and "lab" sessions are quite separate. One schedule-model might be three blocks of roughly three hours per week. It is estimated that Sequence B would require the equivalent of four to six full-time faculty in each of its three semesters. As the College comes to a level of full student strength, it should be possible for advanced undergraduate science students to serve as paid research associates or teaching assistants in Sequence B.

## (3. *Science as Inquiry: Sequence C*

This one-year sequence would be completed in Division I. Certain entering students will have strong non-science interests and are likely to pursue them in humanities and the arts. As with other students, these young men and women will have taken basic college preparatory sciences and mathematics in secondary school and will have presented scores on relevant College Entrance Examination Board tests prior to admission to Hampshire. It is assumed, therefore, that they will enter the College with some degree of background in these fields. It is also expected that they will stand for the Division I field examination in the Natural Sciences. Again an arbitrary assumption about enrollment size is made: the projection used in this model is that forty per cent, or 144 entering students, would opt for Sequence C.

With these characteristics, assumptions, and expectations in view, Sequence C would afford the entering student an election which would increase his general literacy in science and mathematics without making demands on him which would be irrelevant to his long-term interests. Students in Sequence C would enter a program with two large group lectures a week and a minimum block of two hours weekly in laboratory-discussion sections with enrollments of approximately twenty. The lectures would include demonstrations and other presentations. The laboratory sections would be occupied with problem-solving, group and individual projects and experiments, and analytical discussion led both by instructors and students.

The first semester would be concerned with the nature of mathematics, and would be organized to introduce students to the nature of mathematical thinking. It would treat mathematics as a separate discipline and seek to help students discover a sense of its elegance and poetry. The first semester of Sequence C would not aim at "training for mathematical proficiency." Instead, it would pursue—according to the judgment and interest of the faculty responsible—a limited series of manageable topics in some depth. The purpose of such exercises would be to engage students with some of the joy and sense of structure in mathematics which are too often obliterated by bad teaching. Here the style of the brilliant work of David Page at ESI in introducing ten-year-olds to higher mathematics-without-jargon, and the work of Professor Patrick Suppes at Stanford might be helpful for faculty to consider.

In the second semester, Sequence C would turn from mathematics to the nature of science. Again, the approach would be to catch some awareness of the human and artistic elements that reside in the conceptual processes and structures of scientific inquiry. Something of the part "the intuitive leap" plays in scientific research; something of the fact that a cut-and-dried "scientific method" is regarded as a laughable myth by scientists, and why; something of the emergence of a true single-language (in the sense, for example, of mutually respected and understood canons of verification) world community of scientists—these are things the second half of Sequence C might try to get at. Again, the method of pedagogy should rest on selected topics or case-studies in depth, not on "coverage" or proficiency training. Again, the pedagogy of both the lecture and the section should aim at as much direct engagement with problems and materials as possible. The topics and subjects chosen would depend on the instructor's interest and his own discipline.

It is estimated that Sequence C would require the equivalent of 1.65 full-time faculty members each semester.

Implicit in the foregoing discussion of Sequences A, B, and C is that the Division I School field examination in the Natural Sciences would have a somewhat different level of difficulty for each Sequence.

c. *Division I Seminars and Tutorials in Humanities and the Social Sciences*

The *New College Plan* of 1958 introduced the notion of the freshman seminar, principally as a means to help the entering student at once to gain greater academic independence and maturity. The Plan called for two freshman seminars in the first fall term: one in humanities and one in the social sciences. The concept was a bold and original one a decade ago; it has had application and a considerable testing at other institutions in the intervening years.

As will be seen, Hampshire's academic program adheres to the earlier notion in essentials, but with certain modifications that seem indicated by present circumstances. The College, for a number of reasons, intends to use a sequence of basic seminars in each of the two regular semesters (Fall and Spring) of the Division I year, rather than two seminars in the Fall Term only, as the 1958 Plan suggested. In addition, the College will use individual tutorials in the Oxford sense in conjunction with the Fall Term Division I seminars. Before describing the College's Division I seminar-tutorial system, it would be useful to look back to 1958. A great deal of what was said then about the freshman seminar idea is incorporated into the operation of Hampshire's Division I seminars:

> The New College curriculum is designed to establish a pattern of independent behavior by intensive training in it at the outset, and to reinforce the habit of initiative thereafter by continuing to provide situations which call for it. Hence the very large investment of faculty time in the freshman seminars of the first term and the combination, thereafter, of student seminars with lecture courses: once established, a way of doing things can be kept going with diminishing reinforcement. So the curriculum gives up the customary pyramid which provides a broad base of factual knowledge in survey courses during the early years and an apex of specialized study in the later departmental seminar and thesis, where the student learns the tools of a scholarly discipline. Breadth of knowledge is certainly essential; but really to know goes with knowing how to know. Broad knowledge will not be

pre-digested for New College students; it will come as a natural consequence of exploration, of "getting around" in their subjects.

Methods are best introduced, not in the abstract, but in action. The fall freshman seminars will teach methodology by exploring limited subjects, each teacher deciding on a subject and its limits with a view to best showing a group of about thirteen students how he works, and how they can work, in using his discipline. There need be no effort to be novel, either in the disciplines presented or the topics used, except as novelty happens because of the way the main line of a man's intellectual development is going. . . . In the course of educational experiences there is more probability of developing good intellectual practices if some attention is paid to method as well as to content. But the experience must be specific and clear, rather than broad and diffuse—so the subjects treated in the freshman seminars will be limited in scope. It will be valuable for the teachers of the various different seminars to cooperate, as they see opportunities, in arranging that their students hear lectures together on subjects of common interest, or encounter approaches whose differences and likenesses will illuminate the methods each group is learning to use.

Seminars in History would neither be in "Western Europe from the Fall of Rome to the Atom Bomb," nor yet in "Historiography," but in subjects like "The Civil War," "The Age of Absolutism, 1648-1789," or "The Age of Pericles." Similarly, neither "Beowulf to Thomas Wolfe," nor "Principles of Criticism and Methods of Literary History" would be offered; instead literary history and criticism would be presented as activities by working intensively with limited materials. The curriculum proposed at New College will make the students' first college experience sharply different from what most of them will have had in school—as is too often not the case with present freshman programs. They will encounter a scholar working with materials which are alive for him with excitement, perplexities, alternatives, problems, unexplored possibilities. Instructors will have the advantage of working in areas they have chosen because of strong interests. . . . Students will quickly be assigned work to be performed independently, the instructor designing projects for which the freshman will have or can acquire the necessary frame of reference, and in which he will encounter, as he works, fundamental problems of the topic and the discipline. A problem which all will encounter will be "How to Write." Teachers will have to spend a great deal of time teaching composition, as it relates to their field. . . . The art of behavior in a scholarly group will be taught along with the art of the conduct of the mind.[128]

One institution that, in its own way and for its own reasons, has given an adaptation of the freshman seminar notion substantial trial is Harvard College. In 1963, after four years of experience with freshman seminars as a new form of elective, a subcommittee of the Committee on Educational Policy of the Harvard Faculty of Arts and Sciences reported on an evaluation of the idea in action. The subcommittee's main conclusion was that continuance of the freshman seminar program on a permanent basis was important.[129] Difficulties and problems were found, as might be expected, but it was believed "the College has developed a way of teaching its first-year students that has great vitality and significance." *

The Harvard evaluation commented that the "seminars, in their inquiries, have demonstrated that undergraduates can tolerate ambiguity and that ideas have more impact when they are evolved than when they are given." [130] Several specific points that interest Hampshire in the evaluation's conclusions are these:

Faculty and students have frequently noted what one student called the "multiplier" effect of the seminars—"its effects on my friends and roommates." It may be that the effect operates more powerfully out of seminars than out of other teaching.

There is considerable evidence which suggests that what is learned in seminars is often better retained that what is learned in courses.

The seminars have been "metaphoric." They have served, at their best, to represent to the student more than they have covered. . . .[131]

The Harvard evaluation had been anticipated in 1962 by an objective report written by Professor C. L. Barber,[132] describing the nature and results of a four-college trial of freshman seminars and "student seminars associated with upper-class lecture courses." The latter was another innovation suggested in the *New College Plan*. In 1959-60, a group of some of the best-known faculty at Mount Holyoke, Smith, and Amherst Colleges and the University of Massachusetts experimented with these approaches. The experimentation again was encouraged and sup-

*The subcommittee report contains no reference to the genesis of the freshman seminar notion in the *New College Plan*, but the copy of it in Hampshire's possession does include an unsigned hand-written inscription on the title page "with long overdue thanks to New College"!

ported as had been the New College study, by the Ford Foundation's Fund for the Advancement of Education.

It was the general conclusion of Professor Barber's report that, given the limitations under which the four-college trial was conducted, the freshman seminars and other new approaches were useful. Professor Barber commented that: "Introduced in a scattering of individual courses, piecemeal, the innovations obviously could not be expected to work as they might as regular features of a curriculum." Instructors found that in the new approach "more of their time, rather than less, was required." But the general feeling of the faculty and students who tried the new approaches was that they were good and should be effective within a generally supportive curriculum. Professor Barber's report observed that:

> . . . The general conclusion which can be affirmed, categorically, is that students work well independently only when a clear-cut academic situation has been created for them. If, when they are left alone, they find themselves merely in a social situation, the occasion may amount to little more than ineffectual faculty interference with their social life. When they are provided with a universe of discourse and common awareness of problems, they show readiness to take off and move on their own.

> In the Freshman Seminars, very considerable success was achieved by putting students "in the position of scholars," confronted by a limited range of material to be dealt with in some depth. To do this at the freshman level requires a great deal of faculty supervision: the more they are put on their own by the nature of the problem and the openness of assignments, the more aid and counsel they need. Results are best when the formulation of issues by the instructor is particularly clear-cut, for then the students find for themselves that they need the resources of the discipline to solve their problem. A teacher who has active research interests, on which he can draw, is most likely to succeed in introducing a subject in this way: he is most likely to have the courage to cut his students loose at intervals. Our experience indicates that for such teachers to undertake seminar teaching of freshmen is well worth it, in view of the zest, sophistication and capacity for self-direction which can be developed in the students at the outset of their college opportunity.[133]

The Hampshire College academic program incorporates the notion put forward in 1958 and gives it, plus related tutorials, a central place in the Division I offering.

As the chapter on campus design and college community organization will make clear, Hampshire will decentralize a good deal of its academic work in facilities related to residential clusters called Houses, each in a way a small college. When the College has achieved full strength in its fourth year of operation, each of four House clusters will include approximately 360 students, and approximately sixteen faculty members, representing the four Schools, will have their office-studies in each House's academic building. Of this number, perhaps twelve will be members of the faculties of the Schools of Humanities and the Arts, and the Social Sciences.

The entering class in each House would number about ninety men and women students.

( 1. *The Fall Term Division I Humanities-Social Science Seminars and Tutorials*

In the present illustrative model, the entering class of 360 would enroll in thirty Division I Seminars, approximately evenly divided between the School of Humanities and Arts and the School of Social Sciences. Each House would have seven or eight Division I Seminars of approximately twelve students under the leadership of resident House faculty in the fields of the Humanities and the Social Sciences. These would begin after the two-week Fall Colloquy and would run for twelve weeks. The number of Fall Term Seminars in Division I would be thirty, as noted, offering a relatively wide variety of choice—subject only to enrollment limits—to the entering student. Students could enroll in Seminars either in their own Houses or in other Houses.

The individual faculty member would meet with his group each week for a seminar on a subject of study or research of particular interest to him in his discipline and field.* Scheduling would be at his discretion and the convenience of all concerned, with evening hours a likely time.

*In connection with the Division I Fall Term Seminars led by faculty of the School of Humanities and Arts, it is expected that some of these—as many as the faculty involved would desire to have and be able to staff—would in effect be small workshop or studio groups interested in creative expression in the lively arts. In other words, Humanities Seminars would not all be concerned with matters of academic scholarship.

By now, this kind of pattern is well-established. The Muscatine Report, noting that Harvard and Stanford now offer thirty-five freshman seminars a year, in 1966 urged that Berkeley institute freshman seminars "at the earliest possible moment":

> Such freshman seminars should consist of groups of no more than twelve students, taught by members of the faculty in whatever areas of intellectual discourse a faculty member is inclined to meet entering students. The subject matter of all such seminars need not be strictly determined as long as the orientation is one of dialogue and the spirit of inquiry. Each, faculty member offering a freshman seminar would act as academic adviser to the seminar students.[134]

In the Hampshire program, *each Division I Seminar member would also have a tutorial relationship to the faculty member in charge of the twelve-week Fall Term Seminar which he had elected.* Perhaps in connection with the specific subject matter of the Fall Seminar, but possibly in other reaches of his discipline or School field, the faculty leader would suggest an organized reading program to the individual student and would expect the student to prepare a paper every other week during the Fall Term dealing with an agreed-upon topic related to the reading. The faculty member would schedule half of the students in his Seminar group for individual tutorials each week. The tutorial process preferably would be very like that at Oxford, described succinctly by the Lord Franks Report:

> At its heart is a theory of teaching young men and women to think for themselves. The undergraduate is sent off to forage for himself among a long list of books and journals and to produce a coherent exposition on the subject set. The essay or prepared work is then read by its author and criticized by the tutor. In this discussion the undergraduate should benefit by struggling to defend the positions he has taken up, by realizing the implications of the argument, and by glimpsing the context in which a more experienced scholar sees his problem. . . . [The] tutorial means that the undergraduate has to try his hand at creation under corrections.[135]

The Division I Fall Term Humanities-Social Science Seminar *cum* Tutorial system would require a faculty member to meet once a week for two hours or so with his Seminar group and to meet approximately six hours a week with individual students for tutorials. His tutorial time could be reduced by meeting with two students at once but a good deal would be lost in the process, as the Oxford Report indicates, and the strain on the tutor might well be more rather than less. Probably only one paper could be read at a session; the tutor would then have to arrange to read the other paper separately. Students in sessions who "merely listen and perhaps throw in an occasional opinion are not experiencing a tutorial but merely attending a class." [136]

Between Seminars and individual tutorial sessions, the faculty leader would give two-thirds of his teaching time to this program in the Fall Terms for twelve weeks of a fourteen-week semester.

(2. *The Spring Term Division I Humanities-Social Science Seminars*

During the Spring Term, Division I students would be able to choose from basic seminars similar in organization to those offered in the Fall Term. There would again be available approximately thirty Division I Seminars, about half of which would be in the Humanities and half in the Social Sciences. Each Division I Seminar would once more enroll up to approximately twelve students. There would be enough flexibility in this Term so that seminar size might in some cases go as high as fifteen. This could allow for a limited number of students in other Divisions to enroll in certain Division I Seminars that held special interest for them.

A Division I student would find it advisable usually to enroll in a Seminar offered by a School other than the one which had given his Fall Term Seminar. Thus a student who had been in a Humanities Seminar in the Fall Term of Division I would be likely to take a Social Science Seminar in the Spring Term.

Tutorials would not be given by Spring Term Division I Seminar faculty.

d. *The Division I Case Study of Man: Fall Term*

From the simplified chart of Division I Studies, it may seem that the third course in this divisional sequence is an unrelated mixture of things. Actually, it is instead an organized strand offering all 360 entering students a variety of related initial experiences in the integrative application of different disciplines to complex topics. All four fields of the

College have inter-relationships, and this may best be discovered through studies which tend to exercise the resources of more than one field.

*The pattern discussed here for Division I is again provisional and its curriculum content should be seen only as a set of models of possibility.* But the underlying principle of the third course is a commitment: that, in addition to elections within Natural Science, the Humanities, and the Social Sciences, entering students should encounter studies which reveal the intersection of disciplines and fields.

This is approached in the present model of the third course by (a) an intensive four-week ethnographic case study in the Fall Term which presents a large amount of magnificent data from the most advanced frontier of one very narrow discipline (that of eskimology, or the study of Eskimo culture and language—a field perhaps less than familiar to most American academicians!); (b) an introduction, during the balance of the Fall Term, to topics and problems in language, logic, and value; and (c) a Spring Term lecture-student seminar course dealing with a very limited set of studies-in-depth in language and history. These three portions of the third strand *might* be approached traditionally—but not in the Hampshire program. All invite, if not demand, attention from a variety of disciplines and fields. Hopefully, this will become evident as the models are presented in this discussion. The first portion of the third course—in this illustrative model—is called, for present convenience, A Case Study of Man.

The subject matter of the Case Study is man's life in a preliterate culture. The data concern a full year's cycle in the life of a Netsilik Eskimo family. The data are recorded on film. They are the result of a current major project supported by the National Science Foundation and undertaken by Educational Services Incorporated, with scholarly leadership by some of the most distinguished ethnographers in the world, with extensive filming done in the field by staff of the National Film Board of Canada, and with film editing done at the ESI film studios. It is not hyperbolic in any sense to say that these are probably the best ethnographic films of Eskimo life, representing it as it was before contact with white civilization, in the world. This is not to except Flaherty's classic of forty years ago, *Nanook*.

The films are not didactic. For the most part, while they are photographed in color and are technically near perfection in quality, they carry no sound. No voice of "The March of Time" tells you what you are seeing. You simply *see*. How *much* you see, *what* you perceive, *how* you interpret it, what it *means* to you, the *questions* that the data raise—all are up to the viewer.

There are eight films covering a sequence of four seasons. The films as they stand are basically ethnographic records, anthropological documents. Their principal subjects are the members of a non-fictional Netsilik nuclear family—a man, a wife, a four-year-old son. Each film is more than thirty minutes long; the total of eight is the result of many months of expert scholarly and technical editing of several hundred thousand feet of uncut film. Simply taking the film required expeditions to the Pelly Bay area of far northern Canada over a period of three years. One family, with some kin and others, go through a whole year: spring sealing, summer fishing at a stone weir, fall caribou hunting, early winter fishing through the ice, winter communal life at a big ceremonial igloo.

The films are not yet on commercial open-market sale; they are not yet being used in undergraduate college teaching anywhere. If they are so used in the future, they would ordinarily be seen in advanced study of anthropology and ethnography. The only scholar who has used the films in teaching is Professor Jerome S. Bruner, who has experimented extensively with extracts from the total footage in his studies of learning and instructional theory.

With the impact of culture shock, a contemporary American sees in these films a human world in tremendous contrast to life as he knows it. In the Netsilik world, there are food, work, family, childhood, mutual affection, anger, fun, pain, planning, travel, technology, art, life, death—whatever fundamental dimension of humanity one could name. But the guise these come in, the forms they take, are seldom the ones we know, to say the least. Such data and the questions imminent in them are what Lévi-Strauss calls "that mirror which other civilizations still hold up to us to recognize and study . . . [the] image of ourselves." [137]

The Netsilik material is unlike anything that entering college students will have met before. It is not entertainment. And it is not all just brutal shock for tender minds. Nor is the Netsilik material simply a vivid introduction to one branch of ethnography. Because of its richness and perfection as a record, and because of the almost endless number of doors it opens for cultural contrast and comparison, the Netsilik documentary series is potentially a powerful vehicle for instruction of an integrative kind. It is wide open to analysis by several disciplines and fields.

The material leads one to see that an integrative, multi-disciplinary approach can give a fuller understanding of man than can any single discipline alone. Take the act of hunting a seal and killing it at an air hole in the ice. Simple? Not at all. The act of the seal hunt and kill by a lone man on the stark ice is a microcosm of complexities; it is an economic act; it requires a technology; it depends on accurate knowledge of the physical environment (ice, wind, weather, etc.) and of the patterned behavior of animals; it is closely linked with social structure; it hinges on belief and magic, on a cosmology which accounts for seals and men and how they deal with each other; and it is—as you watch it— both a dance of life or death for seal or man, and for the man a definition of manhood as the living embodiment of courage. This single small episode in the Netsilik material can call into play nearly as many disciplines as you can name.

Such materials, inviting investigation from many disciplinary angles of vision, and with potential for revealing the essential relatedness of knowledge as well, are seldom used in any undergraduate curriculum.

Thus, an illustrative model of the third course in the Fall Term of Division I might begin with an interdisciplinary four-week Case Study of Man in a Preliterate Culture. All entering students would ordinarily undertake the Case Study. The School fields principally drawn upon in the Case Study would be the Humanities and Arts, the Social Sciences, and Language.

One among many ways the Case Study model could be organized is the following. During the first three weeks of the Case Study, the Netsilik documentaries would be seen in sequence by entering students as a whole group. In the first week, there would be one general lecture to the whole group of 360, and two film showings to the whole group. In the second and third weeks, there would be three film showings to the whole group each week. The schedule, as developed by a faculty team, would allow for a brief lecture-introduction to each piece of the filmed data. The main purpose of such introductions would be to begin the raising of questions about the data. After each large-group film session on a schedule determined by the faculty team, students would meet in eight lecture-student seminar groups of no more than forty-five, each under the leadership of one of the faculty team members.

As in other lecture-student seminars, the faculty leader would use some of the time for presentations of his own, perhaps raising further questions of contrast and comparison between Netsilik life and our own, perhaps underlining particular episodes in the film which need analysis, perhaps introducing data from other preliterate societies. But he would *not* spend his time "giving the answers" about the films. His task would be to help make explicit the questions implicit in the data, to instigate analysis by students rather than do the analysis for them. Perhaps most important, he would try to raise the level of question-asking from initial preoccupation with the exotic, bizarre, or shocking features of Netsilik life to the level suggested by Lévi-Strauss, where the questions begin to ask things about ourselves and all men. Much of the time in these sessions would go to discussion in small student-led seminar groups, supervised and listened in on by the individual faculty member but not "run" by him.

In the fourth or concluding week of the study no films would be shown. From the beginning of the Case Study, each student would regularly have received copies of selected primary materials (e.g., myths in translation, etc.); copies of selected research papers dealing with aspects of preliterate cultures—not Eskimo alone; and selected materials dealing with major dimensions of man (as hero, as myth-maker, as technologist, as worker, as artist, as parent, as member of social organization, as an adaptive being, etc.) from the Humanities and the Social Sciences and Language. At the last meeting of the third week a summary *descriptive* reading on the Netsilik past and present would be given to students, along with a list of other suggested readings and references, and a few thoughtfully considered integrative questions about commonalities and differences among men, using the Netsilik data as one point of reference.

In the middle of the fourth week, the forty-five member student groups would meet again for an hour. Students would be asked, from the background of the Netsilik data and their readings and discussions, to write individual analytic and synthesizing papers in the class dealing with contrasts and comparisons between "primitive man" and contemporary technological man. These would be submitted that day to the faculty member in charge of each lecture-student seminar.

The next day, in another hour session, each student would receive another's paper to read thoroughly; then, according to specified criteria, he would write a critique of the paper he had read. This second exercise would be a critical separate essay examining and assessing such things as: use of data from the documentaries and elsewhere, use of logic and analytical method, and use of synthetic interpretation in the other's paper. Again, both papers and critiques would be submitted to the professor.

On the following day, at the last session of the Case Study, the faculty leader in each lecture-student seminar could use a selection of papers and critiques to demonstrate strengths and weaknesses in student efforts at integrative discourse. He could do so in many ways, including having duplicated enough samples of papers and critiques for the whole group to read with him during discussion, or having samples shown on an overhead projector, or by other means. Or he could rely simply on that earliest tool of all, the lower jaw.

In any event, the Case Study would have moved students into direct contact with an enormous amount of data from the current frontiers of one kind of scholarly research, would have exercised them in trying to comprehend it and its implications from a variety of disciplinary viewpoints, and would have given them a touch of the analysis, synthesis, and criticism which go into efforts at educated integrative understanding of complex phenomena.

It is estimated that the Case Study would require staffing equivalent to 1.50 full-time faculty for four weeks. Copies of the Netsilik film documentaries could be secured from Educational Services Incorporated for such experimental use in undergraduate education.

e.  *Division I Seminars in Logic, Language, and Value:  Fall Term*

From the Case Study, the third course in the Fall Term of Division I would shift into approximately eight weeks of Division I Seminars in Logic, Language, and Value. In part, these Seminars are a natural next step after the Case Study, just as the Case Study relates to and intensifies the kinds of thinking begun in a very introductory way in the Fall Colloquy. In another sense, the Division I Seminars in Logic, Language, and Value are a direct initial approach to one of the four fields of the College, that with which the School of Language Studies is concerned.

These Seminars would be conducted in groups of twelve and would be available to all entering students. The present model arbitrarily assumes a total enrollment of 360 students in thirty groups of twelve. As in other Division I Seminars, the work undertaken by each group would revolve around a problem or topic of special scholarly interest to the instructor in charge. For the greater part, the faculty staffing of these Seminars would come from the School of Language Studies, but faculty members from other Schools who were interested in aspects of communication also might offer Seminars appropriate to this sequence. Present projections indicate that these Seminars would require the equivalent of 6.35 full-time faculty members.

While each Seminar would therefore deal with direct investigation and analysis of its own selected subject matter, teamwork and joint planning among faculty engaged in this sequence of Seminars would be vital. This is the case, because one of the principal aims of this sequence is to give all entering students something of a common exposure to fundamentals of logic, problems of meaning in the uses of language, and complexities of the question of value. Planning diversified Seminars which would, at the same time, give students what the University of Warwick in a roughly comparable first-year course calls "a common mode of discourse" useful in all sides of the intellectual life of the institution, would be a genuine curriculum problem for the faculty of the Seminars to resolve.

f. *Division I Spring Term Lecture-Student Seminars in the Language of History*

During the Spring Term, the third course continues as an integrative strand of the academic program of Hampshire. It does so through a large lecture-student seminar course in The Language of History, available to all Division I students. The present model assumes an enrollment of 360. This is not a course in historiography, although the uses of historiography are explored in it. Nor is it a course in the philosophy of history, although philosophic questions are raised, and philosophic analysis as applied to the study of history is central to it. The intentions of this course are to give students an introduction to some of the problems of inquiry in the field of history, some initiation in the uses of linguistic philosophy and its methods in relation to historical knowledge, and some further sense of the long perspectives of man's past.

Professor Morton White, a leading contemporary philosopher, has given much attention to the vivification of a useful connection between modern philosophy and modern life and knowledge. In "A Plea for an Analytic Philosophy of History," Professor White states a good part of the problem with which this course will concern students. An excerpt from his "Plea" suggests one view of the problem:

> It is always refreshing to hear that the historian wants to report the facts as they really are—to tell the truth. But while it is easy enough to announce this as the function of the historian when the truth of isolated statements like "Caesar crossed the Rubicon" is at stake, the matter is wholly different when we have to evaluate total histories or syntheses. All historians agree that Caesar crossed the Rubicon, but not all of them present the same "picture" of Rome. We like to say that some pictures of Rome are superior to others. Why? What is there about two pictures of an historical period that makes one better than the other in spite of the fact that both of them can be shown to be truthful in what they say? [138]

It would be wrong from this to take a dim view of the historian and his proper craft. "Narration is the most typical activity of the historian," and "narrative history is a unique form of human discourse" worth the serious attention of other disciplines that may help it cope with the difficulties it faces.[139] It is the students of languge and logic that Professor White challenges:

> . . . precisely because contemporary philosophers of language tend to concentrate on the logic of *single* statements—whether statements about the past, explanatory statements, logical statements, scientific theories, or moral judgments—they overlook the narrative, which is a special kind of discourse deserving of special treatment. If we succeed in clarifying the logic of narration, we shall have inaugurated a new era in the philosophy of history with the help of the tools of linguistic philosophy.[140]

The Division I course in The Language of History does not quite presume to "clarify the logic of narration" or begin a "new era in the philosophy of history." That had best be left to the linguistic philosophers under the gun leveled at them by Professor White. But the course is connected with the spirit and main direction of his argument.

For one thing, it aims at engaging students in historical inquiry and narrative themselves, using as fully as possible documentary material to reconstruct an event or complex of events. In this sense, the methodology of history as inquiry and expression are subjects of direct use and study. The course aims at comparing different historiographic products that presumably deal with the same phenomena, particularly the comparison of narratives or accounts (including interpretation, as narration must if it is not simply to be chronology) prepared by students.

To these ends, a provisional model of the course might have the following features. It would combine a large lecture once a week to the whole group of 360 students, with thirty-six separate student-led seminars (each with ten students) assisted by Junior Tutors. The course would deal with aspects of three major topics.

The lectures might be given by different specialists (see later discussion of this question) according to the several topics of the course. Lectures on any of the topics would serve best by underscoring or explicating questions inherent in historical study of the topic—in terms of materials available: methods of inquiry most feasible and productive; questions of verification and interpretation; questions of meaning in assumptions and conclusions about the study of the topic; questions of how much is perceived—with what distortion—and how much is missed.

The three major topics in the course could well be drawn from classical, medieval, and Renaissance history, and examined in depth. "Coverage," that is, the chronological widescreen view of the backgrounds of these periods and their connective links, would be left for reading in the multitude of books available. The course would be obliged to provide students with guidance to relevant connective reading. The three topics ought to be relatively narrow, but endowed with enough complexity, depth, and records to allow for considerable exploration. There should also be a reasonable possibility of contrast and comparison among the topics.

The alternatives from which to choose are virtually infinite. Simply as an example of one set, the course might use as its three major topics:

*The Classical Period—"Rome Under the Five Good Emperors, A.D. 96-180"*

This was the Golden Age of the Empire, about which Gibbon wrote:

"If a man were called to fix the period in the history of the world during which the condition of the human race was most happy and prosperous, he would, without hesitation, name that which elapsed from the death of Domitian to the accession of Commodus." Yet as Gibbon well knew, the canker of decay was not far under the golden surface of these eight-four years. Within this complex topic, choices abound for intensive study which might be useful exercises. Full centralization of political power in an emperor who needed only military support and no semblance of senatorial election. A far-flung domain gained and governed by a military system based on foot-soldiers. A decreasing supply of slaves (now that conquests were fewer and captives were fewer) in a technology based on slave-power. Decreasing amounts of booty. A diffuse and uncommanding ideology. Such things were among the dimensions of the happy, prosperous, golden moment of the Empire, fulfilled and at peace. These and others could be investigated in accounts that are readily available. The interrelationships and consequences of such factors have remained a laboratory for historical inquiry and interpretation ever since classical times. Substantive and methodological problems still fill the laboratory.

### The Early Medieval Period—"Charlemagne and After: Why Centralized Government Failed"

The great success of Christianized post-Roman Europe in repelling invaders remains something of a puzzle. As late as A.D. 732, Saracen invaders were only fifty miles from Paris. Yet by 1099 the Christian counterattack against the Saracens had regained Jerusalem. The story is far from bounded by these dates or events, but it is symbolized by the military achievements of Charlemagne, and its limitations are revealed in his ambitious but abortive effort to recreate a universal Roman Empire.

After 814 it became clear that a centralized, large-scale European government could not function under conditions as they were. Even though Christendom could mobilize with military effectiveness against the invading misbeliever, Christendom could not mobilize governmentally to serve its peaceful needs.

The matters available for investigating why this was true again are many. They have to do with a lack of at least three things that Rome at its height had in splendid fashion, things any large centralized government must have: *fast and good transportation* (Rome used the sea even more than its excellent roads; Charlemagne and inner Europe could make little use of the sea and had no adequate system of roads); *fast and good communications* (again a matter of sea-use and a road system, but also a matter of the available degree of literacy); *superiority of offensive weapons over defensive weapons* (Rome had a brilliant infantry system which could enforce obedience; by A.D. 900-1000 the European defensive weapon of the castle was superior for the most part to the mounted knight, unless he could supply a large besieging group for a long period, and, obedience as a result was not quick and easy to enforce). These and other subjects of inquiry relate to the main topic, and provide ample opportunity for its analysis.

*The Period of the Renaissance—"Florence and the Medici: Commercial Capitalism and the Transformation of Culture"*

Again a free-associated example is all that is offered here. But Florence, as a city transformed by commercial capitalism and the rich and powerful Medici of the 15th and 16th centuries, provides abundant material for examining some of the content of a complex historical problem. From Cosimo the Elder, born in 1389, banker and patron of the arts and literature, to Lorenzo, and Catherine, and Cosimo the Great who died in 1574, and the whole panorama of Florence in the midst of change, the story of much of the social impact of commercial capitalism can be vividly sampled and its relation to the transformation of high culture in the arts, scholarship, and science examined.

In its organization for instruction, the senior faculty member responsible would be likely to choose much more useful topics than these, and might well vary their number and length.

It would be most desirable to have the weekly lecture handled by one very able man. He would not have to be an impossible-to-find-and-engage combination of a distinguished ancient historian, medievalist, Renaissance scholar, and linguistic philosopher. In many ways, the best kind of person to organize, lead, and serve as the senior lecturer in this course would be a philosopher of history with a strong interest in applying the point of view so ably expressed by Professor White, and with ability to lecture from this viewpoint effectively. In such a case, the man could build the course around whatever topics he felt would lend themselves best to grasping the language of history and the uses of logic in narrative.

At full College strength, the senior Lecturer would be aided by twelve Junior Tutors or teaching assistants, three assigned to each of the four Houses. Each Junior Tutor would be responsible for supervising and helping three student seminars of ten students each. At first, the Junior

Tutors might well have to be senior students from the other colleges of the Valley or graduate students of the other institutions. Later, the Junior Tutors in this course should be recruited from the ranks of advanced-level Hampshire students. In any case, the Junior Tutors would receive compensation.

Aside from the large weekly lecture, students would meet for two hours of student-led seminar work each week, and would be expected to spend substantial additional time in seminar preparation. The three student seminars under any given Junior Tutor would meet simultaneously in House academic facilities. The task of each student with regard to the three major topics of the course, in addition to extensive reading, would be to prepare individual papers to present to other members of his seminar for examination, logical and historiographic analysis, and thorough discussion. The papers should be concise exercises in narrative and interpretation, dealing with very specific events, relationships, or developments. Ideally, when a student's paper was up for discussion, it would have been reproduced by a duplication process in advance of the meeting and would be available for the other nine members of his group to read and talk from.

The Junior Tutors each would be responsible for:

Meeting weekly in a group of twelve with the lecturer for planning and evaluation;

Attending the lecture each week;

Helping to develop student leadership for each of the three seminars which would be in session simultaneously under his or her general supervision;

Being available for individual or group consultation about seminar work;

Reading, commenting on, and evaluating the student papers for his or her seminars.

For each Junior Tutor this would come to something like six to eight hours a week. An advanced student interested in professional teaching as a possible career could use this experience as a preliminary internship.

### g. *The Midwinter Term*

This innovation, relatively untried at the time of its inclusion in the recommendations of the 1958 Plan, has since had rather widespread adoption in various forms.

In the academic year of the New College as it was described in 1958, a Fall Term of fourteen weeks would end before the Christmas holiday. In January, for approximately four weeks, the Midwinter Term would occur, and the whole College would leave its regular work to concentrate on two general studies, one of an aspect of Western culture, one of a dimension of Non-Western culture. Students of all levels and in all fields would mix with each other in a set of common educational experiences. As the 1958 Plan saw it, the Midwinter Term would require only half of the regular faculty, who would receive extra compensation for their participation. The other half of the faculty would be free to pursue their own studies and interests from Christmas until the beginning of February. The 1958 planners foresaw the Midwinter Term as engaging outside lecturers from neighboring institutions and beyond. Outside faculty would serve for several days or longer, with the understanding that they were general participants in the all-college activities, as well as having special responsibilities. Visits by distinguished scholars and artists appeared to the 1958 group as a natural part of the Midwinter Term, where cogent interchange with students would be more practicable than in visits occurring during the regular Terms.

The 1958 planners saw each of the two major courses of the Midwinter Term as having a faculty director given adequate planning time in advance to develop the course, with the advice of a faculty group including scholars from other institutions; each course as having daily lectures as well as seminars; each with required reading, papers, discussions, and examinations. The two courses of the Midwinter Term would "be equivalent to one of the three courses carried during [regular] term." [141]

When the 1966 four-college Educational Advisory Committee reviewed this portion of the New College Plan they came to somewhat different conclusions, which reflected change in conditions and notions of higher education that had occurred in the eight-year interval. The 1966 Committee agreed with the idea of some kind of break between

Fall and Spring Terms, approximately of the same duration as the Midwinter Term suggested in 1958. But they were reluctant to call it a "Term" or to endow it with many of the attributes of a formal, organized academic enterprise. Instead, the 1966 group spoke of an "Interim" which would be "of flexible design . . . scheduled in a three or four week period between the fall and spring semesters." [142]

The 1966 group felt that a change of pace between semesters would be desirable, particularly if the "interim" were free of formal course organization and allowed students to plan and choose, encouraging "them to give free rein to their individual interests." In advance of each "interim," about five projects would be planned for it by the faculty of each School. In addition, suggestions for individual student projects could be offered. Students would have freedom in the "interim" to "choose to work independently, or to work with other students, or to participate in a faculty-directed project, or indeed to engage in some activity that might not be considered academic work." Projects need not, in the judgment of the 1966 Committee, be in one's special field; they might require travel or living off-campus; they would receive no formal evaluation, require no papers, receive no grades.

The "interim" would be designed to encourage individual work, but it would include, as noted, planned projects by faculty members. Some students might not be ready for, or desire to, undertake independent projects. Some faculty, on the other hand, might be glad to organize short projects through which they could try things out and do some preliminary experimentation in their own fields, both in content and methods.

In general, Hampshire College follows the recommendation of the 1966 Educational Advisory Committee. There appear to be good reasons to do so. One is that it combines provision for students who may want structure and adult-directed programs, with provision for students who are ready to try their wings on independent study at the College or in the air of other places. Another reason is that such freedom could let students try new experiences in the arts, in reading, in other fields which the boundaries of the Fall Term had not included. The Midwinter Term, as Division I is now planned, could be a useful, freeing change of rhythm in the College year.

There are two features of the Midwinter Term at Hampshire which are not to be found in the 1966 recommendations. These are:

(1. Whatever their choice for the Midwinter Term,* all students would be asked to write an evaluation of themselves in terms of this reasonably free period in their lives. The point of this evaluation would not be to provide a means for faculty to judge the student, or for the College to force the student to account for his time, or to coerce him indirectly into seeing that the College expected him to *use* his time "constructively" (i.e., in terms of goals other older people count important for the young, if not for themselves). The point would be to accent self-direction, self-realization, and—in the process—self-evaluation. No artistic fictions would be greeted warmly, any more than would neat accounts of what one did to win a new merit badge in the great scouthood of life. What would be expected would be as much honesty about his Midwinter Term experience and his own part in it as the student could manage: his motivations to do what he did and how they appeared after the fact; how he felt about how he did the things he did; what, if anything, they meant as part of the process of his life; what *his* choice and *his* response to it added up to. The self-evaluation would be *written*.

It would be, in the case of a Division I student, the subject of one post-Midwinter Term private tutorial. For Division II and III students, it would be the subject of a private conference with their academic advisers. The self-evaluation would not be kept by the faculty or the College, but returned to the student. The only criticism that faculty advisers would convey to students in post-Midwinter Term interviews would have to do with the adequacy of the process of self-evaluation shown, not consciously judging the substance of what was done. The exception to the rule would be when a student, after going as far as he could in self-evaluation, asked for guidance or advice, and even then the adviser would try to turn essential questions back to the student, to get him to think for himself.

(2. While the 1966 Committee, and the 1958 one before it, regarded the Midwinter Term in different ways, they agreed in their largely "academic" emphasis. This is true, even though the 1966 group included the possibility of an individual student's tackling something outside the normally academic. Hampshire certainly accepts the latter possibility, too, and would equally pass no moral judg-

---

*All students in all Divisions would be expected to submit their plans for the Midwinter Term to their academic advisers by a fixed date in mid-Fall for consideration and discussion.

ment on the student who chose to spend the month surfing in
Hawaii, on the student who decided to work at Gimbel's and earn
some needed money, or the student who earnestly pursued a directed or independent study on campus. It would be his choice;
all the College would ask is that he rigorously and honestly evaluate himself in living out his choice.

But the College feels an obligation to enlarge his field of choice
beyond the relatively narrow range of taking part in or conducting
an independent study, or reading, or loafing and seeing if Whitman
was right about that helping to "invite your soul," or working for
money. The area of further choice the College will open up has
to do with *concern* and serving where there is human need that
strong young men and women could meet, going beyond themselves
to others.

Thus, copying with no embarrassment at all the quiet example of the
Quakers—and many others—the College will organize at least one
feasible work-service team project each Midwinter Term. The project
could be as far away as a little town in a Southern state where hard labor
was needed to help rebuild a burned church, under the supervision of that
rare man, a skilled "mechanic," as good builders once were called. Or
it could be as near as places of need in the Connecticut Valley. The
project could well involve physical hardship, hard physical work, and
contact across forbiddingly difficult cultural barriers in our own land.
There should be some joy in it, the different discipline of *making* something that people badly need, the discovery of further reaches of oneself
in giving where the giving is not easy.

In many other ways, the College may enlarge the range of choices
students may have in the Midwinter Term.

h.  *The Reading Period*

At the end of the twelve-week regular Spring Term, the College
will schedule a two-week reading period in which there will be no classes,
seminars, or usual academic meetings. For Division I students, each
School will have prepared selected lists which will be useful to read,
work with, and discuss in preparation for the Division's field and integrative examinations.

For students finishing the first year of Division II, reading selections will be related more directly to the nature and scope of disciplines within the School fields. Such students would ordinarily then be in the final process of deciding on a discipline and field in which to concentrate. Their reading would be aimed at helping them review their decision and factors relevant to it, in terms of the nature of the discipline, what it really dealt with, what it really required. In the course of the Reading Period, they would be likely to consult with field faculty advisers for further information and counseling. Reaching a decision at this time, Division II students would propose in writing a program of concentrated study in their chosen discipline or interdisciplinary combination for the latter half (usually the second year of the sequence) of Division II. The proposal would indicate, as well, the courses they wished to take outside their discipline, both in the major field and in other fields.

For Division II students completing the usual second year of that sequence, the Reading Period would be principally related to selections that might be useful to them in standing for the School examination in the discipline in which they had chosen to prepare themselves. In addition, selected readings would be given them in connection with other fields and the integrative process on which they would stand for examination.

A Division III student would use the Reading Period, before which his study or project must have been accepted in the School of his concentration, essentially as a time very early in which his advanced School examination and advanced integrative examination would be taken, and in which he would prepare for graduation.

Other Divisions would present their examinations at the close of the Reading Period. The character the Reading Period assumes will depend heavily on the view the faculty take of it. If their view is that the principal service of teaching is to prepare for short-term quantitative retention of subject matter for display at the moment of examination, the Reading Period could very well be a miserable cram session. If instead, as Hampshire's academic program intends, teaching aims mainly to enlarge a grasp of conceptual inquiry and its principles as applied by disciplines and fields of study in order to reach higher levels of complex understanding, the Reading Period will rightly have a different flavor. It will not be a tense, crowded time of massive factual ingestion to be followed by examination-as-regurgitation. It will be quite different: a

time for very selective reading and a good deal of contemplation and talk
with one's colleagues about the essential things to know if one is to be an
on-going knower, not a temporary receptacle of encyclopedic information.

## 2.  THE PROGRAM OF STUDIES IN DIVISION II

The Division of Disciplinary Studies, as noted earlier, will ordinarily
constitute a two-year sequence. In it, a student will further explore the
disciplines of the four School fields. Part of his self-education, as the
1958 Plan suggested, will be designing his own program of concentration. Well before the Reading Period at the end of the first year of
Division II, perhaps by March 15, a student would have drafted a preliminary essay outlining his proposal for a discipline and field concentration for himself. He would have submitted this preliminary draft to the
Dean of the School of his choice, who would consider it and the student's
level of preparation with the assistance of advising faculty in the School
and possibly in other Schools of the College. In conference and writing,
the student would receive a response to his proposal, perhaps giving it
preliminary approval, perhaps suggesting changes or deferral of decision,
or suggesting that he consider a concentration in another discipline or
field.

In the event of preliminary approval with or without suggestions for
modification, the student would have time in the Reading Period to reexamine his decision. If he then believed he had made a final decision,
he would, as noted, submit his proposal in final form. In the event of
recommended deferral of decision at the point of his preliminary draft,
he might wait until the next year of the Division II sequence to make a
further proposal of program in the same or another discipline of the
same field. Or, depending on his interest and his assessment of himself,
he might at the time of the Reading Period make a preliminary program
proposal in a different field and discipline. Every effort possible would
be made by faculty and staff to enable his decision to be his own, reached
thoughtfully, and yet with the benefit of personal consideration and experienced advice.

In the main, the first of the two usual years of Division II would be
occupied with a balance of elections among the four Schools, intended
to enable the student to see School fields more accurately in terms of

their constituent disciplines. The second year of the Division II sequence would principally be concerned with giving the student intensive training in the elements of conceptual inquiry and actual experience in his chosen discipline or special disciplinary program. He would be expected as well to work to some extent in related disciplines of his field and to elect courses in other fields, as possible.

No attempt is made here to present illustrative models of possible courses a student might take in Division II work. A major responsibility of each School faculty will be to develop appropriate and feasible curriculum offerings at the intermediate level in its own disciplines and field. As a School faculty does so it will be expected (a) to concentrate on curriculum which will emphasize increasing the student's capability in self-education, (b) to aim at achieving high quality with the minimum possible cost in faculty time and facility requirements, and (c) to avoid what Professor Marston Bates once aptly called "the discipline trap," in this case meaning the assiduous avoidance of course proliferation. *The point of the College's emphasis on disciplines-in-fields is to teach the essential tools for continued, competent, and creative conceptual inquiry and expression, not to develop multiple specializations in narrow subject matter "fields."*

The categories or principal modes of courses for Division II have been suggested in the detailed provisional description of Division I. There would be three principal categories, whose nomenclature is only generally descriptive. What these categories would mean in application would depend on each School; the actual form and pedagogical design they would take would be quite different, it is likely, in the School of Natural Sciences and in the School of Humanities and Arts.

One basic category would be the *Division II Seminar,* meaning usually a group of from ten to fifteen students meeting once or more a week. A second category would be the *Division II Lecture-Student Seminar,* which could take a number of forms, would utilize large (often sixty or more) and small group sessions. These commonly would involve increased training and use of students as discussion leaders and teacher colleagues, and the use of abler advanced students, graduate students and others as paid assistants. The third category of instruction would be *Division II Independent Study* under the supervision of regular or adjunct faculty. Again, this is a variable category in terms of what its ac-

tual form and substance would be in different Schools. It is clear, however, that transition into its greater use is vital to the mission of the College
and the welfare of its students, and that the transition must be well
planned and overseen responsibly by faculty for it to be productive.

Norms are entirely hypothetical in advance of operation and without
allowing for the variation of function and operation among the Schools.
But it can be supposed that a student in the first year of Division II
would be likely, in his six courses, to spend one-sixth of his academic time
in Independent Study, one-half of his time in Lecture-Student Seminars,
and one-third of his time in Division II Seminars. In the second year of
Division II, these proportions might shift toward a student's spending
one-third of his time in Independent Study, one-half in Lecture-Student
Seminars, and one-sixth in Division II Seminars. The move would be
steadily toward greater individual responsibility in reading, research, and
study.

To this end, it should be emphasized again that the "norms" touched
upon above are conjectural, that variations would occur, and that indeed
*no* courses are literally required. *An especially able student might move
immediately through this whole divisional sequence or parts of it by examination, rather than by course work. Others perhaps would move,
upon approval of faculty and after thorough consideration, into a considerably higher proportion of Independent Study than the "norms" suggest. Some able students might go into completely Independent Study
for the latter half of Division II and all of Division III.*

Ordinarily, however, something like the conjectured norms would be
the case. The usual pattern (using Independent Study, Lecture-Student
Seminars, and Division II Seminars as operationally developed by the
several Schools and their faculties) might be something like the following
for students in each of the Schools during the Division II sequence:

*Humanities and the Arts*

The equivalent of:

> 7 semester courses in Humanities and Arts
> 2 general elective courses in or out of the field
> 1 semester elective course in Natural Sciences
> 1 semester elective course in Social Sciences
> 1 semester elective course in Language

*Natural Sciences*

The equivalent of:

> 7 semester courses in Natural Sciences
> 2 general elective courses in or out of the field
> 1 semester elective course in Humanities and Arts
> 1 semester elective course in Social Sciences
> 1 semester elective course in Language

*Social Sciences*

The equivalent of:

> 7 semester courses in Social Sciences
> 2 general elective courses in or out of the field
> 1 semester course in the Science as Inquiry Program, Sequence B
> 1 semester elective course in Language
> 1 semester elective course in Humanities and the Arts

*Language Studies*

The equivalent of:

> 7 semester courses in Language Studies
> 2 general elective courses in or out of the field
> 1 semester course in the Science as Inquiry Program, Sequence B
> 1 semester elective course in Social Sciences
> 1 semester elective course in Humanities and the Arts

## 3. THE PROGRAM OF STUDIES IN DIVISION III

The Division of Advanced Studies, as discussion earlier indicated, will most commonly require the fourth academic year for completion. It will be a year in which for at least one-half of his academic time and perhaps a good deal more, a student will develop an intensive single study or project related to one aspect of a subject in the discipline or set of disciplines in which he is concentrating his work. The idea and fundamental plan for his study or project will have to have been drawn up, submitted to his School, and approved before he completes work in Division II. In many cases, the planning of a study or project for later pursuit in Division III will be the subject of Independent Study by the student during the latter part of his Division II sequence.

It was said in the initial description of the divisional sequence of the College that the form of Division III special studies and projects will be a function of the nature of the student's discipline and field. "Disciplines" at Hampshire *generally* refer to *inquiry* in the sense of the earlier abstract definition used in this paper. But they are also taken to include the disciplines of *expression* in that significant part of the Humanities School which is concerned with the creative arts.

This usage may be somewhat less than familiar and comfortable for the symbol-and-analysis oriented scholar. But Hampshire regards *discipline of expression* as a singularly important concept, difficult or impossible as it may be to define in rationalistic, entirely objective, or universal terms. It is as much as anything a sense of virtue in order; or, as a line in the first chapter said, to learn "that it is not the business of art to use chaos to express chaos." There is an evident and admitted bias in this view of things, which Hampshire is happy to defend. The defense rests not at all any view that expression in the college experience should be professionalized or shackled to vocationally acceptable standards. They indeed might be too low! Hampshire's position is that creative expression is most free when it is informed—as indeed good *inquiry* always must be—by insight into method, its limits, its capacity for reconceptualization, and the sense of order it can lend perceived reality.

In this meaning, inquiry and expression are not inevitably two disparate worlds, two dandy parallel lines in liberal education that go forward to infinity without intersection. Both are ways similar at least in their intention to arrive at statements about life and the universe that have meaning, even though their apparent dress for travel are as unlike as farthingale and mini-skirt.

In any event, Division III students, depending on their School, may present a thesis, a paper reporting an original experiment or a useful replication study, a play, a solution to a problem of design, a book of sonnets, or any number of things as evidence of advanced study in their discipline. The crucial requirement is that it must represent the fullest, most mature command of his field that a student can offer, in the judgment of the faculty. Mention was made earlier of the importance of the advanced one-term integrative seminar in Division III, and of the possibility of elective studies as well.

Hopefully, the Hampshire student who completes his work in Division III will not have come full circle to the point where he began in the College. That would mean a long trip around with no upward, lasting rise. Rather, the College hopes that he will have kept with him news of Hampshire's belief that individual man's honorable choice is not between immolation in a senseless society or withdrawal into the autarchic self. It trusts that his studies and experience in the College will confirm for him the choice that only education allows: *detachment and skill enough to know, engagement enough to feel, and concern enough to act, with self and society in productive interplay, separate and together.*

# 6

## THE ACADEMIC PROGRAM:
### *Language and Liberal Education*

*Language is, without a doubt, the most momentous and at the same time the most mysterious product of the human mind. Between the clearest animal call of love or warning or anger, and a man's least, trivial word, there lies a whole day of Creation. . . . In language we have the free, accomplished use of symbolisms, the record of articulate conceptual thinking; without language there seems to be nothing like thought whatever.*

SUSANNE K. LANGER
*Philosophy in a New Key*

IT APPEARS NATURAL, and if anything somewhat belated, to regard language as one of the most relevant special fields with which liberal education now should be concerned. Some of the reasons for this were reviewed in the first chapter, along with reasons a college should be engaged with innovation in information transfer.

Of course it is true that all colleges are already continuously involved with language and information transfer. They always have been, since Plato's founding of the Academy in 385 B.C., and long before. In this, scholars and students have been one with all men, for, as Sapir observed:

. . . Language is an immensely ancient heritage of the human race. . . . It is doubtful if any other cultural asset of man, be it the art of drilling for fire or of chipping stone, may lay claim to a greater age. I am inclined to believe that . . . these developments, in fact, were not strictly possible until language, the tool of significal expression, had itself taken shape.[143]

All learning and living, in the human sense, deal with language and the exchange of information.

Hampshire College proposes to deal with language and information transfer as a major field of liberal education rather than only as a given in the general life of the institution. This field will be the concern of the School of Language Studies.

Education's concern with language, when explicit, characteristically has been limited to certain discrete fragments of the academic program in schools and colleges. Schools, more than colleges, have been preoccupied with the formal grammar of conventional "language" as human verbal communication, and with a relatively narrow view of rhetoric in prose or verse. In mathematics, with noble exceptions among the best teachers, schools and colleges have scarcely been at pains to clarify that the essence of the discipline is that it is a *language*, behind whose symbols "lie the boldest, purest, coolest abstractions mankind has ever made." [144] Logic has fared somewhat better, in the better colleges if not in the schools. Logic usually finds a small home in the collegiate department of Philosophy, and leads at least some students into examining questions of clarity, validity, fallacy, inference, and analysis. A few other students are led into symbolic logic enough to gain a first acquaintance with formal deductive systems, including the propositional calculus, the first order calculus of functions, and some semantics. In college studies of literature, language is treated mostly as rhetoric; and, where anthropology is taught, language may be handled in the run of things as an example of one way to formulate a theory of the structure of human behavior. Most collegiate catalogues in psychology refer directly to language not at all, although course work must deal with it implicitly. Questions of information transfer are assumed in courses on cognition, perception, learning, and motivation, but are not usually dealt with holistically, or as aspects of coherent heuristic systems.

These things are the case in most of undergraduate education. In graduate study at certain universities and in the work of some of the world's leading scholars, the story is quite different. Consider some examples in language for a moment; after these, it may be useful to look at the matter of information transfer once again.

## 1. THE LINGUISTIC REVOLUTION IN PHILOSOPHY

During the past four decades or more, what Professor White calls "a slow and silent revolution in philosophy" has gone virtually unnoticed by those outside the discipline. An earlier era of speculative metaphysics which had produced works on a grand, not infrequently inflated, scale, has given way to a modern concern with analytic philosophy. Analytic philosophers may and do differ in doctrine, but the "temper and tone of the movement is deflationary and critical; its method linguistic and logical." [145]

This change owed much to the revolutionary implications of developments in science in the first decades of the century. At the frontiers of science, observation had become almost wholly indirect, and the sense-data upon which scientific propositions might be proposed were most often not direct observation of actual objects of inquiry but *readings* of index needles, revolving drums, sensitive plates, and other indicators.[146] These data were empirical enough, but they were not the actual phenomena: "what is directly observable is only a sign of 'physical fact'; it requires interpretation to yield scientific propositions." Thus Susanne Langer and others saw the problem of observation as all but eclipsed by the problem of *meaning,* by the fact that in advanced science of the 20th century the available empirical sense-data were primarily symbols whose meaning must be somehow gotten at.[147]

Philosophical books of the 1920's and 1930's had come at the implications of the question of meaning in science with a vengeance. C. K. Ogden and I. A. Richards, Ralph Munroe Eaton, A. J. Ayer, Rudolph Carnap, Gustav Stern, Alfred North Whitehead, Ludwig Wittgenstein, and others had explored aspects of the symbolism of science. Not all, by any means, were qualified to consider the problem of scientific knowledge *as scientists,* but this deterred very few. That the edifice of human knowledge was not a vast collection of sense reports but a structure of facts that were symbols and laws that expressed their meaning, excited the whole intellectual world.

Excitement stirred younger disciples in the universities, in the realization that science (which Cassirer called, with at least a little hyperbole: "the highest attainment . . . in human culture . . . the summit and consummation of all our human activities . . . the most important subject of a philosophy of man." [148]) required new analytic tools to cope fully with its symbolic content. Science, with philosophy's analytic aid, might build up a symbolic universe that would help man "to understand and interpret, to articulate and organize, to synthesize and universalize his human experience." [149] It was a moving prospect; helping build the language of science would build the world anew.

The Bolsheviks of this part of the revolution in philosophy were the logical positivists, whose school, as Professor White reminisces:

> . . . was still a modish philosophy in the 1930's when our young traveling fellows were carrying home the doctrine of the Vienna Circle, but time . . . rubbed off a bit of its bloom and blunted some of its thorns. The philosophy of science, sponsored by positivists when it was a philosophical pariah, is now an important philosophical discipline, and symbolic logic, that natural child of mathematics and philosophy, has become the respectable concern of a distinguished journal. . . . A good deal has happened since those days when it was worth a graduate student's academic life to be caught turning the pages of Carnap, Reichenbach, or Wittgenstein unless he was scrawling nasty remarks in the margins.[150]

The revolution in philosophy has had many other partisan troops than those the positivists have mustered. In America and England there has been a half-century of growing emphasis on logic, on exactness and precision in statements in philosophy and a growing wariness of large-scale metaphysical pontification. Pragmatism asked that any statement be able to stand the test of practical meaning and examination of its empirical consequences. Operationalism, coming out of a physicist's thinking, had significance for language and meaning beyond science, as Nobel laureate Professor Bridgman saw it:

> The essence of [operationalism] is that to know adequately the meaning of a term we must be able to describe what we do when we use it. It is my personal opinion that this way of dealing with meanings has a wide application to all our language, in so far as that language is an activity of intelligence as distinguished from a purely emotional activity.[151]

Professor Bridgman insisted on only one point: that we can always ask what the meaning of any term that we use is, and that, in answering, we must satisfy *some* criterion of meaning. If we can formulate the criterion explicitly, we are in a better position to judge from our other experience whether any term has the meaning we supposed. Often we will find it does not.

Bridgman found this to be the case in physics and thought it might well turn out to be true of terms of a humanistic sort as well. Few of these (e.g., justice, freedom, duty, responsibility) had been, he felt, subjected to rigorous criterion analysis. He did not at all propose discarding such concepts, but rather endowing them, through critical analysis, with a fuller potential of more exact and clear meaning than we usually give them.

Professor Bridgman also saw the grammar of a language as almost compelling certain attitudes. In English and other European languages, for example, reification (i.e., conversion from an abstract concept into a concrete thing) is virtually inescapable in discourse. One cannot say "I do" without implying "I do something," and the "something" then becomes reified. The implications that specific language structures have for cultural patterns are interesting. There are cultural languages in which it is uncongenial or very hard to form universal statements and syllogisms. "It begins to look," commented Professor Bridgman, "as though formal logic, as we know it, is an attribute of the group of Indo-European languages with certain grammatical features." [152]

The excursion which this discussion has taken into linguistic dimensions of modern philosophy is so superficial and fragmentary that it would drive any working analytic philosopher up the wall. Hopefully not all the way up, because its only intention is to underline in a few broad strokes the attention philosophy today is paying to language, not only the language of science but that of the humanistic tradition. Such attention appears of great relevance to liberal education as Hampshire defines it, and argues that the matter is too important to be left to the graduate schools and the philosopher's closet alone. Hampshire will therefore bring linguistic and analytic philosophy, at least in introductory form, into the heart of undergraduate general and specialized education through its School of Language Studies.

## 2. THE EMERGENCE OF PSYCHOLINGUISTICS

The first chapter noted the emergence of psycholinguistics as one of the most interesting intellectual developments of the past twenty years. This alone would not justify attention to it in a new construction of undergraduate curriculum; the "interesting intellectual developments" of the past two decades provide a richness which could not only embarrass the undergraduate program, but overwhelm it. The justification Hampshire College sees in introducing students to psycholinguistics is the same justification which supports an inclusion of analytic philosophy in the new undergraduate field of Language Studies. Both psycholinguistics and analytic philosophy are relevant to conceptual inquiry and the development of clearer understandings of man and his universe. They are intellectual tools of the first order; even though they are far from perfection, they are instrumentalities whose uses men and women should learn in liberal education. To leave an introduction to these tools to the graduate schools would be to confine things of general importance unnecessarily and undesirably.

Mrs. Langer, along with Professor Cassirer and others, distinguished between two conceptions of symbolic communication, as did Bridgman in writing of a kind of language that "is an activity of intelligence as distinguished from a purely emotional activity." Mrs. Langer assumed that one conception of symbolism leads to logic and helps meet new problems in the theory of knowledge, e.g., in the comprehension of science. The other conception she assumed was psychologic, not concerned with assisting science in the quest for certainty, but taking us in the opposite direction, towards understanding emotions, religion, fantasy, and art. Susanne Langer believed both conceptions of symbolic communication had a relevance to human response. Her work was an effort to establish a general theory of symbolic transformation in language which would reconcile these two symbolic modes:

> . . . rather than restricting intelligence to discursive forms and relegating all other conception to some irrational realm of feeling and instinct. . . . The parent stock of both conceptual types, of verbal and nonverbal formulation, is the basic human act of symbolic transformation.[153]

Defined, this "basic human act" was the brain's active transformation of experiential data into symbols which might be communicated in speech, expressed in art, or acted out in ritual. All of these, Mrs. Langer comprehended as language.

Psycholinguistics is itself a bridge among cognitive and affective views of language. Basically, it is concerned—in its presently developing form —with the overlap of linguistics and psychology, just as linguistic philosophy is concerned with the relationship between epistemology and linguistics. In both psychology and philosophy, a number of modern scholars have not been timorous about moving into connection with linguistics. The move is a modern one. It is far from a move congenial to all psychologists and philosophers, but it is certainly where a lot of the action is at present in both fields.

Little has been said here about the *linguists* themselves. Since they are now being related to both by philosophy and psychology, and will have a genuine place in Hampshire's field of Language Studies, the nature of their work is important to note.

The linguist (as distinguished from philosopher and psychologist) attempts to provide a description of a particular language. He deals with its phonology (phonetics and/or phonemics), syntax, lexicon, and, where possible, its history. He may do so as an aid to those who wish to learn a language. His studies of linguistics may be pursued as a guide to other aspects of a particular language-culture. He may study a language in these terms in order to develop an alphabet and written form for it. His linguistic work may aim at supporting the interpretation of a language's literature, or at aiding translation, or at other goals. He has been principally a technical expert in natural languages, considered from a descriptive and classificatory viewpoint. More recently, modern linguists have realized that their own field may gain significantly in sophistication by association with other disciplines concerned with knowing and communication. An overzealous independence reduces linguistics to a kind of cryptographic taxonomy of linguistic forms.[154] The conjoining of other disciplines and traditional linguistics becomes most crucial as problems of *meaning* are faced in natural language.

Psycholinguistics stands in relation to the understanding of social life in a fashion analogous to the relation of analytic philosophy to problems of the nature and interpretation of knowledge, scientific and otherwise. Both fields are concerned with language and communication, and intersect more often than scholars in either field seem yet to realize. Both fields deal to some extent with traditional linguistics as described above. Both deal with mathematics on occasion, as well they might.

Psycholinguistics, like linguistic philosophy a bit earlier, is considered a puzzling newcomer by its own larger discipline. Psychologists most often simply take for granted the fact that language is the form of communication that above all others best supports the complex workings of our social order. For many of them, language is a basic undefined term of their science, from which to go on, without stopping for detailed analysis, to their special interests. For others, and this is very relevant to the role of Language Studies in a liberal curriculum, the *effects* of communication have been the attractive objects of study. Thus social psychology has produced research in persuasion, propaganda, content analysis, mass media, and rumor which can contribute substantially to a multi-faceted program of Language Studies.

The major contribution of psycholinguistics to undergraduate study, however, is in raising questions about the linguistic *processes* people use and depend on. Psycholinguistics is an exciting field because it is almost wholly in the question-asking stage of its development. It might be argued that this is abundant reason to keep it *out* of the undergraduate curriculum. Hampshire disagrees. There is no thought, and it would be foolish if there were, of trying to bring into undergraduate study the kind of research that Professor Miller is carrying on in psycholinguistics at Harvard's Center for Cognitive Studies. But there seems every reason to introduce interested undergraduates to psycholinguistic questions and a degree of content they can usefully work with, even as a field for concentration.

Questions and content, appropriate to undergraduate instruction in psycholinguistics, might be drawn from such parts of the field as the following: phonology, syntax, and semantics; the biological capacity for language; early grammatical speech; change in child language; the growth of transformations; the role of parental speech; the Whorfian hypothesis that man's personal experience of the world he lives in is shaped by the language he speaks; linguistic universals; paralinguistics (the function of cues, tempo, loudness, and other aspects of speech not connected with grammar); kinesics (communicative body motions, gestures, and the like, that add a visible dimension); linguistic reflections of social structure; and the heterogeneous experimental methodology (not methodolatry!) of a varied and lively field.

### 3.  INFORMATION TRANSFER AND THE TECHNOLOGY OF LANGUAGE

The first chapter of this paper argued that revolutionary technological and conceptual developments in information transfer cannot intelligently be ignored by any part of higher education, including collegiate instruction. The society as a whole cannot afford to ignore or mis-use such innovations. The fact that responsible and enlightened educational leadership in America *will* respond to the immense new technological opportunities for the diffusion of knowledge and culture was dramatically illustrated by an action of the Ford Foundation on August 1, 1966.[155]

On that date, President McGeorge Bundy of the Foundation submitted a statement to the Federal Communications Commission presenting a possible model for the use of synchronous space satellites in a non-profit system which would guarantee the nation adequate access to non-commercial and instructional television, as well as to commercial television. The model was not presented as a formal proposal. But its technical feasibility, legal basis, economic validity, and television programming practicality had been tested in highly expert studies. The model suggested, in a brilliantly ingenious combination of social engineering and the bold use of satellite technology, a new broadcasting plan which would so assist commercial television that the latter would be impelled by self-interest to fund educational television at a sufficient and stable level. Mr. Bundy commented that

> satellite communications may permit a revolution both in the technology and in the economics of television. Intensive exploratory studies have convinced us that . . . these revolutionary possibilities offer the promise of building a cost-free highway system for multiplied regional and national non-commercial services—and also of providing a large part of the new funds which are desperately needed for non-commercial programming at every level.[156]

The Ford Foundation's model is now under close study by the FCC and other groups. It is opposed by Comsat and AT&T, and apparently favored by the three commercial networks and National Educational Television (NET).

The Ford brief on satellite technology and its social uses demonstrates that creative educational leadership *can* intervene to invent striking new ways to exploit the remarkable communications technology now available and still to come. The huge scale of the Ford Foundation proposal should not obscure the clear implication that its fundamental style of bold imaginativeness has for the approach education generally should take to newer technologies. The point, for Hampshire College, lies in a matter of attitude and understanding of necessities. The College proposes, as the second chapter of this paper indicated, to be bold in exploring the potential educational and economic advantages of new technologies for information transfer. The College intends not only to *use* new technologies where it is sensible and economically possible to do so, but to introduce its students to their meaning and use as a part of liberal education in the present age. In the process, Hampshire College will explore possible relationships that could be developed with industry, government, and private foundations.

In the following chapter, some of the features of the College's design for incorporating INTRAN (a modified acronym for information transfer) as an integral component of the institution are presented. The shorthand name may easily suggest an erroneous conception; e.g., *intran*sigent, as in devotion to gimmickry. Hopefully, it will carry more of the flavor of *in transitu,* since through INTRAN, a function physically and conceptually located in the School of Language Studies, the College will try to be "on the way," in terms of understanding and exploiting technology that will help its program. The spirit of INTRAN at Hampshire will be experimental and innovative; from the beginning, however, it will be a generative point for systematic service to faculty and students. The College will not indulge itself in a kind of science-fiction fantasy at the "Gee, whiz!" level. But it will deliberately develop its technological information-transfer capability as far and as fast as economic feasibility and the criteria of liberal education established in this paper will allow.

Among other specific things, this means that Hampshire College will be concerned through the instrumentality of its INTRAN Center with:

   a. *Open-Circuit Television.* The College has been in consultation with
      Mr. Hartford Gunn, general manager of WGBH, Channel 2, for
      the past year. Mr. Gunn and his staff operate what in many ways
      is the best educational television station in the United States. The
      station is operated in connection with the Lowell Institute Coopera-
      tive Broadcasting Council, a group of fourteen leading educational
      and cultural institutions, including most recently in its association,

Yale University.* Hampshire will continue to explore with Mr. Gunn the possible uses open-circuit television may have in its program. The new Ford ETV proposal may greatly increase the availability and repertoire of ETV for college instructional purposes.

b. *Open-Circuit Radio.* Hampshire is aware of the contribution already being made to the Valley by WFCR, the FM station operated under the joint auspices of the Four Colleges. This station originates some of its own programs, but it makes heavy use of taped material, of high quality, from WGBH-FM in Boston. The College hopes to have an active relationship with WFCR and will investigate ways it may contribute to this shared enterprise.

c. *Closed-Circuit Television.* This system involves coaxial cable interconnection of points on a single campus, or of points on several campuses. The coaxial cable can be capable of carrying a great deal more than television signals. At Harvard, as the first chapter noted, a $100,000 network has been installed this year, connecting forty different locations. Among these are the Widener and Lamont Libraries, the Littauer Center, the Computing Center, and the Loeb Drama Center. The Harvard installation is what is called "a wideband information transfer system." This means that the same cables that carry television signals can also carry pulse data for computer operation and transmittal. The cables have been run underground, in the same tunnels that distribute steam for heating Harvard buildings. The main production studio and technical center for the Harvard hook-up is WGBH, whose facilities are on Harvard land rented for a dollar per year.

The possibilities for present use at Harvard are simple; they are principally the piping of conferences, demonstrations, lectures, and ceremonies from one part of the campus to other parts. But future possibilities—not far off—are great and varied. President Pusey foresees that the development of such local systems may open the way "for extensive interuniversity co-operation"; such a vision provided the main reason for Yale's recent decision to join the Lowell Institute Broadcasting Council.[157] Uses of the Harvard closed-circuit cables for computer-access, library-access, and many other purposes in the relatively near future are foreseen. As these things occur,

*Present members of the Council are the Lowell Institute, Boston College, Boston Symphony Orchestra, Boston University, Brandeis, Harvard, MIT, Museum of Fine Arts, Museum of Science, New England Conservatory of Music, Northeastern, Simmons College, Tufts, and Yale.

it will be possible for one wired campus to hook-in to another as needed, thus strengthening the total resources of both institutions. Hampshire will make provision for coaxial cable interconnection on campus from the beginning, including in consideration the possibility of interconnection direct to student carrels in residential rooms.

The basic purposes that wide-band coaxial cable interconnection could serve are evident. Fundamentally, it should provide students with greater access to materials and experiences; it should enable teachers to demonstrate and display material to large groups with films or tapes that communicate sound and motion; it should make the educational process more flexible by making access to material easier and by making it duplicable or repeatable on command; and it should relieve teaching of repetitive, time-consuming tasks that are better and more cheaply done by electronic-mechanical means.

The best known, most widely applied tool of information transfer in undergraduate education is the language laboratory. The designs are very similar everywhere: a large room filled with student stations, usually as semi-carrels built into large table tops. The student has earphones and a microphone. A central source, with greater or lesser flexibility, transmits the lesson to the headset via magnetic tape. Students can respond and replay and hear their responses. In some places the language laboratory is also used as a playback device for music courses. The next logical step, as Hampshire sees it, is to equip each student's room with a language laboratory station and make the languages available to him whenever he chooses to study. Educationally, such access could mean that a language would be learned wholly without "courses," and that competence would be measured by examination, satisfactory completion of which is a prerequisite for graduation, as in the Hampshire plan. Further, it is technically possible to build into the student's room a more versatile and flexible unit consisting of a tape recorder, microphone, headset, television screen and oscilloscope, all tied to a central resource center, making available to the student on demand tapes (video, audio or both) of lectures, films, recordings of plays, music, readings, language materials and the capability of doing some "laboratory" experimentation. IBM, for example, has developed course programs in biochemistry and other disciplines for use through teletypewriter connection to a central computer. The IBM programs of computer-assisted instruction (CAI) can be developed and modified by teachers themselves; to make this possible without being a computer expert, IBM has developed a simple "Coursewriter" language which a teacher can readily learn and use in translating what he wants taught into material the computer can use. Hampshire is already in close touch with IBM on these and other developments, and plans to remain so.

Another example of a tool of information transfer being used increasingly is the short moving picture. The problems ordinarily associated with showing films in classrooms are well-known: broken film, burned out bulbs, ill-adjusted machines, and other burdens. Now, through closed-circuit television, a film clip (from archive film for a history lecture or a carefully prepared, expertly done laboratory demonstration, as examples) can be previewed in the teacher's office and can be signalled for during the lecture to be projected from a resources center on a reflecting screen or a set of television monitors. Or, without using television at all, it is possible to show short closed-loop single concept films on automatic cartridge-loading projectors now available.

The full utilization for any one college of information transfer systems depends on the creation and accumulation of files of suitable materials in central facilities and the creation of distribution networks to bring resources and users (users usually have resources) together. Eventually, for instance, great distribution centers may be built in several spots in the United States, as the current Ford Foundation model suggests, with networks among the centers and subnetworks interrelating the libraries, universities, colleges, museums, and other resources and users with each other and, if necessary, with any other source or user in the country.

There is little science-fiction in any of this. Great institutions, great foundations, and great corporations would not be moving towards these kinds of information-transfer capabilities if there were. To get a realistic but eye-opening view of what is coming, one may read dispassionate and informed discussions such as those presented in the *IBM Research Reports* (e.g., the January, 1966, issue on "Computer Assisted Instruction"); in *The Revolution in the Schools,* edited by Ronald Gross and Judith Murphy;[158] and in William Clark Trow's *Teacher and Technology.*[159] Or to be very local, one may take a second look at *The Amherst Record* of August 11, 1966. The lead article on page one concerns the installation of a Centrex telephone system by the New England Telephone and Telegraph Company designed to serve all University of Massachusetts students directly in their rooms, and all Amherst College faculty and staff. In passing, the local telephone executive comments, somewhat wistfully it seems, that "these room telephones offer potential for sophisticated learning techniques such as access to language lab tape banks, registering by phone, and, eventually, access to computers."

### 4.  THE SCHOOL OF LANGUAGE STUDIES AT HAMPSHIRE COLLEGE

Considerations of the kind touched upon in the foregoing discussion and in the first chapter have led Hampshire and its advisers to decide that one of the four major fields of liberal education in the College will be that of Language. The School of Language Studies will require much further study and discussion in its development than can be accomplished in the present paper. But some of its main lines are clear. Language will be regarded as a comprehensive rubric including aspects of linguistic philosophy, psycholinguistics, information transfer, the history and nature of natural languages, and studies in foreign languages as described in the fourth chapter.

Hampshire feels that Daniel Bell was too tentative but on the right track when he said of general education at Columbia that:

> The question of 'language' is so important that the question may be raised whether or not in coming years that a course in *language*—dealing with the nature of symbolism, communication theory, psycholinguistics (and computer languages), structural linguistics—should be a basic course, required of *all* students, as the foundation for many different lines of study. The striking advances in linguistics itself—raise this as an important question.[160]

Hampshire College was challenged to a bolder line in regard to Language by the 1966 Report of the Educational Advisory Committee. One of the most original and persuasive recommendations in this thoughtful document was that the College should establish a fourth division, dealing with Language:

> It should be the function of the division of languages to promote an understanding of the variety of languages that have been developed as instruments of human communication and as intellectual and artistic tools. . . .

It is understandable and inevitable . . . that the great majority of Americans have not even considered it necessary or worth the time it takes, to know anything much about the origins, background, history and development, the multiplexity as well as the paradoxical constancy and mutability of their own language and thus the fascination of it, not to mention its importance and wide-ranging influence. Such a rich subject need not be left to scholars who communicate only with other scholars, nor has it been entirely. But the study of it needs to become more widespread. It would in fact seem wise to persuade our whole educational system to be permeated by a knowledge of the nature of language, our own language and concomitantly the languages of other peoples.

Such a radical innovation will, of course, not be introduced, much less elaborated on, in one year or even one decade within our total educational fabric. But it could easily become part of the curricular scheme of a new educational venture like Hampshire College, which in its own way will be educating not only future community and regional, but also national and perhaps even world leaders. It would seem evident, then, that Hampshire College students will not be able to afford to neglect the story and study of language and the diverse functions of language, including primarily language as a means of multiform communication—language, therefore, as a potential power to keep or to liberate men and minds from stubborn, stifling provincialism that can lead, at best, to sterile or, at worst, to explosive, even tragic encounters between people and nations.[161]

The 1966 Committee considered that, in addition to their being connected with one of the other three fields, certain faculty members would serve in Language Studies. The Committee foresaw a need for a Languages faculty including philosophers, mathematicians, linguists, computer theorists, and others. Courses suggested by the Committee were thought of in an earlier framework of "freshman seminars," non-major courses, and courses for majors, as follows:

*Freshman Seminars*

> Game theory
> Linear graph theory
> Philosophical analysis
> Geometric inequalities
> Irrational numbers
> Logic in use

Theories concerning a hypothetical language
Language as word, sound, or sight; *and* as symbol
Grammar and culture
Grimm's Law of Consonant Shifts and other significant linguistics laws
Assumptions concerning the place of origin of the Indo-European family of languages
The Germanic Language groups, including English

## Courses for Non-Majors

Finite mathematics
Computer linguistics
History of languages
Semantics
Foundations of mathematics
Linguistics
Language and psychology

## Courses for Majors

Symbolic logic I
Symbolic logic II
Metalogic
Linguistic analysis:  Metaphysics
Linguistic analysis:  Epistemology
Linguistic analysis:  Value theory
The syntax of language
Topology
Modern algebra
Number theory
Geometry
Advanced calculus
Statistics
Complex variables
Computer theory

The recommendations of the Committee will be discussed further during the whole period in which the School of Language Studies takes form. The essential point will not be lost:  Language, in this broad sense, will be a new major undergraduate field at Hampshire College.

Further, the School will signify the College's strong interest not only in knowledge about communication, but in improving information transfer capabilities at the collegiate level. Hampshire College is far from being committed to any idle notion that gadgetry will do the job in liberal education. But the College is not going to try either to repeal the 20th century or revive the 12th. Its eye is on the human uses of technology in education of the kind this paper describes—with a strong orientation toward maintaining high quality, developing individual capacity for self-education throughout life, and economizing sensibly at the institutional level where instruction occurs. Hampshire College will use the new technology of education whenever it will serve these things. Assignment of responsibility for continuous awareness and evaluation of developments in information transfer is made directly to the School of Language Studies and the INTRAN Center within it (see next chapter). The College will design its physical facilities and review them continuously in order to achieve the greatest possible flexibility for the installation or adaptation of genuine technological improvements in education.

In doing these things, Hampshire will serve its own students more fully. The College hopes that the School of Language Studies will be seen by students of the other institutions of the Valley as offering them an opportunity to share in an exciting new field of undergraduate study.

# 7

# HAMPSHIRE COLLEGE AS A COMMUNITY

*. . . You can climb*
*Back up a stream of radiance to the sky,*
*And back through history up the stream of time.*
*And you were given this swiftness, not for haste*
*Nor chiefly that you may go where you will,*
*But in the rush of everything to waste,*
*That you may have the power of standing still—*
*Off any still or moving thing you say. . . .*

ROBERT FROST
*The Master Speed*

POETRY may well provide, as Robert Frost once said, "the one permissible way of saying one thing and meaning another." The lines from his sonnet, "The Master Speed," suggest that the meaning of swiftness lies, paradoxically, in a greater power for stillness. Speed is not just for haste's sake, nor for that of caprice, either. "This swiftness" means a greater range for detachment, for "standing still," for seeing and thinking. Frost's paradox (to say nothing of the lovely, clean lines in which it is set) seems relevant to the question of what a college should mean and be in the swiftness of young lives.

On the other hand, the driving pressure in much of American higher education today, as in the secondary schools, is for intensive performance, the criteria of which are professional competence, quantifiable output, and haste. There is precious little elbow room for standing still, looking around, thinking about something that catches your mind's eye but isn't

173

in the fast-running program. In this sense, education reflects what Jules Henry called the *drivenness* of our general technological society. As Nevitt Sanford put it, "the American college, and American institutions of higher learning generally, are imbedded in our culture. . . . They are expressive of persistent trends, and persistent conflicts, in the American value system. . . ." [162] Because this is the case, performance pressures, which the society feels, are understandably visible in its schools, colleges, and universities.

The likelihood that the pressure to perform will be reduced generally in higher education in the near future would be a worse bet than wagering a dray-horse against Man o'War. A technological society of the kind we have now *needs* competence; precise, skilled, technical competent manpower-production, on a rapid assembly line basis, is in many ways the fundamental job our society has assigned to education. Large-scale change in education towards a higher function than this may come, but only as and if our society's operation and values change.[163] It would seem, as Kenneth Keniston says, that while one of the functions of the liberal arts college should be to provide an education and an environment that encourage students to gather intellect, ethical sense, and action into one related whole, and that while graduate education should assist the pre-professional to connect his inner self with the vocation that will occupy his life, "this too rarely happens." [164]

There are new and old institutions, however, where students do find high academic performance and an active connection between intellect and life very much a part of the college community. It is this fact that is hopeful. It shows that the great current, running in society and education, *can* be channeled to serve more than manpower training needs, that colleges, while imbedded in the culture, are not bound entirely by it. The fact that some colleges do enable students to "gather intellect, ethical sense, and action into one related whole" gives credibility to the thought that swiftness can have the meaning that Robert Frost meant, in the context of a new college.

The community of Hampshire College is founded on this belief. The form of the community is designed with the intention of supporting the kind of college culture, academic program, intellectual life, and moral concern touched on earlier in this paper. Some of the features of the College community are described or suggested here.

## 1. THE STUDENTS

It is necessary to describe a community according to its constituencies; in the case of Hampshire this necessity is regrettable, since it is the College's intention to emphasize an openness of relationship among individuals, younger and older, in community with each other.

The greatest number of Hampshire's individuals manifestly will be its students, in the term's usual meaning. But Hampshire hopes that the dominant spirit of its community will be that *all* within its precincts are students, in the sense that the community is one of people, whether young or old, sharing a common quest. This is not to deny differences in age and background, in achievement and experience, in authority and responsibility. It is to say that the understructure of these is an enterprise in which all have in common the pursuit of things that can only be pursued and never wholly gained.

Present plans, as a later section on campus design explains, call for Hampshire College to have approximately 1440 students when it reaches full strength. As nearly as possible, there will be a fairly even balance between numbers of men and women students. Hampshire will be the first coeducational private college among its sister institutions in the Valley.

a. *The Hallmark of the Hampshire Student*

The students who will find Hampshire College right for them are likely to have some very important things in common, no matter how diverse their backgrounds or interests. One of these is that they will have good minds; they will be people who respect intellect not as an end but as a means. Another is that they will have had preparation for entrance which Hampshire judges to be at least equal to that of students at other colleges of high quality.* A third is that they will be capable of handling a steady opening up of increased independence, responsibly and without undue anxiety. They will be young men and women who *want* to combine intellect and creativity with ethics and action, and who have a ca-

* Emphasis here is on Hampshire's judgment, not on necessarily standard test performance, secondary school course-completion, and similar criteria, although these will certainly be taken into account in most cases.

pacity for pride in the self-discipline and honesty that such a combination requires. They will have an instinct for civility, as that term was earlier used in this paper. They will be strong enough to stand critical discourse, to argue and be argued with, to hold their own convictions and act on them, to know the difference between courtesy and being either square or manipulative.

They will not be unbelievable paragons of all the virtues. The best of young American men and women really have these kinds of characteristics. And Hampshire proposes to begin with the best in these terms. None of these things demands a homogeneity of high test-scores, of uniform interests, or of social, economic, or ethnic backgrounds. Hampshire will be right for a great heterogeneity of students in kinds of intelligence, lines of creativity, fields of interest, and types of background. But Hampshire students will be a special kind as well, distinguished most by a strong reaching for maturity. If, in this, they represent a minority, they may be not so much set apart, as simply ahead of the majority in a general change. "It is the minority," Richard B. Sewall suggests, "that generally sense and sometimes set the tone and mood of a culture, or define what may really be stirring among the inarticulate many." [165]

Hampshire College is selective in its choice of students; it is so on these kinds of grounds, which are much more difficult to specify and assess than SAT scores or athletic prowess. The students Hampshire selects will not be those for whom the term "experimental," as the 1958 New College Plan said, has "the implications that discipline is unnecessary, that the arts offer a way of life that can elude normal obligations and limitations, that the educational community should be set up in opposition to the society as a whole. . . ." [166] The students the College actively seeks are not unlike those capable of enlarging the vanguard Professor Sewall has described in discussing what he sees of the undergraduate culture:

> Its hallmark is neither rebellion nor negation. It is not the familiar story of the new generation denying the values of the old. Rather, it is a reaffirmation of values which the old still preach but fail to practice. In this sense, it is faintly conservative, even nostalgic; it is radical in that it goes to the roots of things. It wants to know why. If it seems to defy authority, the intention is not so much to dispossess authority as to remind it of its proper job. It will work happily under any au-

thority that provides a decent scope and opportunity for the realization of certain basic ideals. It wants to see justice done . . .; virtue rewarded . . .; morality, honesty, and the principles of democracy applied to international as well as domestic affairs. It has passed beyond the romantic self-expression of The Roaring Twenties, and beyond the nihilism of the beatniks, to the sense of an external world which it can and should influence, and to this extent it is much more politically sophisticated than my generation was. It wants to be a part of that world, not to run it, but to be heard in it. Just as it wants to break down the barriers that made the old undergraduate world a thing apart, so it attacks the barriers that make for divisiveness and separatism in our culture as a whole: it is increasingly interracial, interdenominational, intercollegiate, international, interclass, and coeducational.[167]

Implicit in Professor Sewall's description, but not directly expressed by it, is the fact that, for all the disparagement of "leadership" that tends to be fashionable in the academic world of professionals and students, this vanguard of his is expressing in its own way a healthy aspiration to take the reins.

Hampshire intends to kindle as much interest in leadership and as much understanding of its necessity and responsibilities as a college can. We cannot, as John Gardner put it, choose not to have leaders, but we can have the kinds of leaders we want in the world of larger action. Deprecation of leadership as a factor in society is as wasteful as it is silly. Hampshire is not founded to serve a leaderless society. As an institution, the College wants to share in a reconstruction of the concept of leadership in the community of men, and help its students become effective and morally responsible leaders themselves, for the needs of their time.

b.  *The Education of Men and Women at Hampshire College*

One of the most complex and interesting opportunities that Hampshire has is to try to redefine coeducation in terms that will make sense in our kind of society and culture. Doing so at all effectively is beyond the reach of the present paper; it will require intensive study and planning from now until the College opens, and continuous planning, innovation, and evaluation beyond that. The chief thing that can be done now is to underline Hampshire's awareness of a primary responsibility in this connection and an intention to do something about it.

In particular, the College will reexamine the question of the position of women in American society and the relation of education to their needs. Esther Raushenbush, President of Sarah Lawrence College, has been generous in giving Hampshire the benefit of her experience and wisdom in this matter. A number of women educators in the four colleges have given valuable assistance over the years to the development of plans for a new college. In the summer just ended, Hampshire has gained very useful suggestions and reactions from consultation with a number of women concerned with education, including Laya Wiesner, Elizabeth Hall, and Sister Jacqueline.* The writings of Alice S. Rossi, Edna G. Rostow, Jean D. Grambs, Esther Peterson, and others have helped shape Hampshire's present understanding of some of the dimensions of the question. These and other leaders will be worked with, if their interest and time permit, as the College continues its planning.

Hampshire is convinced that, while coeducation has no exclusive claim as The Way for colleges (and indeed has its own present share of deficits and difficulties), the education of men and women together is proper for the vision the College embodies. It is hard to see how growth towards human understanding, and the intellectual, affective, moral, and enactive realization of "self in society"—Hampshire's vision of liberal education—can be achieved without an educative community of men *and* women. The commitment of the College to coeducation involves at present at least the following views:

> That coeducation *as is* in most colleges cannot be accepted as a given in its patterns or assumptions.

> That coeducation, both in academic program and the community life of the College, is a proper concern for reexamination, innovation, and reconstruction.

> That sex differences in human behavior and outlook in our culture run deep, and need to be considered in planning education for men and women.

> That women face inequalities in our society which cannot be justified because of inherent differences and which may be productively dealt with by education.

*President of Webster College, Webster Grove, Missouri, and a spirited force in education everywhere.

That women, as well as men, should increasingly assume responsibility for their own decisions, being encouraged to think ahead to a whole life span in which marriage and parenthood are one thread among many in their lives.

That women, as well as men, should be able to find something of what Erik Erikson once called a "psycho-social moratorium" in college life, free not to make intense commitments across sex lines, and free to explore the dimensions of identity.

That education should help women see marriage and motherhood as a significant potential part of self-realization but not as its exclusive basis.

That education has a profound responsibility to help make it possible for women to lead lives of expanding independence; in which marriage and child-bearing are a genuine choice rather than a compulsion; and in which, if motherhood is chosen, there can be purposeful, independent, and satisfying life beyond it.

c. *Innovations in Admissions*

The College will rely heavily for guidance in the development of student recruitment procedures and admissions policies on the great reservoir of experience and understanding of these things among its sister institutions in the Valley. These institutions have the benefit of a long history, of being accustomed to look for quality in its many forms among prospective students, and of leadership by some of the best admissions officers in the country. Hampshire will be grateful for the advice and assistance that these institutions give it, on admissions as in other matters.

Thought will be given as well to new possibilities in admission, and these hopefully may be tested in discussion with officers of the other four institutions. Some of the possibilities presently in mind, without commitment to action on any, are mentioned below.

( 1. *The Policy of Guaranteed Delayed Admission*

As discussion indicated earlier, the College will seriously consider the feasibility and desirability of allowing students to be accepted but to delay their actual matriculation until a period as long as twenty-four months has gone by. The basic intention would be to allow the student, who wants and can benefit by a moratorium between secondary school and college, to have it. The experience colleges had with returning G.I.'s after World War II was that they had gained a degree of purpose and maturity which set them off markedly from young men who had not been away. It would be unwise to generalize extensively from the G.I. phenomenon, but colleges indeed learned something from it.

It appears to Hampshire that it would be very useful to some of to-day's high school graduates to leave the academic world for a few months, a year, two years, or conceivably longer, before tackling college. Work, military service, travel, or hibernation for a while, could well let a student come on to college afterwards with a clearer sense of himself. The problems any single institution would have in applying such a policy may make it unfeasible, but Hampshire intends to study the matter carefully and perhaps try it on a limited scale.

### (2. *The College Before College*

An intensive summer program for entering freshmen who, while able, are regarded as high risks because of lacks in their cultural background and in the quality of secondary schools they attended, is reported by the Carnegie Corporation as being very useful.[168] Certain "high risk" students, who have been admitted to college, enter an eight-week pre-college workshop in the summer preceding their freshman year. They live on campus and have an active experience with the way academic life goes. For a relatively small group (as few as thirty to thirty-five), an institution may assign five regular faculty members and six tutors, who are advanced undergraduates. Pre-freshman students are given slices of college-level course-work in such fields as sociology, history, philosophy, science, and the nature of ideas. Of even more importance, perhaps, tutors work with them closely in learning or improving such skills as listening to a lecture, taking notes that are usable, taking examinations, and organizing their time effectively. Hampshire regards pre-college summer training for selected entering students as an advisable thing, especially for young men and women from inadequate backgrounds.

### (3. *Very Early Identification and Encouragement of Students with College Potential*

This area of consideration falls into two parts, one of which is definite enough to be a clear line of action, the other of which is in a most tentative state. Neither can be more than suggested here.

The first has to do with the very early identification and encouragement of able but disadvantaged boys and girls who are capable of benefiting from higher education. Ordinarily, colleges seriously consider students for admission only when they are in the final year of high school.

For the most part, colleges are then dealing with middle-class youth who have been encouraged (some, indeed, pushed) by their families to expect to go to college. The encouragement usually begins before the child is aware of it, and "preparation for college" is simply a given, an implicit assumption of the whole family environment. The middle-class child comes to realize early both that he is expected to go to college and that, one way or another, it will be possible. In a real sense, the family *guarantees* college for him, culturally and financially.

Quite the opposite is true of many very able children in lower-income families. Negro boys in low-income families of urban or rural slums, for example, are likely to have no such expectation or encouragement, regardless of their ability. Often, as in the Boston schools, their academic performance falls steadily during elementary school, reflecting school, familial, and societal failure to support their intellectual growth. Thomas Pettigrew of Harvard has commented in discussion of this to the effect that, by the age of ten, "most Negro boys know what the score is and know it's for them." Professor Pettigrew means that Negro boys, by the end of the fifth grade, often have concluded that school really doesn't want them—and that they in turn do not want school.

The result at minimum is psychological withdrawal from any but apathetic involvement with school. In many cases apathy shifts to hostility, hostility is expressed in anti-social behavior, and the behavior leads to "dropping-out" or being dropped out. This happens with many very bright Negro boys of low-income families, as well as with many more who have less ability. The phenomenon is, of course, not at all limited to a single race, although in the case of Negro children of low-income background the factor of poverty is complicated by racial discrimination.

The upshot is that, by the time the last year of secondary school arrives, the boy is either not in school at all or, if he is still there, he is so ill-prepared and diffusely motivated that college is a poor bet for him if it is a bet at all.

Thus far, colleges for the most part have tried salvage operations with such youth only after the twelfth grade, or, at the earliest, a year before.  Hampshire is certain that this can work for some disadvantaged students, but that it is far too late for many others.

The College therefore proposes, on a limited trial basis, to identify a small number of high potential children of disadvantaged homes in their tenth year, and guarantee the families involved that their children will have full scholarships at Hampshire, *if* the children proceed through the remainder of their schooling at an acceptable level.  To this financial incentive, the College will also supply children so identified with voluntary tutorial help by Hampshire students during the seven years before their high school graduation.

Hampshire leadership believes that such a program of very early incentive and encouragement will demonstrate the utility of a totally new approach to admissions for children of poverty.  To wait until the senior year of high school is to wait too long.

The second approach to early identification is so tentative that it can be formed only as a series of questions.  Three assumptions are required.  One is that total charges for private collegiate education will continue to rise in the foreseeable future.  A second is that many if not most families would find it financially helpful to spread such costs over a period of years longer than the years of actual college attendance.  Evidence of this lies in present bank-connected insured tuition payment plans which allow a family to spread payments *beyond* the graduation date for a period of several years.  A third assumption is that some boys and girls might have a more productive and healthy secondary school experience if they were assured of a college place from the eighth grade on, and were able to work up to their levels of interest and ability without constant anxiety about standardized test scores and the junior-senior "college-entrance" lottery.

Given these assumptions, a question Hampshire will investigate is whether it might be feasible and desirable to enable a family to arrange for provisional acceptance of a child at twelve years of age, conditional upon (a) the child's later decision in the twelfth grade that Hampshire was indeed the college of his choice, (b) assessment by the College of the adequacy of the young person's preparation and development at the twelfth grade, and (c) the family's participation in a tuition payment plan beginning when the child is twelve and continuing through his college years. Such an arrangement could be abrogated by any of the parties involved at any point up to matriculation with no loss of capital by the family, except for insurance and bank handling charges. Abrogation after matriculation, if needed, would provide for suitable reimbursement to the College.

If such an arrangement—considered most tentatively here—proved both workable and desirable—it would help the parent or other source of funds by spreading tuition charges over a period of at least nine years, with continued full insurance coverage. It would help the College by stabilizing to some degree its tuition income. And it would help the student by freeing him from a good deal of the pressure for extrinsic rewards that now fills the high school years.

## 2. THE FACULTY

Teaching in American colleges today faces a number of hazards, pressures, and opportunities.

One of the hazards, which American faculties are not notoriously loath to name, is that of over-administration. Discussion will return to this question in the next section.

Another hazard, touched on at the beginning of this paper, arises from the commanding position of the various disciplines and their associations and the condition of the academic marketplace. In these communities of the professional, the central preoccupation is professionally recognized scholarship; the most prized membership often is not in a community principally concerned with the education of young men and women, but in an association where life's prizes are won at the annual meeting and in the pages of the professional journal.

Much good, of course, results. There is a constant challenge to faculty to be scholars, to share in pressing the edges of human knowledge forward. In many ways this helps to place today's American college teachers among the most highly informed and actively knowledgeable professors in the world. Students gain in consequence.

Professionalization in the disciplines, however, can move the instructor's principal allegiance from the campus and classroom to the quarterly. Competition with colleagues in one's discipline can become more basic than discourse with students. In the process, community within the institution is not nourished. These tendencies are more commonly encountered in the large universities than in the colleges.

Hampshire's sister institutions in the Connecticut Valley have been singularly able to avoid an unnecessary conflict between teaching and research and to achieve a coherent sense of community. These are institutions with a tradition of fine teaching *and* excellent research, whose testament is found both in their graduates and in distinguished contributions of faculty in the sciences, the arts, and public service. One of the challenges before Hampshire College is to build a faculty which can match this tradition.

Guidance for Hampshire lies in what the 1958 Four-College Committee had to say about the faculty of what was then called the New College. Present leadership of Hampshire cannot improve on what was said eight years ago.

The College must offer:

> salaries on a scale at least equal to that of any of the sponsoring institutions, tenure in accordance with the joint recommendations of the American Association of University Professors and the Association of American Colleges, substantial help in the purchase of homes or rental of apartments, and regular research and study leaves. The prospect of taking part in a fresh start should certainly draw able people. And a committed, indeed, dedicated faculty will be essential to make the program work. But at the same time it will be necessary deliberately to avoid, here as with the student body, a group entirely composed of experiment-minded people. Variety and reliability will be as important as dedication.
>
> An important factor in attracting substantial scholars can be a generous provision of opportunities for research. The New College curriculum requires people who are vitally interested in teaching, ready to devote time and imagination to attending to the *students'* thinking, not just to their own. But there need be no dichotomy be-between teaching and research. During the twenty-eight weeks of the fall and spring terms at New College, the teaching demands on the faculty will be very heavy. But during the midwinter term, fifty per cent of the faculty in any given year will not be involved and so will be free to pursue their own studies from before Christmas until early in February. This should prove a substantial attraction to research-minded people.

Since the heaviest demands on faculty time come in the fall, when the freshman seminars are being given, most leaves of absence will probably extend over the whole period from before Christmas to the following September. Those who do take part in the midwinter term each year (probably about half of the faculty) will also have a stimulus to learning, for along with extra pay they will have occasion to explore subjects of fresh general interest, or to push further, in delivering lectures and preparing readings, etc., their understanding of what is general in their own specialty. . . . Individual offices, properly equipped, should be provided for all faculty members.

. . . The midwinter term will be an occasion for interchange with visiting scholars. The Committee believes that for the fall and spring terms also a certain part of the faculty—not more than 10%—should consist of visiting teachers from other sections of the country, brought in to observe the New College program by taking part in it. This device would spread information about the successes and failures of New College while bringing criticism and fresh perspectives to its faculty. In addition to such full-time visitors from a distance, there should be a considerable amount of part-time visiting by members of neighboring faculties. A number of courses can be given simultaneously at New College and neighboring institutions, sometimes in the same form, sometimes in two different forms, so as to provide experimental parallels.

The emphasis in the curriculum on student initiative will provide a basis for a much wider use of students as teaching assistants than is usually possible. It is proposed that every member of the faculty and administration enlist, as his paid assistants or aides, one or more talented and congenial upperclass students to work with him in reading papers, gathering data for lectures or research, perhaps sometimes giving lectures and conducting seminars. Such student assistants would constitute an intellectual elite—and their experience might well lead a good proportion of them to enter the teaching profession. Their wages would in many cases function as a supplement to scholarship funds, though ability and willingness rather than need should be the basis of selection. In certain situations, for example in the case where an upperclass lecture-seminar course has a particularly large enrollment, it will be valuable to employ several student teaching assistants to assist one teacher.

. . . A substantial proportion of the faculty needed for the first class should be appointed a year in advance. . . . In the first four years of the College, as class after class is added and staff procured, it should be possible for the decisions as to the representation on the faculty of the various disciplines to be governed in a measure by the pattern of student demand as it emerges.[169]

Earlier discussion mentioned the desirability of providing semester sabbaticals at full pay for faculty after every third year of service. Another feature of faculty time is that a usual teaching program would be the equivalent of three courses. Such steps are intended to free faculty for frequent self-renewal and for participation in the College as a community of people.

Both the 1958 and 1966 Committee studies proceeded on the assumption that the New College could be organized to provide a high quality of education with a faculty to student ratio of 1 to 20. This is in contrast to other private colleges of high quality in America where ratios are often less than half this. If the ratio expected by the study committees were achieved, this would mean that Hampshire could have, at a full student strength of 1440, a faculty of 72. The question of whether such a ratio and a high quality of education are genuinely compatible remains to be resolved. If the total number of full-time faculty is 90, as suggested in the preceding chapter, the ratio would still be 1 to 16, or very substantially greater than that at nearby private colleges.

The College plans to have the greatest number of its faculty be men and women who are at the beginning of their careers, engaged at the instructor and assistant professor level. Young scholars and teachers can bring with them a degree of enthusiasm about their material which makes it as vivid and exciting for students as it is for themselves. The next largest group will be established scholars at the level of professor. The smallest of the three groups will be men and women in mid-career, with the rank of associate professor.

A possibility, discussed tentatively, is that unlike other colleges, Hampshire might begin with only two faculty groups or ranks. A senior group of full professors, distributed in the four School fields of the College, would be one of the two. These would be men and women of mature experience in the academic world, with demonstrated achievement in scholarship and teaching. Their positions would carry tenure and perquisites comparable to those of full professors at leading American colleges and universities. The second group, perhaps three times the first in number, would be made up of very able young men and women who were in the process of completing doctoral programs, who had just done so, or who had recently completed other graduate study or special work relevant to the teaching program of Hampshire.

The College will emphasize in every way it can usefully do so, the integration of faculty with students and administrators in a genuine community. Faculty will not be asked to submerge their lives in incessant "life" with students. Good faculty would refuse, as they should; and students would not want it. A "genuine community" in Hampshire's sense means among other things that faculty and students will have *opportunity* for a substantial degree of informal contact outside the classroom.

The campus design explained in the last section of this chapter is intended deliberately to make faculty and students easily available to each other, and yet to protect the independence and privacy of both. Student housing is decentralized into villages or clusters known as Houses. Each House or village cluster will have its own identity, as one might expect. In addition, a good part of the academic facilities of the College will be decentralized into the Houses or village clusters: some classrooms, lecture halls, seminar rooms will be a part of each. And most of the College faculty will have their private office-studies in the academic facilities of the Houses; faculty of each of the four Schools thus will be largely dispersed among the Houses, rather than quartered in central offices of a "departmental" kind. Some junior and senior faculty will live in college residences of their own within each village cluster or House, but their residences will be separate and as private as faculty would wish them to be.

### 3. Community Organization and Government

One of the minor hazards of the academic community is that of over-administration. We have a peculiar American genius for organizing and engineering virtually everything from the automated production of automatic transistorized widgets to soft landings on Mars. This organizational and engineering genius of ours is wedded everywhere in our society to a kind of metastatic growth of bureaucracy which puts earlier

German models to shame and demonstrates that C. Northcote Parkinson may be the social Einstein of our time. Bureaucratic or not, administration has come to be a massive component of American collegiate and university education. There is a tendency in American colleges and universities to increase the administrative staff and the administrative detail out of proportion to the essential responsibility of teaching. This development has not gone without consequences or notice. Last year, John Gardner commented in California that "administrators" had become something of a dirty word in recent campus troubles, perhaps the only dirty word at Berkeley not spelled with four letters.

Perhaps as dangerous as over-administration is its opposite, where leadership is too late and too little. The fact is that there is an absolute need for bold and decisive administrative leadership in the college community. If there had not been such leadership in American higher education in the 1950's, working hard and under great pressure, America would not have the college and university resources now at its command in the 1960's. Real danger comes when administration becomes an end in itself, as most human activities tend to be if let alone, when it tends to multiply and bureaucratize, or when it tends to vacillate, run to ambiguity, and fail to help a community define and articulate its limits and its aspirations.

Hampshire College aims to be a community which is not over-administered, and not one more illustration of the correctness of Professor Parkinson's several laws. Within the community, a deliberate effort will be made to avoid a centralized bureaucracy, out of keeping with either the College's human concerns or its size. To a substantial degree, administration will be decentralized in several ways. Access to the administrative structure of the College by students and faculty will be as open as possible.

On the other hand, Hampshire College does not intend to be inoculated with what Mr. Gardner has called the "anti-leadership vaccine" commonly urged as the basic specific for true democracy. Perhaps Walter Prescott Webb was too extreme in once defining a committee as a group of people who individually cannot solve a problem, and collectively decide that there is no solution. And perhaps, as a senior professor and historian, he extended his extremism even further when he said that "God so loved the world that He did not send a committee, and for that we should all be thankful."*

Hampshire College is traditional in that it has an organized Board of Trustees with ultimate policy authority under State charter for the governance of the institution. Hampshire is also traditional in the sense that, under the policy-making power of the Board, authority and responsibility for operating leadership of the College is given to its chief executive officer, the President. His responsibility and authority are not solely negative, nor in practical terms could they be. It takes more than vetoes to build a new institution, particularly one which will be dedicated to a vigorous and imaginative reconstruction of private undergraduate education so that it may survive at a level of high quality in the face of unpromising and difficult conditions for all small, independent colleges.

Hampshire College begins with confidence in itself as an idea produced over the years by daring men and women of the four colleges, as a bold act of faith by its organizing trustees, and as an institution which must now be defined in fact by decisive action. Leadership in this new academic community cannot take refuge in the modern art of reaching a decision without really deciding. It cannot justify itself by sending out questionnaires, requiring reports, gathering statistics, using new and expensive machines, and finally escaping the solution of its own problems by appointing committees. As the institution takes form and continues, its leadership must have all the facts and guidance that it can get. But:

> after the facts are in, the leader must in some measure emulate the little girl who told the teacher she was going to draw a picture of God. The teacher said, "But, Mary, no one knows what God looks like"; and Mary said, "They will when I get through."**

Again, the example may be exaggerated to make a point. Colleges certainly cannot afford to be led by Men of Destiny who believe they know

---

* Professor Webb made these pungent comments in "A Letter to a New College President," in the *Graduate Journal* of the University of Texas, Fall, 1960.

**John W. Gardner used this not too unlikely story in his essay. "The Anti-Leadership Vaccine," included in the 1965 *Annual Report* of the Carnegie Corporation of New York.

all the answers. Neither can they afford to be led by Nervous Nellies, who will flutter with every wind that blows.

The organization of Hampshire College as an institution and as a community is intended to permit active participation in processes of planning and operation by faculty, students, trustees, and administrators. It should be possible for innovations and evaluation to be freely initiated by any member or group in the community. It is not intended that a multiplicity of permanent committees be established, but that a very few representative committees should have considerable responsibility for helping to shape the nature of the College. It is also intended to have a simple, clear, decentralized administrative structure in which lines of specific responsibility and authority will be effective channels through which information, decisions, and services can flow.

Organization charts are one of the banes of modern society which fall in the category of artistic fictions. By and large, human relationships and institutional problems are always more complex than any organizational chart can disclose or accommodate. With this assumption understood, the organizational chart which is included here may be seen as a provisional approximation and not as something ready to be graven in stone.

The President, of course, is directly responsible to the Board of Trustees and serves at their pleasure. At Hampshire College, the President is assisted by two chief administrators who report directly to him. One of these is the Dean of the College or Academic Vice-President; the other is the Administrative Vice-President. In addition, the President of the College is aided by a Student Assistant to the President. The Student Assistant to the President is exactly that: an executive assistant who works closely with the President, assisting him in every reasonable kind of responsibility. The Student Assistant to the President is chosen by the President from a group of three senior students elected for consideration by the general student body. The Student Assistant's experience could be an intensive internship in educational leadership undertaken by him as the special study which would ordinarily require at least half of his time in any case during the Division III year.

The Dean of the College will have under his supervision all of the academic activities of the institution. Reporting directly to him will be

THE ORGANIZATION OF HAMPSHIRE COLLEGE

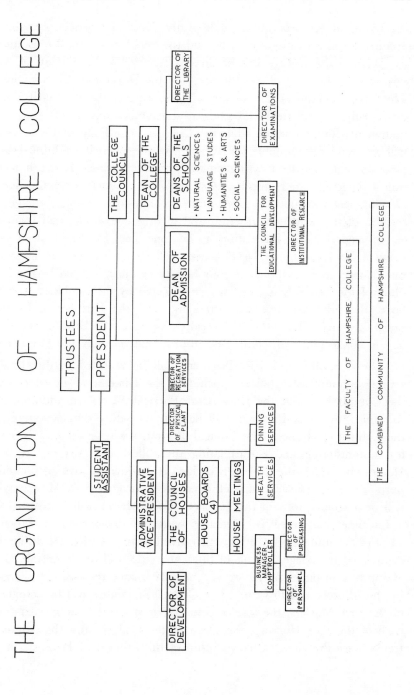

the Deans of the separate Schools of the Natural Sciences, Language Studies, the Humanities and Arts, and the Social Sciences. In addition, the Dean of the College will be directly reported to by a Dean of Admissions, the Director of the Library, and the Director of Examinations. The latter position is one which will be required by the institution's heavy emphasis on field and integrative examinations as the basic requirements for graduation from the College. The Dean of the College will also have responsibility for oversight of the Council for Educational Development, described earlier on the basis of Professor Kenneth Keniston's suggestion to Hampshire College. The Council for Educational Development will function to maintain a continuous review of the effectiveness of the academic program and to originate, study, and forward recommendations for innovations to be considered by the faculty. The Council for Educational Development will be chaired by the Dean of the College, and composed of four faculty members elected by the faculties of the four Schools, two students elected by the combined student body, the Administrative Vice-President, and the Director of Institutional Research. The latter will report directly to the Dean of the College in connection with continuing institutional research and evaluation.

The Administrative Vice-President will be reported to directly by several administrative officers, including the Director of Development, the Comptroller, and the Director of Physical Plant. In addition, the Administrative Vice-President will be charged with general oversight of the Council of Houses. The Council of Houses will be the basic agency for administering and co-ordinating the collective affairs of the four Houses into which the College is divided for residential and instructional purposes. Each of the House clusters will be headed by a Master, who will be a senior professor in residence. Each Master will be assisted by a full-time administrative executive with the designation of Proctor. Most of the student-related administrative functions which are ordinarily centralized in college (Deans of Students, etc.) will be decentralized at Hampshire through the House system, with major responsibility carried by the Masters and Proctors. The Council of Houses will be composed of the four Masters, the four Proctors, four students (one elected from each of the four Houses), the Dean of the College, and the Administrative Vice-President. Chairmanship of the Council of Houses will be rotated yearly among the four Masters. For administrative purposes, the Chairman of the Council of Houses will report to the Administrative Vice-President. A College-wide Director of Recreation Services will be under the general oversight of the Administrative Vice-President but will report directly to the Chairman of the Council of Houses and will be an ex-officio member of that Council. It is expected that each of the four Houses will have its own student-faculty governing board and will make appropriate arrangements for House meetings and student participation in government of House affairs.

The third major Council of the College will be known as the College Council, of which the President will be Chairman. This body will be intended to provide a central representation for all of the principal elements of the College for regular consideration of College needs, programs, planning, evaluation, and questions of policy affecting the community as a whole. The College Council will be composed of four faculty members elected by the School faculties, four students elected by the student body at large, the Chairman of the Council of Houses, one Proctor elected by that group, the Dean of the College, and the Administrative Vice-President.

It is expected that each of the separate Schools of the College will organize its faculty as seems best to the Dean and his colleagues. Further detailing of arrangements of faculty participation in the development of decisions and for student participation in all-College life of the community will be a matter for concentrated further study as plans for the College move forward.

## 4. HAMPSHIRE COLLEGE CAMPUS DESIGN: A MODULAR APPROACH

The work of site planning and development on the 450 acres of beautiful land which is the Hampshire College campus is in its initial stages. The firm of Sasaki, Dawson, and DeMay is proceeding with a staged series of site studies and landscape design which will accomplish several things of importance to the College's future. Hideo Sasaki and his associates have completed a fundamental survey-assessment of Hampshire College land resources.* They have examined the surrounding

*See appendix material for the Sasaki analysis.

community environment of South Amherst to determine its principal
current characteristics (in terms of zoning, land use, traffic, commercial
services, etc.) and have projected what these characteristics may be in
the future. They have tried to estimate the impact the College will have
on the changing South Amherst community, and how the surrounding
environment will affect Hampshire in the years ahead. Further work
of Professor Sasaki's firm will assist the College in developing a coherent,
functional, economical, and attractive master plan for the use of its
land.

To design and develop the buildings of Hampshire College, the Board
of Trustees has chosen one of the foremost of modern architects, Hugh
Asher Stubbins, Jr. Mr. Stubbins heads the versatile and distinguished
firm of Hugh Stubbins and Associates, Cambridge, Massachusetts. The
recipient of many honors and awards for architectural design in America
and Europe, Mr. Stubbins has demonstrated keen understanding and
creative insight in dealing with the architecture of academic institutions.
He has executed important commissions for Bowdoin College, Harvard
University, the Massachusetts Institute of Technology, Princeton University, the University of Massachusetts, Mount Holyoke College, Brandeis University, and other public and private schools and colleges. In
addition he has designed major modern television facilities, office buildings, churches, museum quarters, and other structures.

In undertaking the commission for building design and development
at Hampshire College, Mr. Stubbins has an unusual opportunity to help
shape a whole institution from the beginning. In terms of site selection,
master planning, and landscape design, Mr. Sasaki has a similar opportunity. From the start, Mr. Stubbins and Mr. Sasaki will cooperate
with each other closely. The College is fortunate to have the interest
of such a distinguished architect and such an outstanding authority in
landscape design.

These men and their associates will have direct responsibility for
design and development in their distinct but related fields. In addition,
but separate from actual project work, the Trustees and College administration have been privileged to secure the services of Mr. Pietro
Belluschi as the Board's architectural adviser and consultant.

Policy decisions about architecture and campus design are being considered by the Trustees and the College administration. Several principles are implicit in present planning and development:

The campus design should express in every possible way the distinctive social and educational character of Hampshire College.

The campus design should provide variety within a coherent context, not rigid sameness of style or appearance.

The campus design should respect and enhance the natural beauty of the land.

The campus design, while helping state the distinctive identity of the College, should not present the institution as a walled tower but as an "open city," with a sense of relatedness to the surrounding world in which it exists.

The campus design should contain a substantial flexibility in order to allow for adaptation to possible *change* in the College's functions and *growth* in the size of its enrollment.

The campus design should capture some of the variety and richness of city life, in the spirit of the city so well expressed by Jane Jacobs, some of the quality of small, coherent living communities, and some of the serenity and openness of the rural scene.

The campus design should enable the institution to use the automobile, *not be used by it.*

The architecture should be modern and beautiful, without being monumental or externally uniform in a rigid sense.

The architecture should be of economical and flexible design, probably using modular economies of the sort suggested by the School Construction Systems Development project sponsored by the Educational Facilities Laboratory. The architecture, in any case, should consider radical departures from usual college construction engineering.

The architecture, while varied in expression, should (a) give a sense of over-all harmony when the campus is seen as a whole; (b) utilize some materials (e.g., brick and wood) which have a historical continuity in the culture of the Valley; and (c) *not* be a series of unrelated "statements" by architects more interested in self-expression than the needs and intentions of the institution.

These and other principles guide present thinking about the physical nature of the Hampshire College campus. At present, operating decisions

about over-all design and specific architecture are in the making. What
follows is a description of a provisional schematic model of campus and
physical organization which College leadership has developed. It is
*provisional,* it should be emphasized, and not yet explicated in terms of
design applications. The reader should understand that the following
is a highly simplified model, which will be considered by the College
among other alternatives.

a.   *The College as a Metaphor of Metropolitanism*

The essential feature of the campus design for Hampshire College
presented here is a combination of *centralization* and *decentralization,*
both *capable of substantial expansion.* A metaphor which has its hazards is that, in microcosm, the campus design should resemble a metropolitan area with an urban core city and surrounding suburban communities. This metaphor features the College's physical design as having
an "inner-city" core or College Center, with major facilities and variegated campus-wide services and opportunities efficiently but interestingly
centralized, surrounded by a series of relatively small residential-academic coeducational clusters, called Houses. Both the size of the College
Center and the number of House-modules should be capable of expansion within certain limits. There should be economical and easy access
from House to House, and from House to the College Center. The essential feeling the campus design should convey to students and faculty
is that there is interesting life and work to be found in its satellite communities (the modular Houses) *and* in its central core complex.

There should be a "home base" feel about the Houses; the combination of life and work there should provide students with a sense of
identification with a comprehensible community in which they are
members, and in which they feel the morale of membership. At the
same time, the complex of central facilities should provide students
with many things that cannot be found in the life of the House. Among
these would be richer intellectual resources, interchange with students
and faculty from all of the other Houses, opportunities for shopping in
small privately operated shops in the central complex, the full resources
of the central library and all that goes with it. The central complex
would not be simply a monolithic administrative convenience (although

in many ways it would provide for administrative economies and efficient arrangements), but the coherent "urban" heart of the campus. Its design, while having strong underlying features of efficient organization (in terms of engineering, transit, conduits, etc.) should have the feeling of variety and surprise that Jane Jacobs describes in the city.

b. *The Essential Features of the House Module*

For the immediate future, Hampshire College would have four Houses in its satellite ring surrounding the College Center. All of these would be modular, in the sense that they would incorporate in their *underlying* organization and structure certain standard features. But in their overt physical expression and community style, each would be unique and distinctive, with its own identity. Each House would have a membership of approximately 360 students. These would be equally divided, as far as possible, between men and women. Each would include residential components and certain basic academic facilities.

(1. *The House as a Residence*

Residential facilities might be somewhat similar to the University of Rhode Island housing complex developed by Belluschi, Sasaki, and others. That is to say, the residential facilities of the House may feature clusters of cottages or row houses.

There would be two related clusters; one for men, one for women.

Each cluster would be made up of four cottages housing approximately 45 students each.

Each cottage would have five suites for nine students.

Each suite of nine might include three doubles and three singles, all having individual desk carrels as at Rhode Island. (The carrels would be a special feature here, designed not only for as much privacy as possible, but also for maximum immediate and long-term development of on-line and electronic service.)

Each suite would have a furnished living room, a tiny kitchenette, and toilet facilities adequate for nine.

Each cottage would have a separate entrance and a downstairs lounge and kitchenette.

Each of the House modules would have related to it a separate duplex with apartments for two faculty members and their families.

In addition, the housing of the module would include a separate but related, commodious, and attractive residence for the Master of the House. Further, there would be a smaller, attractive residence for the Proctor, who will serve as full-time administrative officer for the House under the supervision of the Master.

### (2. *The House for Dining and Social Activities*

The House module would have one dining hall capable of serving 360 students, with major food preparation facilities centralized for two Houses or more. The dining hall should be convertible to social purposes, and it should be supplemented by an adjoining lounge.

### (3. *The House as a Place for Decentralized Academic Work*

The House module would have certain academic facilities closely related in a physical sense to the housing clusters and the dining-social facilities. The academic facilities of the House should be highly flexible for many and varied uses. These facilities would provide two principal sections: one for flexible use with small and intermediate sized groups, and the other for flexible use with groups of larger size.

The section for use with smaller and intermediate groups would be comprised of two separate rooms, each with a total student capacity of 75. Each of these two rooms should be easily convertible into three seminar-classrooms of 25. Each also should be readily convertible into one room of 50 capacity and one room of 25 capacity. This section, then, should give each House two rooms of 75, or six rooms of 25, or two rooms of 25 and two rooms of 50. The section would have a maximum total capacity of 150 students at any one time.

The second main element in the academic facilities of the module would be one large enclosed area with a capacity of 200, which could be easily converted into two lecture rooms with a capacity of 100 each.

Great attention should be given in the design of these rooms not only to *flexibility* but to *soundproofing* with flexibility. In addition, all of the rooms should be equipped for audio-visual uses, with provision of modular electric outlet grids, coaxial connection with college-wide operation from a central studio laboratory, rheostatic overhead light control, window-darkening, and the like.

Approximately sixteen faculty members would be assigned to office space in each House's academic facilities. Each faculty member should have a private study-office useful for tutorials and other academic work.

The academic facilities also would include administrative offices for the Master (who would be expected to spend half of his academic time overseeing the study and life of the House) and for the Proctor. The Proctor of the House would be a full-time administrative assistant to the Master, charged with over-all supervision of day-to-day life and arrangements of the College. The term "Proctor" is borrowed, with some modification, from Oxford usage. It is likely that in each House the Master would be a senior male professor, and the Proctor would be an academically well-qualified woman interested in college administration and counseling.

The academic facilities for each House should include one relatively small (perhaps 1,000 square feet), quiet library-reading room. In addition, the academic facilities should include a small lounge for faculty and students, with civilized equipment for having coffee and talk, or tea and sympathy.

### c. *The College as Four Houses*

Four House modules of the kind described would house 1,440 students, eight faculty members in duplex apartments, four Masters in separate residences, and four Proctors in separate residences.

Seen College-wide, the academic facilities of the four House modules would provide a large number of variable uses for the College's 1,440 students. The House academic facilities would provide for approximately 64 faculty-study offices. The four large lecture-multipurpose rooms would have a total combined capacity of 800. The 8 lecture-demonstration rooms of 75 capacity would be convertible to 24 seminar rooms of 25 capacity or 8 lecture rooms of 50 capacity plus 8 seminars of 25 capacity. The total full-use capacity of these 8 rooms would be 600 students. College-wide, the House modules would provide a total of eight administrative and clerical offices, four small library-reading rooms, and four small academic lounges.

College-wide, the combined dining and social facilities of the four House modules would provide dining hall capacity of 1,440 minimum. These dining halls would be convertible to social and community purposes of the several Houses or of the College as a whole and would be connected to four lounges offering additional study and leisure space.

d.  *Central College Facilities Serving the House Modules*

A basic principle is that all central services should be economically, functionally, and attractively *convenient* to the modules. Another basic principle is that all central services should be planned *with expansion in mind.* This means that *at the beginning* some of the central facilities should be already larger than the demands that would be put upon them by the four House modules. It also means that all central facilities and services should be planned from the beginning to be readily capable of structural and other enlargement as the College grows.

(1. *The Library and College Center*

In a highly schematic fashion, not at all representing the kind of originality of design which it would require to execute the intentions expressed in the above paragraph, the chart opposite will suggest something of the functional nature of the Library and College Center, as well as its relationship to the Houses. The College Center is a coherent, connected complex which in various ways would house nearly all of the central facilities and central personnel of the College. Among other things, its underlying structural coherences are intended to accomplish economies in many kinds of operations. The Library and College Center complex will house the library proper; the College's main administrative and service offices; the headquarters and central facilities (some conference rooms, laboratories, offices, studios, workshops, etc.) of the College's four principal Schools (the School of Language Studies, the School of Humanities and the Arts, the School of Natural Sciences, and the School of Social Sciences); ground level shops; coffee shop and/or coffee houses; if possible, a below-grade auditorium for college-wide activities and performances; central heating, electrical, and other services for the whole complex; malls, terraces, walkways, and the like. This is asking a lot, but it is the kind of dense, variegated, "urban" mix that Hamp-

# HAMPSHIRE COLLEGE

A SCHEMATIC FRAMEWORK SHOWING A HIGH-DENSITY COMPLEX OF CENTRAL FUNCTIONS SURROUNDED BY SATELLITE RESIDENTIAL - ACADEMIC MODULES.

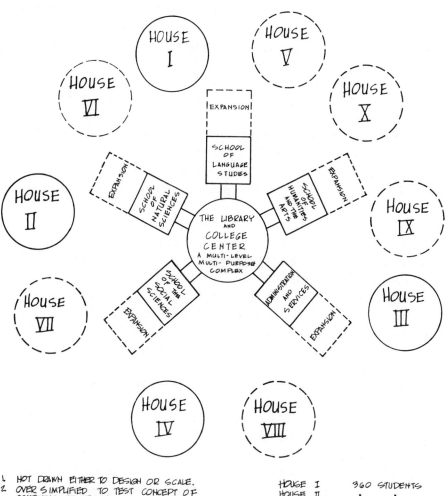

1. NOT DRAWN EITHER TO DESIGN OR SCALE.
2. OVER SIMPLIFIED TO TEST CONCEPT OF COMBINING CENTRALIZATION AND DECENTRALIZATION

LEGEND:
——————— SOLID LINE = IMMEDIATE PROJECTION
- - - - - BROKEN LINE = POSSIBLE EXPANSION

| HOUSE I | 360 STUDENTS |
| HOUSE II | . . |
| HOUSE III | . . |
| HOUSE IV | . . |
| | 1440 STUDENTS |
| HOUSES V - X [360 EACH] | 2160 |
| | 3600 TOTAL PROJECTION WITH TEN HOUSES |

Labels within the figure:
HOUSE I, HOUSE V, HOUSE VI, HOUSE X, HOUSE II, HOUSE IX, HOUSE VII, HOUSE III, HOUSE IV, HOUSE VIII

EXPANSION
SCHOOL OF LANGUAGE STUDIES
SCHOOL OF NATURAL SCIENCES
SCHOOL OF HUMANITIES AND THE ARTS
THE LIBRARY AND COLLEGE CENTER A MULTI-LEVEL MULTI-PURPOSE COMPLEX
SCHOOL OF THE SOCIAL SCIENCES
ADMINISTRATION AND SERVICES

shire College's distinctive character requires at the heart of its campus.

As the schematic drawing shows, the individual Schools and the administrative headquarters of the College should be physically connected to the total complex and capable of horizontal and/or vertical expansion. Ways must be found to make it possible in original planning for the Center itself to be expanded; it seems likely that this would need to take the form of vertical expansion. Because active interplay between the satellite House communities and the College Center is a prime consideration, it will be a crucial, practical consideration to provide easy circulation of people between the Center and the satellite Houses under all conditions of weather. Similarly, it will be important to make practical plans for relatively easy circulation among Houses, either directly from House to House or via the College Center.

The schematic drawing indicates immediate projection of four satellite Houses with a total student population of 1,440. The diagram indicates a possible future decentralized increase of satellite Houses to a total number of ten, at which point the student population of the College would be 3,600. This is probably the maximum growth the College could reasonably contemplate without going beyond the limits of feasible expansion of the Central complex.

The Library proper is far more than the ordinary conception of a library. It is the educative aorta of the College. It should be by far, in every sense, the major building on the campus. It will be physically the biggest construction of the College Center, and it will have to be capable of sizable expansion and modification, etc., as educational needs change and as the College creates additional modules. It should not be monumental, but it must be beautiful and alive, with promise of the excitement of learning, with the civilized pleasure of being with other people who are learning, and with being in the midst of treasures of intellect and culture. The Library will house the College's main collection of books and periodicals in the usual sense. The Director of Library Services should be a very able man in terms both of traditional librarianship, bookmanship, library display, and pioneering in the new. The Library will aim from the beginning to acquire materials *selectively* to avoid unnecessary duplication with the other four colleges and to support the nature and purposes of Hampshire. The Library will also strive to be *financially economical* in its selection of materials, both in acquisition of an initial collection and in seeking the best possible alternatives to standard letter-press books that present technology can provide. The Library should have general and special reading rooms, a limited number of reading carrels not electronically equipped, and a limited number of private research rooms for faculty and advanced students who are undertaking special studies dependent upon the Library's resources.

### (2. *The Administrative Wing*

The Administrative Wing should be an "official" entrance to the College for protocol purposes. The Administrative Wing would house the President of the College and his secretary; the Vice-President for Administration and his secretary; the Academic Vice-President-Dean of College and his secretary; main administrative services (e.g., development, records, bursar, admissions, etc.); and facilities for official and unofficial college visitors. In addition, the Administrative Wing should have a Board room which can be used for meetings of the Trustees, meetings required by the President and Vice-Presidents, and meetings of major College committees. The Administrative Wing likewise should provide an office, with access to secretarial help, for the principal elected student leader of the College. The offices of the President, the Academic Vice-President-Dean of College, and the Administrative Vice-President, should be large enough and appropriately furnished to accommodate small group meetings.

### (3. *The Social Science Wing*

The Wing for the School of Social Sciences should provide a suitable office for the Dean of the School, an office for secretarial assistance, and an adjacent seminar-conference room for meetings of the Social Science faculty of the College, for committee meetings, and for advanced study seminars. Upper division and advanced major study in the social sciences would be principally undertaken in this Wing and would require appropriate lecture room, seminar room, and laboratory facilities. It appears desirable for the School initially to have an enclosed teaching space which would allow for conversion into six seminar rooms of 25, two lecture rooms of 75, two classrooms of 50 plus two of 25, or into a large lecture hall of 150.

(4. *The Natural Science Wing*

The Wing for the School of Natural Sciences would have similar requirements for the Dean of the School, his secretarial support, and faculty conferences. In addition, it is expected that the majority of the science faculty of the College would have their offices in this Wing. The other members of the science faculty would have their offices equally divided among the four Houses. Each of the four Houses should have in office-residence at least one natural scientist and one mathematician. The Science Wing will require lecture-demonstration rooms capable of handling 100 students each; it seems likely that two such rooms would be immediately needed. In addition, the Science Wing will require laboratories for physics, chemistry, and biology. These will be principally needed for the Division I and II unified science programs. Provision will have to be made, however, for flexible laboratory installations to accommodate the needs of a limited number of natural science majors who concentrate their work on the Hampshire campus.

(5. *The Humanities Wing*

The Wing occupied by the School of the Humanities and the Arts will be designed to accommodate the functions of the approach to arts in the humanities that Hampshire College has chosen. The Dean of the School will require office, secretarial support, and conference facilities similar to those of the other Deans of Schools. In addition, the School of the Humanities and the Arts will require space for a varying faculty in music, graphic arts, plastic arts, drama, dance, and creative writing. It is not yet decided whether all of these fields will be covered in the School of the Humanities and Arts, and it is likely that some of the Arts staff will be part-time and from off-campus. For the time being, three private offices for individual faculty members and a multi-purpose office room for occasional faculty would be satisfactory. In addition to the arts fields noted, Hampshire may offer opportunities for creative expression in the cinema and study in that field. In any case, this Wing should provide a seminar-sized classroom for music theory and other art theory instruction, and perhaps eight small instrumental studios. All music facilities, including the seminar room, should be soundproof. Cubicles for listening to recorded music will not be provided, since it is intended to make the music tape resources of the Library available by wire to headsets in student carrels in the residential rooms. With flexibility to allow for change in the developing program of this School, the principal balance of its space should be given over to studios for individual and group work in the several arts mentioned. The School should have at least one flexible room with a total capacity of 75, similar to those in the satellite House academic facilities, capable of easy conversion to three seminar rooms of 25 capacity or two rooms of 50 capacity and 25 capacity respectively.

### (6. *The Languages Wing*

The School of Language Studies would occupy a Wing with complex and changing requirements. The Dean of the School will require office, secretarial, and conference facilities similar to the other Deans. The School should also have a 75 capacity convertible room similar to that just described for the School of Humanities and the Arts. In addition, the School of Language Studies will have special needs, specifications for which will be complex and technical, with space and other requirements which cannot fully be foreseen at this stage. Certain of the following needs would be met immediately; others would be met over a period of time as research and project funds became available:

### (a) *The Foreign Language Laboratory*

This should be no less than a 50-station laboratory with as advanced console control, tape service, and feedback mechanisms as the College can manage. The laboratory will require an office for the Director of Foreign Language Studies, secretarial space, and its own convertible 75 capacity classroom. A special study of office and classroom needs for the intensive summer programs in foreign languages and English as a second language (for foreign students entering the United States) is required.

### (b) *The INTRAN Center*

It is important to emphasize that the INTRAN Center may well become the central nervous system of information transfer for the whole College, particularly including interconnection with all student carrels in residential quarters. From modest beginnings, but with adequate space for its developing activity, this *information transfer center* (INTRAN) will engage in the following things:

Conducting applied research and development to maximize the effective use of new technologies for information transfer in the College as a whole, with particular attention to increasing the resources and usefulness of the Library, increasing the electronic availability of information on call at student carrels in their rooms, increasing the same for professors in their own studies and teaching, and increasing administrative effectiveness in handling information with regard to the life, management, and evaluation of the College. For these purposes and others, it will be essential for the INTRAN Center to concentrate its attention on finding ways and means to achieve computer utilization in storage and retrieval.

Operating information transfer services such as closed-circuit television to student rooms and classrooms; wire transmission of recorded lectures, reviews, music, etc. Here, in addition to developing computer services for the College, INTRAN will need to plan, develop, and operate other electronic systems for information selection and distribution.

Serving a demonstration function for students exploring the field of information transfer and as a vital training laboratory for advanced students in the School of Language Studies.

Providing a workshop where students and faculty can learn to develop and construct graphic and oral materials for communication.

In cooperation with the Library director, developing and helping to maintain:

Collections of electronically and photographically recorded material;

Special equipment for access to such materials in the Library: e.g., eight millimeter closed-loop cartridge-loading film projectors, etc.;

Central rooms for individual and group viewing and listening in connection with audio-visual materials which are not practical to decentralize to student carrels or to class-rooms. The function here is similar to that of the remark-able new audio-visual center at Phillips Andover Academy.

Collaborating actively with the other four Connecticut Valley institutions in exploring the possibilities of information transfer, and developing them on an interinstitutional basis. The aim here would be to achieve as *great economy and as little dupli-cation of effort* as possible, and to move toward pooling via information transfer techniques as much as possible of the sep-arate intellectual and cultural resources of the several institutions so that such resources may be more accessible to all members of the interinstitutional community.

INTRAN obviously will require time, money, and leadership for its development. Of crucial importance will be locating an extra-ordinarily able Director and developing a highly competent staff.

The functions of INTRAN touched upon here would provide many opportunities for students to become intern staff members of INTRAN, and in the process develop fields of concentration in this area. It should be possible for the School of Language Studies to offer students at the other four colleges the opportunity to take advanced work in this field.

The space requirements of the Center are, at this stage, diffi-cult to specify. They are likely to be relatively small at the begin-ning but to require ready access to additional space for expansion. For this reason, it would be sensible to allot to INTRAN from the beginning more space than its immediate needs require. At the least, this would mean providing the Director with an office, secretarial space, space for at least three double offices, and an engineering room which from the beginning would be intercon-nected with the Library, the other Schools, and the academic and residential facilities of the four Houses. In addition, it would be desirable for INTRAN to have a small soundproofed television studio equipped both for two-camera, video tape recording and closed-circuit transmission. Further, as a reserve and for instruc-tional uses in the immediate future, it would be desirable for INTRAN to have a convertible 75 capacity room useful for small, medium, and larger groups.

The computer requirements of INTRAN and the development of wide-band interconnection systems for decentralized multiple self-instruction and group instruction purposes are being actively explored with corporations, other institutions, and individual consultants.

### (c) *The Linguistics Laboratory*

This additional part of the School of Language Studies will be a laboratory and workshop for advanced study by students and research both by them and by faculty in psycholinguistics, games development, simulation development, perception studies, semantic and philosophic analysis. Ideally, this laboratory should be a very flexible area of space and should be reasonably accessible to the Dean of the School of Language Studies. The Dean and other faculty in the School of Language Studies will use this laboratory principally in connection with the work of students who are entering a concentration in the field or carrying on and completing advanced work. For games development, simulations, experimental studies in perception, and other purposes, it would be desirable to have a workshop room of approximately 1,600 square feet, capable of multiple-purpose use, assisted by swingout partitions which can be easily operated, by multi-outlet electric grid for the easy connection of various kinds of recording and other equipment, by as thorough acoustical control as possible, and the like. In addition, the laboratory should have at least one permanent seminar conference room with a capacity of 30, plus one 75 capacity room convertible to smaller units.

### (7. *Other Considerations of Physical Design*

With regard to sports and recreation, the College would plan to build a large, enclosed multipurpose area at the lowest cost designed to provide a simple, heated (and cooled) area for a wide variety of intramural recreational and sports activities in inclement weather. This would not be either a gymnasium or field house, but something simpler and easier to maintain than either. The simplest example, only for illustration of intent, would be a large geodesic dome of Buckminster Fuller design over bare earth. This facility would be physically related to central separate shower facilities for men and women and to an adjoining swimming pavilion.

The enclosed swimming pavilion would be as much a social and recreational place for the college community as an athletic one. If it is possible to achieve this facility, it should not be dominated by the large public bathroom aesthetic of most institutional swimming pools. Instead, it should be as attractive as possible, with opportunities around it for students to relax and talk and mix and have fun. It would be of especial importance, in view of the intensive use planned for the Hampshire College campus during the summers, to design the swimming facility so that it would not only be warm and comfortable in the winter, but could be to some extent opened to the air and sun in the summer. This is possible to do, as present construction of swimming facilities at resorts and hotels in the northern part of the country demonstrates.

In further connection with sports and recreation, the College would plan to make simple field sports possible on playing fields adjacent to each of the Houses. This does not mean constructing a full-scale playing field for each House, but being sure that near each House is some reasonable room for the playing of softball, touch football, tennis, volleyball, and outdoor basketball. With land on the Holyoke range, the College will be able to make some skiing available to students. It would be particularly pleasant if a skating pond could be located on the campus relatively near the Houses, equipped with a warm-up hut and night lighting.

No suggestion is here made for health services and their location, but they should be central. The head of health services at the University of Massachusetts has offered to advise Hampshire College in connection with developing its own unit. Possibilities exist for cooperation with the University in the area of health maintenance.

No mention either is made here with regard to the location of grounds and buildings services, but it would seem that these facilities should be well out of view of the main community. The Director of Physical Plant at the College, however, should have his office in the administrative wing of the central complex.

The present discussion does not mention the question of automobile access, transit, and parking. The notion of a centralized-decentralized campus discussed here would seek to keep all private automobile circulation and parking on the perimeter of the House clusters and the College Center around which they revolve. Two exceptions to this would be the need for delivery access to the College Center, which could be designed to be handled as unobtrusively as possible, and the need for one major in-and-out automobile access route to the official entrance to the College Center. Beyond this, it is hoped that planning would make it possible for people to move within the campus system easily and comfortably on foot.

(8. *The Campus: Micropolis in a Context of Developing Urbanism*

It would be easy but incorrect to infer from the discussion and schematic drawing in this section that, contrary to its announced principle, the College would be far more of an enclave closed to the surrounding community than an "open city."

It is true that the model being considered for Hampshire College has none of the complete monolithic "urban" character of the new Scarborough campus of the University of Toronto. And the Hampshire model is equally unlike Harvard Square, in that it intends not to be at the mercy of automobile traffic.

The dangers of most exurban campus designs have been elegantly depicted by Ervin Galantay of the Columbia University faculty in architecture. Professor Galantay comments that:

> The campus becomes a ghetto neatly walled in by a ring road, parking and buffer zones. It may be adequate as a hive for learning and perhaps mating; but not a single shop is permitted on campus, let alone a bar, discothéque, cinema or motel. The same two-dimensional mentality triumphs in the unquestioned segregation of undergraduates, graduates, married students and faculty. Yet great universities thrive on a cheerfully overlapping relation of town and gown, students and masters.

> The entire concept of the exurban campus should be rethought.*

While the Hampshire model intends to keep the disruptive automobile outside the House clusters and the College Center as much as possible,

* *The Nation,* June 27, 1966, pp. 789-790.

an inventive approach to design should make it possible for people to come and go easily between the college community and its surrounding world. The exclusion of random automobile traffic does not necessarily mean a circumferential anti-automobile wall around the College. It should be easy for cars to come and go as far as proximity to the Houses goes. This occurs in the Claremont Colleges now. In Hampshire's case, each House area would in effect be a gateway to the campus, providing openness in both directions.

Further, the "urban" metaphor expressed by the notion of the College Center gives opportunity for the creation of shops, discothéques, movies and the like in the middle of things. Hopefully, just as Hampshire students would find it easy to go out into the Valley and its other institutions, students from the other four campuses and people from the general community would find things worth coming into the College Center to enjoy.

# 8

# A FEW BOLD INSTITUTIONS:

## *Interinstitutional Cooperation and the Larger Community*

*Another opportunity lies in much greater interinstitutional cooperation. . . . Voluntary arrangements should be encouraged to go farther than they have as yet. . . . [No] single university can any longer hope to be a universal university, and . . . all must group themselves into communities of universities and colleges. Within such a community each institution could take pride in the accomplishments of the whole and in its contribution to that whole.*

DAEL WOLFLE
*Science*, November, 1965

*The Northeastern seaboard of the United States is today . . . an almost continuous stretch of urban and suburban areas from southern New Hampshire to northern Virginia and from the Atlantic shore to the Appalachian foothills. . . . [The] urban growth experienced here generates many contrasts, paradoxes, and apparently contradictory trends. . . . Are its results for the better or for the worse? It is not for our generation to moralize on the matter, but to strive to make the outcome be for the better, whatever obstacles may be in the way. Megalopolis stands indeed on the threshold of a new way of life, and upon solution of its problems will rest civilization's ability to survive. In the search for such solutions there will be found no easy keys to success. . . . Solutions must be thought out, ironed out, and constantly revised in the light of all the knowledge that can be acquired by all concerned.*

JEAN GOTTMANN
*Megalopolis*

THE FORMING OF HAMPSHIRE COLLEGE occurs in a time of remarkable opportunity for higher education to strengthen itself through inter-institutional cooperation, and to renew itself through more active civic involvement in the life of the larger community. Both of these opportunities were reviewed in the first chapter, and in the second were cited as two of the specific challenges Hampshire College proposes to face. Indeed, a new private liberal arts college in the Connecticut Valley of Massachusetts has no choice but to do so. The survival of the idea of Hampshire College as a new institution of high quality ultimately depends upon cooperation with the sister institutions which brought the idea into being in the first place. The development of Hampshire College as a new institution in the relatively rural landscape of South Amherst cannot occur without affecting the social and physical environment which surrounds it, nor can Hampshire help being affected by the changing nature of that environment in the years ahead.

What is true of Hampshire College with regard to interinstitutional cooperation and interrelationships with the larger community is true in its own way of each of the older institutions in the Valley. Perhaps their survival will not absolutely depend upon cooperation, but their strength and quality in the future are certain to be influenced by the kind and quality of interinstitutional cooperation they achieve. Similarly, the future of the older institutions is bound up with the human ecology of the Valley. Urbanization is swiftly overtaking the Valley, growing, as Professor Jean Gottmann of the University of Paris has said, "amidst an irregularly colloidal mixture of rural and suburban landscapes. . . ." [170] The question for all of the institutions in the Valley is not whether they will be affected by the onset of urbanization, but how they will respond to it, and whether they will seek, individually and through cooperation, to influence the process.

The founding of Hampshire College could provide a "take-off point" from which it would be possible for the institutions in the Valley to move strongly toward increased and more productive interinstitutional cooperation in academic matters, and with equal strength toward playing an active, vital part in helping shape the urban transformation of the Valley now already under way. In both instances, Hampshire College represents a moment of truth for the academic constituencies which have brought it into being. Hampshire is a symbol of the beginnings of interinstitutional cooperation in the Valley. Without such cooperation, there would be no new college in process at all. At the same time, Hampshire is symbolic —in its need for nurture as a newborn, and in its existence as a new factor in the Valley environment—of the new era in which all of the other institutions here find themselves.

Academically and otherwise, New England has a notable and noble history of individual enterprise. In education, its tradition of independent private enterprise has been, and is, stronger than anywhere else in the country. Only in the present is public higher education emerging as an equal kind of enterprise in this important region of the nation. The virtues of individualism in enterprise and achievement are as important to maintain among institutions as they are among people. So, too, is a healthy balance of private and public education as alternatives available to American youth. But the tradition of separatism and individualism in New England education will not suffice alone for the years ahead. The New England region is ripe for a bold demonstration—by what Dael Wolfle calls "a few bold institutions"—of the great new strength that can be found in interinstitutional cooperation, without losing the historic values of individual difference. It is important throughout the New England region for such a demonstration to be made, showing how advantageously private institutions can work with each other and with public institutions, and with what full effect, both in terms of academic improvement and active influence on the civic realities of swiftly changing community life.

1. Past and Present: Interinstitutional Cooperation in the Connecticut Valley

In February, 1955, the Ford Foundation's Fund for the Advancement of Education provided a grant to Mount Holyoke, Smith, and Amherst, and the University of Massachusetts for a study of the possibilities of cooperative educational activities among the four institutions. Under this grant, a Committee on Cooperation was established to study the problem and report on it to the presidents of the four institutions; its members included leading faculty representatives from each of the colleges and the university.* The Committee understood that its function was to

---

*The members of the Committee were Professors Charles J. Hill, Smith College; Gail Kennedy, Amherst College; Bruce R. Morris, University of Massachusetts; and Stuart M. Stoke, Mount Holyoke College.

take into account any topic which was relevant to the joint interests of
the four institutions. It is said that the members of the Committee accepted their assignment dutifully, but with misgivings: *"Could* anything
really be done and why; after all, aren't things just about all right as
they are now?" [171] During the course of its year of study, the Committee
on Cooperation lost its misgivings and became convinced that some things
could "really be done" and that the status quo was not "just about all
right":

> . . . as the Committee proceeded its interest in the project grew.
> Moreover, a thorough-going plan of cooperation among these four
> institutions, if it could be devised and put into effect, might be of
> more than local importance. It might provide an example and indi-
> cate a pattern of action which could be successfully followed by other
> group of colleges and universities. And, in particular, establishing an
> example of cooperation between public and private institutions might
> be of value. . . .[172]

When their report was submitted to the presidents of the four institutions in June, 1956, the Committee submitted recommendations for
increased cooperation in undergraduate education, in graduate work, in
faculty utilization, in interchange of students, in teacher education, in
campus-to-campus transportation, in area studies, in FM radio and educational television, in coordination of special events (lectures, concerts,
art exhibits), in establishing a joint calendar, in studying the problem
of remedial reading instruction, in providing speech therapy, in adult
education, in audio-visual aids, in statistical services, and in cooperative
recruitment of staff.

In its conclusions, the Committee asserted that growth toward cooperation would be stimulated by increasing pressures upon all four
institutions. These pressures would arise from the expansion of the college
student population and would result in drastically increased demands
for more student housing, more classrooms, and more laboratories. The
Committee did not advocate cooperation just for its own sake, however,
nor as a response to pressures alone. Steps toward cooperation were urged
"as a safeguard for the future," and to offer a long-term strengthening
of educational resources and quality in the Valley.

The Committee urged that, if cooperation were to attain any considerable proportions, a separate corporation be set up. This corpora-

tion could receive and use funds from foundations and other donors. It could make agreements for the cooperating institutions with other organizations or individuals more easily than the separate institutions could handle such matters. Further, it was felt that such a new corporation could take the initiative in developing new forms of cooperation "without arousing the jealousy that might come from extensive leadership on the part of one of the member institutions." [173] A separate corporation could serve as an arbiter among the institutional members, could simplify administrative tasks for all of them, could oversee the operation of co-operative enterprises, be "free from a great deal of the institutional inertia of its constituents," and could serve as a convenient holding and operating agent for affiliated enterprises.

In retrospect, the efforts of the 1955-1956 Committee on Cooperation appear imaginative, bold, and sensible. Several of their recommendations have been implemented with considerable success.

In its spirit and work, the Committee on Cooperation was carrying forward a long tradition of cooperative activity among the Connecticut Valley institutions. On an informal basis, cooperation had existed since the beginning of the institutions.

Edward Hitchcock, President of Amherst from 1845 to 1854, was an outstanding figure in the early establishment of close and neighborly relationships among the institutions. President Hitchcock was a founding trustee of Mount Holyoke College, and served on its Board from 1836 until his death in 1864. While President of Amherst, he taught and lectured at Mount Holyoke. President Hitchcock was also a major influence in the founding of the University of Massachusetts, and in urging its location in Amherst. In the spring of 1850 he toured Europe to study agricultural schools abroad on behalf of the Commonwealth of Massachusetts. He returned to submit a recommendation and plan for a publicly supported college of agriculture to be located in Amherst, so that it would be able to share instructors and equipment with Amherst College.

Throughout the years, graduates of each of the colleges have served as presidents, deans, faculty members, and trustees of the other colleges. Although the history of cooperation has not been well documented, records indicate that the first joint appointment of one professor to the faculties of two institutions in the Valley took place in the 1930's.

Five years before the report of the Committee on Cooperation, the first formal cooperative venture of all four institutions was undertaken. This was the Hampshire Inter-College Library Center (HILC), which was formed to serve specialized library needs of the faculties at the four colleges and the Forbes Library in Northampton. HILC today is a repository, housed at the University library, for monographs, journals, and periodicals, the limited use of which would not warrant duplicate accession by all of the other libraries. The HILC collection, therefore, is more complete and valuable, in terms of its special holdings, than any one of the libraries would be likely to afford alone.

After the Comimttee on Cooperation had made its report, one of the first of its suggestions to be carried out was the appointment in 1957 of a coordinator of cooperative activity and the establishment of a co-ordinator's office. Transportation among the colleges, a joint calendar, an FM radio station, and interchange of students and teachers were developed with a modicum of success. In addition, a number of coopera-tive activities not initially conceived of by the Committee on Cooperation have developed.*

The most widely known and significant cooperative activity at present is the interchange of students among the four institutions. This is ac-complished through an agreement among the colleges by which a student, with permission of his dean and the course instructor, may elect one or more courses at one of the other institutions. The number of students enrolling in interchange courses per year has grown steadily since the program's inception in 1957-58. The interchange courses provide an admirable example of the way in which cooperation can extend edu-cational opportunity and amplify institutional resources. The growth of the interchange enrollment program may be seen in figures from the last four years of four-college cooperation

| Year | Enrollment |
|---------|-----------|
| 1962-63 | 253 |
| 1963-64 | 320 |
| 1964-65 | 336 |
| 1965-66 | 578 |

* The 1964-65 report of the present coordinator, Acting Dean Robert C. Whitney of Amherst College, lists 27 cooperating activities among the four institutions. A copy of Dean Whitney's report is included in the appendices of the present docu-ment.

The present status of cooperation among the four colleges may be divided for convenience between those academic activities which are essentially the sharing of one institution's resources with the others, and those activities which are creative combinations. The most significant of the shared activities are the interchange courses, the extension of library facilities, and the interchange of faculty. Cooperative activities which represent creative combinations (i.e., combinations which create results greater than any one institution could offer) are cooperative courses, joint faculty appointments, a computer center, the FM radio station, and the *Massachusetts Review,* a scholarly quarterly. In cooperative courses, the institutions combine to establish a joint course; for instance, the History of Science program is such a cooperative endeavor now, offered for students at all institutions.

Formal cooperation was given additional stimulus by the Ford Foundation's Fund for the Advancement of Education in 1958, as this paper indicates in reviewing the consequences of the work of the four-college committee which developed *The New College Plan.*

It seems reasonable to assume that, even without Hampshire College and its needs, cooperative activities among Amherst, Mount Holyoke, Smith and the University of Massachusetts would continue at least at their present level. New activities of cooperation have not appeared in profusion, but there is a definite record of success and longevity among those cooperative innovations that have been tried. The success and longevity of innovations in cooperation can be attributed in some good part to the deliberate care with which the institutions have worked them out and assessed them. For example, evening bus service among the four colleges was discussed for several years and finally instituted on a trial basis during 1965-66. After several weeks' run and a careful analysis of the results by the coordinator, Mount Holyoke College decided that it did not wish to continue to participate in the service. The other three institutions found the service valuable and continued it until the end of that academic year.

## 2. FUTURE POSSIBILITIES OF INTERINSTITUTIONAL COOPERATION

At present, the possibility clearly exists for an increase in the variety and intensity of cooperative activities. The pressures which the Committee on Cooperation noted ten years ago have indeed increased and are felt by all institutions, not only those in the Connecticut Valley. Most commentators on higher education today, like Dael Wolfle, speak of cooperation as a necessity for meeting pressures of time, expense, and complexity, and as a major way to increase the general strength of higher education.

The direct impetus for further cooperation may come most strongly from students. In the Valley, students increasingly require more variety and specialization in course work, resources, equipment, and extracurricular activities than any one institution, even the University of Massachusetts, can possibly offer.

The advent of Hampshire College provides a unique moment when the long-standing tradition of informal and formal cooperation among institutions of the Valley could be dramatically reasserted and usefully extended. If it were not for this tradition of friendly association, it might appear presumptuous for Hampshire, as the newest college in the group, to come out strongly for increased cooperative endeavor. It might simply seem that Hampshire, as the newest and neediest of the colleges, is making a case for sharing with others their hard-won resources. This is not Hampshire College's view of itself, nor is it believed to be the view taken by the older institutions of the Valley. Hampshire is the result of an act of cooperation; it represents and will seek actively to express a view of cooperation as creative collaboration, in which all concerned can find advantage.

Straight sharing can be a successful short-term solution for a problem of scarcity, stretching resources that are already normally used. But this can tend to threaten faculty, and it does not contribute to creative expansion of the aggregate educational resources of cooperating institutions. Creative collaboration is not a piece of fancy terminology designed to cloak the impositions of one college on another. The ground on which creative collaboration stands is, by definition, mutuality. The structure that can be built on this ground can enrich programs, enlarge opportunities, and extend resources for all of the partners in the collaborative endeavor. Genuine collaboration cannot be a voluntary or involuntary act of charity whose chief end is to provide a makeshift answer for conditions of scarcity. Instead, it is a new departure for higher education which can materially increase academic abundance by collective action, while maintaining institutional autonomy, integrity, physical organization, and size among its individual partners.

Cooperation among the Valley institutions, even though supported by tradition and specific achievements, still remains much more a potentiality than an actuality. The degree of hard commitment that fully productive collaboration requires, in terms of well-supported leadership, funding, and systematic organization, is relatively slight. The current four-college coordinator, for example, has had to carry this responsibility as a part-time burden on top of his responsibilities as Acting Dean of Amherst College and professor of chemistry. A conscientious and able man, devoted to the concept of interinstitutional cooperation, he has had to define his leadership in modest terms of communication, promotion, steering, and evaluation.

The full value of creative interinstitutional cooperation in the Connecticut Valley is not likely to be realized if things continue to stand as they are at present. The tradition and its achievements are positive indeed, but a relatively slow tempo is not adequate for present and emerging conditions in higher education. It is quite possible, for example, that the superb and unique opportunity for a public university and distinguished private colleges to cooperate in a really meaningful way could be lost in the next decade unless imaginative, vigorous steps are taken with all deliberate speed. The explosive growth of the University of Massachusetts in size may tend to obscure the fact that, at the same time, the University is of necessity growing in other ways which will affect its relationships with nearby colleges. If strong collaborative efforts are not made in the near future for joint planning of the development in such resources as those of libraries, laboratories, computers, coaxial interconnection, and the like, the University will necessarily proceed on its own, and is indeed already doing so. As this happens, it is quite possible that the University, without willing it, will grow away from the other colleges, that unconsciously but irrevocably there will be a setting in of new patterns which tend to diminish the possibility of cooperation, and that one of the greatest opportunities for collaboration between public and private higher education in America will be lost. There is needed, before it is too late, a fundamental reassertion of the idea of cooperation that the four-college committees of the 1950's argued for with such conviction.

A strong extension of the principal of cooperation in the Valley may not turn out to be possible. Frederick Rudolph, the best of our historians of higher education, concluded after reviewing the whole American record that:

> resistance to fundamental reform was ingrained in the American collegiate and university tradition, as over three hundred years of history demonstrated. A historian of the University of Rochester described the traditional policy of his institution as one of 'wise conservatism modified by a spirit of liberal progressivism when warranted by circumstances.' This was also, except on rare occasions, the historic policy of the American college and university: drift, reluctant accommodation, belated recognition that, while no one was looking, change had in fact taken place.[174]

But Hampshire College, meaning its Board of Trustees and academic and administrative leadership, believes that the new College and its sister institutions must not let the moment for a vital strengthening of cooperation go by because of drift, reluctance to do more than accommodate, or unawareness of change. In the hope that the moment may be seized and greater interinstitutional collaboration gained, Hampshire puts forward a proposal for joint action, to coincide with its own establishment.

Several things are very clearly needed for the kind of interinstitutional collaboration that the times call for in the Connecticut Valley. Most of these things are comprehended under the single word *leadership,* which in turn is readily translatable into some very concrete matters.

The basic proposal that Hampshire College makes for guaranteeing that interinstitutional cooperation in the future will match both tomorrow's needs and the expectations that are inherent in the four-college tradition, is for the creation of a new instrumentality which will give strong leadership to the development of collaboration. The instrumentality proposed is a new interinstitutional Center for Cooperative Development, designed to serve the institutions of the Connecticut Valley.

Hampshire College proposes that the Connecticut Valley Center for Cooperative Development in Education should be governed by a corporation representing the administrative and academic leadership of the constituent institutions. Under the Hampshire proposal, the new Valley Center would be independently financed, would have its own professional leadership and staff, and would be sheltered in its own physical quarters. The functions of the Center would be several:

To propose to the five colleges, or any combination thereof, or to other institutions later associated, programs of cooperation and collaboration.

To coordinate the initiation, execution, and continuous evaluation of such programs as now exist and as may be initiated in the future.

To undertake, from time to time, with the agreement of the constituent institutions, programs which none of them can or will undertake alone or in combination, and from which two or more desire the benefits.

To seek, with the agreement of member institutions, financial support for certain cooperative activities.

It will be seen that the Hampshire College proposal for a new Valley Center in many ways echoes what the 1955 Committee on Cooperation said would be necessary in order to implement the kinds of active cooperation that it recommended. The Valley Center would be autonomous in a legal, administrative, and financial sense, although in the beginning some financial priming from its constituent institutions might be necessary, along with foundation support. The Center would depend, initially, on the five colleges and their interest for its existence. In time, however, it might be appropriate for the Center, operating under policy made by its interinstitutional governing Board, to include in collaboration, if they desired it, such other institutions as the Greenfield Community College, Holyoke Junior College, Springfield College, American International College, and Western New England College. It is also possible, as one trustee of Hampshire College has further suggested, that the Center might in time develop collaboration with public and private schools of the Valley.

The Center's first concern, however, would be to provide initiative, support, and service for the further development of collaboration among the presently associated institutions. To this end, flexibility in the operation and physical location of Center facilities would be essential. For example, it might be logical for transportation services among the colleges to be administered and headquartered at the Center. On the other hand, a major computer facility, financed by and available to all of the colleges, might be at the University, at Amherst, or elsewhere in the community of institutions. The Center might have assisted in securing funding for the computer facility, it might serve by handling administrative arrangements for the sharing of the computer among participant institutions, and it might be responsible for assisting with the funding and administration of remote facilities.

The Center would not, therefore, be one massive, centralized super-institution, but it would be essential for it to have an adequate, permanent building of its own, centrally located, and capable of expansion if needed in the future. The physical headquarters of the Center would provide offices for the full-time administrative staff, including an executive director. In addition, the Center building would provide adequate and comfortable space for interinstitutional committee meetings, for small and large conferences, and for other purposes. It would be essential for the physical headquarters of the Center to be easily accessible to personnel of the cooperating institutions, for it to have adequate maintenance, and to have suitable parking areas and other conveniences.

Hampshire College is prepared to supplement its proposal for the establishment of a Connecticut Valley Center for Cooperative Development in Education by offering to donate the land on which the physical headquarters of the Center could be built. The Hampshire College campus, as those familiar with the geography of the Connecticut Valley know, is in a central location with regard to the other four institutions. Its land uses are only now being planned, and it would be quite possible for site development to include the selection and separation of a suitable area of land for the purposes of the Center. If this offer is accepted, Hampshire College would turn title to the land so donated over to the corporation under which the Center would operate. In addition, Hampshire College wishes to demonstrate its confidence in the value of this proposal by including a request for the Center's initial physical construction and basic operating costs in, or as an item closely related to, an application by Hampshire College for major foundation support. While Hampshire College takes the initiative in making the proposal for the Center, and in offering land for its construction and assistance in securing funds for its establishment, it should be clearly understood that Hampshire College would welcome the same initiative from any other quarter in the Connecticut Valley and would plan to have no connection with the Center in any way different from that of any other cooperating institution concerned.

The possibilities for creative collaboration in the unique complex composed by the five Valley institutions are great indeed. It is not exaggerating to say that, through increased collaboration, the public and private institutions of the Valley can collectively constitute one of the most useful concentrations of higher education in the United States, far more than the several institutions could do as an only casually related group of individual entities largely going their own way alone. In 1962, Professor Stuart Stoke commented that:

> there are many practical problems awaiting solution if the ultimate values of cooperation are to be reached. Among these are better coordination of scheduling, closer agreement of calendars, and improved transportation. Also needed is a reduction of the resistance on the part of faculty members who are loyally fighting rear guard action in defensive positions which are already being overrun. But the development of effective cooperation is a success of continuing effort rather than a fiat and a resting. Good will, intelligence, and persistence will produce solutions to many of the problems cited; and, in the light of current trends in higher education, cooperation should become increasingly valuable.[175]

The Hampshire College proposal for a Center for Cooperative Development in Education is an expression of belief in what Professor Stoke calls the "process of continuing effort" that is required. The effort needed now, and in the future, will be more than it has been in the past.

### 3.  URBANIZATION: THE COLLEGE AS A CORPORATE CITIZEN

Hampshire College is in an area of great natural beauty which has been further enhanced by the creations of man. A perimeter line drawn to connect Amherst, Smith, Mount Holyoke Colleges and the University of Massachusetts, Hampshire's four cooperating neighbors, traces a trapezoidal shape. The trapezoid is roughly two, ten, six, and seven miles on its four sides, and encloses roughly twenty-five square miles. Hampshire College is on the edge of the perimeter on the longest leg, as appendix map material shows. The trapezoid includes much of the Mount Holyoke mountain range, a five-mile stretch of the Connecticut River, and a varied and pleasing landscape, with lovely meadows, rolling hills, dense woods, and outcrops of ledge. Man has added the fragrance and beauty of apple orchards and hay, the precise and colorful checker-boarding of bottomland tobacco fields, the strong contrasts of white frame houses, red barns, and mellowed tobacco barns. Man has added, too, the brick, stone, concrete, glass, playing fields, lawns, and trees of four leading institutions of higher education.

To the east rise the Pelham Hills, undergirded with gneiss and giving little quarter to the farmer or homebuilder. To the north and west are rural communities, back roads and abandoned mills, providing a visual, and in some cases too literal, flashback to 19th-century rural America.

The four established institutions within the trapezoid have a rich tradition of accomplishment in American education. Their tradition of accomplishment is served today by unusually extensive resources. Among the four institutions there are today 1,300 scholars, 1,600,000 books, $134,000,000 in endowment funds, and 17,000 students. Two of the institutions are among the most distinguished women's colleges anywhere. One is one of the very best private colleges for men in this or any other country. The public university is in the midst of revolutionary growth and rapid progress toward excellence.

Over the Mount Holyoke range to the south, and through the corridors of the highways, a great wave of urbanization is coming to crest. The trapezoid itself is more a part of megalopolis than it knows, and within fifteen miles of Amherst rampant urbanization is in full view, with all of the trappings: exhaust smog, traffic jams, water pollution and water shortage, racial tension, slums, tract housing, industrial blight, and the rest—a dramatic contrast to bucolic Amherst and Hadley.

The fact is that things are not all that bucolic in Amherst and Hadley either. The Hampshire trapezoid is in a stage of incipient urbanization, catalyzed by the rapid development of land that is more available than land to the south, spurred by new roads, and nourished by the rapid, inexorable growth of the University of Massachusetts.

The result in Amherst, where there is the greatest pressure, is a large number of new home starts (many in tract housing of mediocre design), a rising tax rate (already as high as any in the Commonwealth of Massachusetts), and dramatic increases in road traffic, land costs, and the rate of commercial development. Suddenly, within a stone's-throw of the University and Amherst College are the evidences of instant Los Angeles transplanted: large shopping centers with enormous parking areas, drive-in theatres, motels, automatic car wash establishments, and similar man-ifestations.

The Hampshire trapezoid is in the early stages of a cycle of urbaniza-tion which can lead to planless sprawl, ugliness, noise, and short-term profit-taking which does violence to the priceless land. But the cycle has, if men and institutions are wise enough to make it so, the potential of achieving urbanization without wanton destruction of the essential loveli-ness of the Valley, even as the order changes. Man here could truly be the architect of his urban environment.

It has been demonstrated in this country that uncontrolled growth results in uncontrollable problems. So, as it begins life in a dynamic and changing community, Hampshire College asks: what opportunity is there, and what responsibility does this new college have to influence the development of its environment, to preserve and maintain its natural and man-made advantages while still accommodating inevitable growth? How can we have urbanization without becoming candidates for urban renewal?

In the first chapter, the challenge for higher education to play a more active part in the urban community was described. In the second chapter, it was emphasized that Hampshire College intends to accept this challenge in every way that it sensibly can. The following instances provide two specific examples of action that Hampshire College has already taken with regard to the larger community in which it will live. Perhaps these examples will indicate the stance that Hampshire will take in the future as a citizen of the larger community of the Valley.

a.  *The Mount Holyoke Range*

The Mount Holyoke Range is verdant, soft, and majestic. It dom-inates the landscape, even though its highest peak, Mount Norwottuck, is only a shade more than 1,000 feet above sea level. In the Far West it would be a foothill of the Sierras, but in this gentle, pleasing valley area it is sizable and important. Today, the virtually unbroken slopes of the Mount Holyoke Range are taken for granted, despite a house here or there and the merciless exploitation of gravel banks and trees by small entrepreneurs. Tomorrow it could become like the Santa Monica moun-tains above Los Angeles, with house piled on house, each perched higher

than its neighbor, and the natural contours of the Range cut away by
tireless bulldozers. Its now clear brooks would be polluted, its woods
gone, and while a private few had gained a remarkable view for their
picture windows, the public would have lost a priceless asset of open
country.

Hampshire College has purchased seventy acres on the Range, all
the land formerly in private ownership between a one-hundred-acre tract
belonging to Amherst College and 268 acres which are a watershed for
the Town of Hadley. As a result, this planned buying has produced a
contiguous parcel of nearly 450 acres which is now in the control of
ownership with a sense of basic responsibility to the public interest.
Stewardship of the watershed, the Amherst College land, and that belonging to Hampshire can include the possibility of providing public or
semi-public access to the land for recreational purposes. Although the
area is of some potential advantage to the educational program of Hampshire College, ownership is *primarily* justified on the ground that preserva-
tion of the Holyoke Range is in the public interest as well as in the private
interest of the College.

b.  *The New Roads*

The majority of the local and regional automobile traffic in the
Amherst area travels east and west, using either the old Bay Road in
South Amherst (once the Boston to Albany Post Road) or State Route
#9 through the center of town. The great increase in automobile traffic
volume in recent years has caused the Department of Public Works of
the Commonwealth of Massachusetts and the Town of Amherst to study
the need for new roads. A principal question involved in the study is
the problem of locating routes, particularly in east-west transit, that will
facilitate automobile travel and not injure the community in doing so.

The development of Hampshire College's land holdings coincided
with growing concern over the road problem. In the course of purchasing
a site, Hampshire leadership kept themselves informed of the thinking
of various officials responsible for road planning; the officers of Hampshire
College wished to avoid locating in a place that might upset existing
plans, or where new roads might bisect the College campus.

As public interest in the future of the road question intensified, the

College administration decided to assume, for the first time in its young life, a role of active corporate citizenship. The College initiated and encouraged action by others in the community on a matter of major importance to the future of the environment in which the College was to develop. Hampshire leadership proposed to the Amherst Town Manager that a study group representing the town government and its various appropriate departments and committees (Highway, Planning, Zoning), the University of Massachusetts, Amherst College, Hampshire College, and the Massachusetts Department of Public Works be invited to consider the road problem together and to work toward three objectives. These objectives were:

(1. To assemble and organize factual evidence about the need for, and alternate routes for, new roads.

(2. To reach a consensus as to the most desirable route or routes for new roads.

(3. To communicate consensus to the Massachusetts Department of Public Works in Boston in an effort to influence a decision of great importance to the Town.

After an initial meeting of this study group, Hampshire College asked its planning consultants, the firm of Sasaki, Dawson and DeMay, to make an analysis of the problem. The analysis was offered to the Town Manager, who asked to have it presented to the study group. A thorough presentation was made by one of the planning consultants, and the study group had a useful discussion of data about automobile routes, neighborhood impact that various routes would have, the interests of the University, Amherst College, and Hampshire College in connection with the proposed automobile routes, etc. The presentation was reported on the front page of the local newspaper and wide discussion of factors in the selection of new automotive routes occurred within the community. Interest was aroused and information was made available publicly; the planning process was moved to a point where the matter is now under the jurisdiction of the Amherst Planning Board, with public hearings scheduled. There is a feeling in the community that a consensus can be reached, made known to authorities of the Commonwealth, and that decisions about the projected road development can be affected by the views of the local community.

This is a slight and simple example of what Hampshire College means by taking the initiative as a corporate citizen within its own community environment. The effort in this case may come to naught, but efforts often do. For the present paper, the example is important because it underlines the characteristics that will mark Hampshire's stance toward active involvement in the changing, urbanizing community around it. Hampshire's stance will be to:

Take the initiative in community affairs whenever it seems responsible and sensible to do so.

Cooperate willingly and actively with combinations of private, public, institutional, or individual interests working toward the solution of environmental problems.

Help, insofar as it is able, to contribute to the analysis of and solution of environmental problems as they arise.

The example of the new roads illustrates all three of these characteristics: Hampshire College took the initiative; Hampshire cooperated willingly and actively with a wide combination of interests in tackling the road problem; and Hampshire contributed information to the general welfare which its planning consultants had developed in connection with studies having to do with Hampshire's future.

## 4. A Look Toward the Future

Interinstitutional collaboration and active engagement with community life are two of the main challenges which the opening chapter discussed. The present chapter has touched briefly on the past and present of both these challenges in terms of the local conditions of the Connecticut River Valley as Hampshire sees them. Discussion also has suggested the stance that Hampshire College will take toward both interinstitutional collaboration and community involvement. In neither case will Hampshire College presume that in its innocence and youth it can add nearly as much as older institutions and interests in the area can contribute. On the other hand, Hampshire College looks toward the future in connection with these things, as in connection with its own role as a change agent in undergraduate education, with a certain freshness and vigor that are virtues of being young and relatively unencumbered. In this, Hampshire may be useful to the other members of the academic and general community in which it intends to live.

A long time ago, St. Benedict set as a rule for his monastery, the following:

> As often as any important business has to be done in the monastery, let the abbott call together the whole community and himself set forth the matter. . . . Now the reason why we have said that *all* should be called to the council, is that God often reveals what is better to the younger. . . .

Hampshire will not confuse itself with the abbott, nor expect that being young assures revelation, but it will be very much a part of the whole community, willing to help with important business, and unafraid to pass along whatever revelation comes its way.

# 9

# FINANCING HAMPSHIRE COLLEGE

*By education and the arts we mean something more than better school buildings, higher teachers' salaries, and more scholarships for the intelligent. We mean a reorientation of our ideals and tastes, the strenuous stretching of mental and artistic talent, the exaltation of excellence above social approval, and of mental achievement above quick material success. We mean, in short, new standards of respect and reward for intellect and culture. And we mean more stable financing for basic research, more concern for advancing knowledge for its own sake. We mean cooperation with other communities of scholars and creative thinkers . . . in order that our pursuit of truth may be an adventure we share with all mankind. And we mean that the pursuit of truth in itself is the highest activity of man.*

*Here, then, in all its ramifications of expense, of standards, content and opportunity is a top priority for a great new America and a national purpose few would dispute.*

ADLAI STEVENSON
*The National Purpose*

M ONEY DOES NOT MAKE a good college, but it is difficult to make a good college without money, and lots of it. Lack of money is one of the major obstacles to starting a new college; achieving quality in any educational enterprise, new or old, requires truly *adequate* financing.

More new colleges are being started in this decade than at any time in our American history. All will have moments of anxiety about money. The publicly or church-supported may find nearly enough funds to realize many of their dreams, and a few of the new private colleges will. But the majority of the private endeavors will be sustained more by the parsimony and hope of their founders than by an abundance of funds. Founded on a few thousand or a few hundred thousand dollars, their programs will be under-financed, forcing compromise to the point where the thick broth of intellectual ferment becomes a water-thin gruel. In these cases the "educational" leadership of the college must devote the majority of its harried existence to searching for the funds to simply keep the place alive, knowing that "only keeping alive" spells academic oblivion.

Although nearly $1.5 billion in philanthropic support was given to higher education in 1965, according to estimates of the Council for Financial Aid to Education, the majority of these funds went to established institutions, making the "rich" richer, and dramatically verifying the old fund-raising rule that it is easier to raise money to reward a performance than to resolve a problem.

This is not to suggest that any American college or university is over-financed. The leading institutions are struggling, too, and their leadership is vitally important to new institutions, to education in the large, and to America. But this support alone does not broaden or diversify educational opportunity in the ways that new institutions must and can, if supported.

The new branches of the public universities—particularly in California, Illinois and New York, where an integrated program of higher education at public expense has been carefully developed and where there is a long tradition and long experience with public higher education— are in a highly advantageous position vis-à-vis the private institutions. The legislatures in recent years have taken a rather expansive and generous view of the needs of education and as a result a number of spectacular new campuses have been approved and constructed. Examples are the University of Illinois at Chicago; the University of New York at Stony Brook and Albany; and the University of California at Irvine and Santa Cruz.

However, new university branches don't assure a future for higher education that will satisfy all the students, all the teachers, the parents or educators. Although new, well-financed and staffed with talented teachers and researchers, these institutions, for the most part, are still bound by the dictates of legislatures dealing with the hard facts of public higher education in an egalitarian society. Despite some valiant efforts to the contrary, they are, as Allan Cartter points out about Santa Cruz, "being permitted only that degree of deviation from the University pattern that can be shoe-horned into the standard budgetary formula." *

So the opportunity is left for the private colleges, and particularly the new private colleges, with their disestablishmentarian views, to achieve a new kind of academic community, one that throws the balance of concern toward consideration of problems—social, intellectual, moral and spiritual—that affect society en masse but will be solved through exertion of educated, concerned, thoughtful and intelligent leadership. And, to go back to financing, only if the private institutions seize that opportunity, will the never-ceasing quest for capital funds be fulfilled, and, by the by, will the inevitable price differential between private and public institutions be justified.

Whether this College, Hampshire College, justifies its own ambitions regarding the task of higher education, is what this document is about. The specific plans the College has for financing these ambitions is what follows here.

## 1. Current Operations

Although there are interrelationships and interdependencies at many points, it is convenient to think about the financial fortune of a new college by discussing separately *current* and *capital* funds.

Hampshire College has the great good fortune of starting life with a $6,000,000 nest egg, the gift of Harold F. Johnson, to be expended without restriction to get the College started. The advantages of having a relatively large initial sum are several. It has enabled the purchase of a large, scenic and well located site. It has provided adequate salaries to attract an able staff. It has allowed for the retention of professional consultants to help plan early phases of the College's development. Most of all, it is enough money to help make Hampshire College a credible

* *Pricing Problems for Higher Education,* Allan M. Cartter, former Vice-President, American Council on Education. Paper prepared for the College Scholarship Service Colloquium on the Economic Aspects of Higher Education, May 23, 1966, Lake Geneva, Wisconsin.

idea, sufficiently real to merit the interest of a distinguished board of trustees, and to bring inquiries from prospective faculty and staff members, students, architects, designers, reporters, building contractors and others from all over the country.

The $6,000,000 is expected to be enough to underwrite the developmental expenses of the College until income from student fees is received in the opening year, to make up the operating deficits projected for the first two years of operation after classes begin, and to contribute approximately $2,500,000 to the capital funds needed to build the campus. A summary of these projections is included as Exhibit I at the close of this chapter.

Mr. Johnson's gift is not an endowment. Most new colleges have little prospect of raising enough money to meet all their obligations *and* have an endowment fund, too.* Hampshire College has no illusions for itself on that score, and, in fact, intends to make a virtue out of the necessity of operating primarily on income from tuition and fees, by attempting to illustrate that the cost (in an institutional sense) of education can be reduced without sacrificing quality. The original 1958 New College Committee was charged with drawing a plan which would provide "education of the highest quality at a minimum cost per student." Much of the spirit of that statement permeates the thinking about Hampshire.

The knottiest problem in planning the ongoing operation of Hampshire College is how to have a large enough faculty to make the educational program possible, and to pay them well without making exorbitant charges for tuition and fees. Since the early 1960's faculty salaries have shown the most dramatic increases among the various items in the educational budget. The increased salaries have been reflected by increased tuition charges, which are generally related to the cost of teaching or "instruction." Instruction represents as much as fifty per cent of the educational and general budget for many colleges. Therefore, a change in the salary level or a change in the number of faculty members exerts great leverage on the total budget.

* The average endowment income for all private colleges is about $150 per student per annum. Distribution is heavily in favor of a few institutions. In 1963, twenty-six of sixty-five endowment funds studied by the Boston Fund over a ten-year period held 82.5 per cent of the total funds.

It has been assumed that faculty salaries at Hampshire College would be competitive with the salaries of our institutional partners in the Connecticut Valley. It has been assumed, also, that high-quality education could be achieved in circumstances such as Hampshire's (where cooperative programs are available), with an over-all ratio of teaching faculty to students 1:16. A student body of 1440, then, would mean a teaching faculty of about 90. Even at this relatively (conventionally) high ratio, it is exceedingly difficult to operate successfully, in a financial sense, without the benefit of endowment income.

Tuition and fee charges at the better-known colleges and universities have been rising about $100 per year, on the average, in the last ten years. Announcements by colleges about future levels indicate that the $100 annual average increase will continue at least early into the 1970's. The increases have raised many difficult questions among parents of students and among educators, particularly in the private colleges. Among these are the following:

> How high can student charges go before a major shift in demand occurs between public and private institutions?

> If there is a shift in demand, will the character of the undergraduate body change, erasing the efforts the elite private schools have made to democratize?

> Are the large scholarship grants characteristic of the well financed private colleges vestigial remnants of a Puritan ethic, with the maintenance of middle-class living standards for the family of the recipient the main result?

In an attempt to shed light on some of these and similar questions, Allan M. Cartter, in a recent paper entitled *Pricing Problems for Higher Education,* discusses realistically many of the apprehensions and misunderstandings about tuition charges. The gist of Mr. Cartter's statement is:

> The real costs of higher education have not risen drastically in the last thirty years. Most of the significant rise has been a result of increases in faculty salaries since 1960.

> Tuition charges have increased rapidly in the last ten years, reflecting the increases in faculty salaries.

There are nearly twice as many students from relatively affluent families ($10,000 family incomes, 1964 dollars) compared with the number of places in colleges as there were twenty-five years ago.

Financing a college education, despite increasing real costs, is easier than ever because of a diversity of funding programs, increasing attention to the need, and a striving by the colleges to achieve social and economic diversity through generous scholarship programs.

The ratio of private to public education costs continues to change in favor of the public institutions, meaning a greater challenge to the private colleges to account for their higher charges in terms of qualitative contributions to their students and to the progress of education in the broad sense.

Mr. Cartter's contributions to clear thinking about college pricing are many. Of special concern to Hampshire College and, most likely, to any new college, is his analysis of the change in the real cost of higher education and his conclusion that the change is relatively modest. While that is reassuring to a prospective purchaser of educational services, it is not the whole answer for a new college, simply because "price" and "cost" are not equatable in the mysterious economics of private higher education. The "price" to matriculate at Harvard College, or any of dozens of the excellent institutions, is not reflective of the "cost." Although the price at Harvard may be little different from a hundred other colleges, the expenditure per student by institutions varies a great deal. The difference, of course, is endowment income. Although the real cost, in Mr. Cartter's analysis, has not increased astronomically, the effect of other income, which has increased in many institutions, has not been considered.

Mr. Cartter, therefore, both encourages and discourages the Hampshire planners. He encourages in the assertion that tuition charges can still go up (at least in theory) because America's families have the wherewithal; he discourages in not considering (rightly, for his purposes) the role that rising endowment incomes have had in helping disguise the real change in the cost of higher education.

As indicated in the budget projections (included as Exhibit II at the close of this chapter), Hampshire College proposes student charges in 1969 of $3300, increasing in 1971 to $3500. At these levels, the College can "make it" financially. Given the present assumptions, the prices appear to be realistic.

In support of this conclusion, Mr. Cartter's paper is helpful. Further substantiation is available through an examination of the tuition levels of other colleges and universities, many of which are charging in the $3000 range in the fall of 1966. There is no obvious reason to expect the roughly $100 average increase in charges to be reversed or to stop. Hence the projection to $3300 by 1969 and $3500 by 1971 follows.

As an unendowed institution determined to compete in the arena of high faculty salaries (a necessary commitment to quality) Hampshire College will be challenged, budget projections or not, to demonstrate how an institution reliant solely on student fees for income, can expect to achieve quality on a par with the richly endowed institutions. Also, Hampshire will surely be challenged to differentiate itself sufficiently from good public institutions to justify its existence at the highest permissible level of tuition charges.

In planning, Hampshire has chosen to answer these challenges, in part, by saying that with a smaller than usual faculty, a cooperative opportunity within a complex of institutions, and a new and organized vision, education of quality and distinction can be achieved. The budget (included at the close of this chapter) prepared for the first four years of Hampshire's operation reflects these assumptions.

As one of the elements in its new design for undergraduate education, Hampshire College proposes a major departure in scholarship philosophy. Unlike many of the established colleges, Hampshire starts life free from the inheritance of a scholarship program with taproots in the 19th century. Then, the absence of great public institutions prompted generous benefactors to provide endowment funds to the private colleges to aid the pious and indigent young men and women whose talents would otherwise be wasted. The growth of the low (or no) tuition public institutions in this century lessened the need for private colleges to fulfill a public responsibility to educate a broad spectrum of American youth.

With that, the old argument for scholarship aid was no longer strong enough to justify such major expenditures of funds. A new form of the old rationalization was found in the argument that scholarship aid was necessary to insure a diversified (and thus democratized) student body.

Diversity of student population has become one of the ten commandments of the admission policy of most private colleges, and adherence to that commandment is assured, in turn, by the existence of endowed scholarship funds.

Hampshire College believes that there is a certain amount of speciousness to the present-day argument; that, in fact, much of the money that is dispensed in the name of diversity and democratization is, in fact, subsidy to families that could afford to pay full tuition and fees if the colleges offered them no alternative. In that sense, scholarship funds have been diverted from their original purpose.

Large sums from private sources to endow scholarship funds are likely to be less available in the future, partly because of federal and foundation support on a current basis, and partly because of the needs of the institutions themselves for funds for faculty salaries and for buildings.

The major departure that Hampshire College will make in the early identification and encouragement of young people with great promise and impoverished families was discussed in some detail in Chapter VII. Radically early identification and long-term encouragement of the kind described in that chapter have not been undertaken hitherto by American colleges. In academic 1966-67 Hampshire will identify fourteen* boys and girls now in the fifth grade with the intention of guaranteeing them full scholarships, provided the conditions discussed in Chapter VII are met, for 1974-1975 and their college years thereafter. A similar group will be identified in 1967-68, and in subsequent years. If attrition reduced the annual group to ten students, by 1977-78 Hampshire would have 40 such students in residence under full scholarship, and the number would stay constant thereafter. Aside from early identification and long-term encouragement, the principal point of the College's policy on scholarships would be to give *full* scholarships only, and then only to students of great promise and profound need. Pursuing this point prior to the academic year 1974-75, when the first "early identification" students will arrive, Hampshire plans to give full scholarships to ten new students of great need and promise in each academic year from 1969-70 to 1973-74.

---

* Without solid data from which to project, an attrition rate of over 28% is assumed, with perhaps ten of these students actually enrolling at Hampshire at the end of high school.

These will be students identified by more usual procedures in the last year or two of their secondary school years. Scholarships for these students will be $3600 per year during 1969-71 and $3800 per year during 1971-73.* Scholarships for these students will be drawn from private funds, as things appear now. In addition to these *total* scholarships, there will be federal scholarship monies, loans, and work opportunities for other students.

Hampshire College regards its proposed departure in the scholarship aid program as a significant way to unburden the operating budget and as an expression of convictions the Hampshire College administration holds about current scholarship practices and the potential opportunities for creative deployment of limited funds within a college budget. Through its proposed scholarship aid program, Hampshire College will demonstrate the value of combining the early identification of talent with a long-term full scholarship commitment based on great need. As a program, the idea is readily transferable to other institutions. Therefore, it has the potential of multiplying its impact manyfold, should its merit be demonstrated.

## 2. CAPITAL FUNDING

Plans for the Hampshire College campus and physical plant will be developed to express, support, complement, and reinforce the organized vision that is the College. This new approximation, which is expressed in the preceding eight chapters, is the basis on which physical planning will proceed. Henceforth academic and physical planning will tend to merge as one intermingling stream, occasionally being separated for administrative convenience, but generally working together to achieve an integrated and harmonious whole which will become Hampshire College.

Mr. Hugh Stubbins, as architect, and Mr. Hideo Sasaki, as master planner, are now actively engaged in the basic design of the campus and its buildings, assisted by their separate organizations. In addition, as noted earlier, Mr. Pietro Belluschi counsels the College trustees and administration on architectural matters as needed. The capital projections at the close of this chapter were constructed prior to the time these

*Tuition and fees plus an average amount of $300 for travel and incidentals.

experts entered into a full engagement with the College. In consequence, these capital projections are at present to be regarded only as useful but very general approximations, designed to serve as starting points for intensive and comprehensive planning.

Exhibit III summarizes the translation of the modular approach to a Hampshire College campus design (from Chapter VII) into the spaces needed to properly house the functions of the College and then, in Exhibit IV, expresses these needs in dollar terms. Recognizing the provisional nature of these specific expressions of Hampshire's goals, and acknowledging that analysis and planning are in an early state, it nonetheless appears likely that Hampshire College will need funds on the order of $29,000,000 to plan and build a campus for 1440 students.

### 3. THE SOURCES OF FUNDS

The best estimates that can be made at this time of the money needed to pay the day-to-day expenses of the development of Hampshire College (aside from capital costs) are subject to many imponderables. The rate at which a staff will be developed depends less on a plan than on finding, recruiting and appointing the right people. It took six months to enlist a president and a year had to pass from the time the search began until he could assume leadership of the College. The contractual nature of academic commitments means that as much time or more could elapse before a dean and other key academic leaders are appointed.

Having acknowledged the imponderables which accompany recruiting first-rate leadership, estimates of the operating cost for the next three years (1966-67, 1967-68, 1968-69), the ones until the College has income of its own, have been made on the basis of the expected staffing and expenses *necessary* to prepare for opening the College in 1969.

If these calculations are reasonable, the $6,000,000 gift from Harold F. Johnson will, by June 30, 1972, have paid for operating expenses in full until July 1, 1969, will have covered the operating deficits (as reflected in the budget) for the first three years of operation, and will have contributed $2,500,000 to the capital resources of the College, presumably toward development of the campus and plant.

Additional sources from which Hampshire expects to obtain funds are the Housing and Home Finance Agency (for loans for dormitories and dining halls), and the Higher Education Facilities Commission (for grants for some academic facilities). Eligibility for such funds depends, in part, on an accreditation qualification for which Hampshire College is not eligible under the present rules of the New England Association of Colleges and Secondary Schools. Hampshire is working with the Association to effect a modification of the rules. (For an elaboration of the accreditation problem, please see Appendix materials.)

The combination of Mr. Johnson's contribution and expectations of federal funds provides a sum of $14,000,000, leaving $15,000,000 to be raised from private sources (Exhibit V).

The private sources of funds for Hampshire College are not yet apparent. A systematic and comprehensive analysis of the possibilities has just started. It is expected, however, that a campaign to raise money shall be undertaken.

To solicit from the alumni of the supporting institutions would be robbing Peter to pay Paul (and might cause some hat-shuffling among the Hampshire College board of trustees!). With the exception of Mr. Johnson, who has made the College a possibility with his unusually bold and generous act, the trustees are men of relatively modest circumstances, and multiple charitable responsibilities. No doubt they will support Hampshire College, but they will not contribute $15,000,000.

Clearly, then, in addition to federal support, Hampshire College will turn to private foundations, to corporations, and to individual donors who may become excited enough by the vigor of a new venture to want to brave participation in a perilous journey in the hope its rewards may be as large as the promise it holds.

## 4. THE VALLEY CENTER FOR EDUCATIONAL COOPERATION

Central to Hampshire's redefinition of undergraduate education is the issue of unlimited demand and limited resources. Hampshire's proposal to help define, clarify, communicate and resolve this issue is, in part, a separately financed, housed, administered and governed organization to be called the Valley Center for Cooperative Development in Education. The aims of the Center, which have already been defined elsewhere in this document, are to encourage, stimulate, and facilitate cooperation among educational institutions in the Connecticut Valley to help the limited resources better meet the unlimited demand. At first, such co-operation would be mostly among the five colleges. Ultimately it could draw on and contribute to all educational institutions in the Connecticut Valley from Springfield to Greenfield.

Implementation of the Valley Center proposal will require imagination and enough funds to assure that strong and independent leadership can be enlisted and can work with effect. An estimated operating budget and an approximation of the capital funds needed to bring the Valley Center to vigorous fulfillment are included at the close of this chapter as Exhibit VI. The projections are for a ten-year period.

Hampshire College, the dreamchild, is coming to life. In the next ten years Hampshire College will grow into a strong young institution, contributing to and benefitting from the cooperative efforts among the five institutions, working through the Connecticut Valley Center, and establishing further their association as a unique and significant enterprise in education.

# EXHIBIT I

## HAMPSHIRE COLLEGE

### Allocation of Initial Financing
### Balance Available for Capital Purposes

| | | |
|---|---:|---:|
| Initial Funding (H. F. Johnson Gift) | | $6,000,000 |
| Expended through June 30, 1966 | $ 356,000 | |
| Balance July 1, 1966 | | 5,644,000 |
| | | |
| *Less* estimated expenditures July 1, 1966-June 30, 1967 for current operations | 190,000 | |
| Balance July 1, 1967 | | 5,454,000 |
| | | |
| *Less* estimated expenditures July 1, 1967-June 30, 1968 for current operations | 500,000 | |
| Balance July 1, 1968 | | 4,954,000 |
| | | |
| *Less* estimated expenditures July 1, 1968-June 30, 1969 for current operations | 1,000,000 | |
| Balance July 1, 1969 | | 3,954,000 |
| | | |
| *Less* estimated operating deficits (as reflected in budget) | | |
| 1969-70 | $ 899,400 | |
| 1970-71 | 511,200 | 1,410,600 |
| | | |
| Available for capital purposes | | $2,543,400 |

# EXHIBIT II

## HAMPSHIRE COLLEGE

### Proposed Operating Budget
### 1969-70 through 1972-73
### Notes and Assumptions

The following notes and assumptions apply to the proposed budget:

1. *Economy*—The United States will continue at its present level of prosperity, making affordable to an increasing number of American families the charges necessary to support private college education.

2. *College population*—An increasing proportion of the eligible age group will go to college; at least 5% of the group will prefer a high-quality, independent private college, thereby continuing the present high proportion of applications to acceptances.

3. *Interest rates*—Will continue high, making feasible short-term investments as indicated.

4. *Number of students enrolled:*

    | | |
    |---------|------|
    | 1969-70 | 360  |
    | 1970-71 | 720  |
    | 1971-72 | 1080 |
    | 1972-73 | 1440 |

    Except in the graduation fee, loss of income from student attrition has not been considered.

5. *Student Aid*—An average number of ten students from each class will receive full scholarship support plus a modest allowance for travel to and from home and for incidental expenses. Loans and jobs as shown.

    | | *Scholarships* | *Loans* | *Jobs* |
    |---------|-----------|----------|-----------|
    | 1969-70 | $ 36,000  | $20,000  | $30,500   |
    | 1970-71 | 72,000    | 40,000   | 33,500    |
    | 1971-72 | 114,000   | 60,000   | 41,500    |
    | 1972-73 | 152,000   | 80,000   | 50,000    |

6. *Comprehensive fee*
The breakdown of the comprehensive fee is as follows:

|  | *1969-71* | *1971-73* |
|---|---|---|
| Tuition | $2200 | $2400 |
| Activity fee | 100 | 100 |
| Board | 600 | 600 |
| Room | 400 | 400 |
| Total | $3300 | $3500 |

7. *Faculty-student ratio*—Eventually a ratio of 16 to 1, counting teaching faculty only. The ratio will not be developed lineally, however:

|  | *# faculty* |
|---|---|
| 1969-70 | 42 |
| 1970-71 | 60 |
| 1971-72 | 78 |
| 1972-73 | 90 |

8. *Faculty salaries*

| *Average salary* | *Professor* | *Assoc. Prof.* | *Asst. Prof.* | *Instructor* |
|---|---|---|---|---|
| 1969-70 | $19,500 | $14,700 | $11,500 | $ 9,500 |
| 1970-71 | 20,500 | 15,500 | 12,100 | 10,000 |
| 1971-72 | 21,500 | 16,250 | 12,700 | 10,500 |
| 1972-73 | 22,500 | 17,000 | 13,300 | 11,000 |

Aggregate salary costs are based on distribution of faculty by rank as follows:

| Professor | 20% |
|---|---|
| Assoc. Prof. | 25% |
| Asst. Prof. | 35% |
| Instructor | 20% |

Average faculty salaries by year are:

| 1969-70 | $13,500 |
|---|---|
| 1970-71 | 14,200 |
| 1971-72 | 14,900 |
| 1972-73 | 15,600 |

9. *Social Security*—Premiums calculated at rate of 4.9% on maximum salary or wage payments of $6600 per year.

10. Total salary payments on which 5% increases were calculated:

|  | Payments | Increase For year | Cumulative* |
|---|---|---|---|
| 1969-70 | $1,169,500 | — | — |
| 1970-71 | 1,424,100 | $ 58,500 | $ 58,500 |
| 1971-72 | 1,711,300 | 74,129 | 132,600 |
| 1972-73 | 1,914,400 | 92,200 | 224,800 |

*As reflected in budget.

11. *TIAA-CREF—Annuity premium payments*—On the basis of 10% of annual salary to be paid by the College, covering all faculty and officers above the rank of instructor at time of appointment, and all other employees after attaining age 30 and a minimum of three years of service. Immediate coverage of any individual who is already a participant at time of appointment.

12. *Other fringe benefits*—Sums included for moving allowances for new faculty and administrative officers, tuition grants for faculty children attending college elsewhere, major medical and group life insurance.

The College will own housing and will subsidize its operation in the amount of $500 per unit per year. College housing to be occupied as follows:

| 1969-70 | 15 | @ | $500 | $ 7,500 |
|---|---|---|---|---|
| 1970-71 | 20 | @ | 500 | 10,000 |
| 1971-72 | 30 | @ | 500 | 15,000 |
| 1972-73 | 40 | @ | 500 | 20,000 |

13. *Interchange courses*—Hampshire College students to be eligible for interchange courses at other institutions in the Valley. Estimate each student will take one semester course each year at one of the other campuses. Tuition costs would be:

|  | Annual Semester course enrollments | Tuition costs* |
|---|---|---|
| 1969-70 | 360 | $ 54,000 |
| 1970-71 | 720 | 108,000 |
| 1971-72 | 1080 | 162,000 |
| 1972-73 | 1440 | 216,000 |

*@ $150 per semester four credit hour course interchange charge established among four colleges.

14. *Business office*—The business office will operate with a minimum of personnel. It is expected that the rapid mechanization and automation of accounting functions will make practicable the purchase of such services from one of the other colleges. The office would also aim at cooperative enterprise in purchasing, auditing and staff personnel procurement. Funds are provided under general institutional expense.

15. *Health services*—Health services will be purchased from local doctors. The College will not appoint a full-time staff physician.

## HAMPSHIRE COLLEGE
### Budget Summary

| | | 1969-70 (360) | 1970-71 (720) | 1971-72 (1080) | 1972-73 (1440) |
|---|---|---|---|---|---|
| **I. Estimated Income** | (Students) | | | | |
| Student fees: | | | | | |
| Comprehensive fee | 3300 | 1,188,000 | 2,376,000 | 3,780,000 | 5,040,000 |
| Comprehensive fee | 3500 | | | | |
| Application fee | 15 | 15,000 | 15,000 | 15,000 | 15,000 |
| Graduation fee | 10 | | | | 3,250 |
| Miscellaneous fees | | 1,000 | 2,000 | 3,000 | 4,000 |
| Total Student Fees | | 1,204,000 | 2,393,000 | 3,798,000 | 5,062,250 |
| Interest Earned - General Funds | | 6,500 | 12,000 | 17,000 | 22,000 |
| Total Income | | 1,210,500 | 2,405,000 | 3,815,000 | 5,084,250 |

| | | 1969-70 (360) | 1970-71 (720) | 1971-72 (1080) | 1972-73 (1440) |
|---|---|---|---|---|---|
| **II. Estimated Expenses** | (Students) | | | | |
| Educational & General | | | | | |
| General Administration | | 207,100 | 207,100 | 207,400 | 207,400 |
| Student Services | | 159,900 | 172,000 | 184,100 | 204,600 |
| External Relations/Fund-raising | | 38,700 | 38,800 | 38,900 | 40,000 |
| General Institutional | | 67,500 | 72,500 | 79,500 | 86,500 |
| Staff Benefits | | 153,700 | 198,700 | 242,200 | 288,400 |
| Instruction | | 791,000 | 1,096,600 | 1,441,800 | 1,693,000 |
| Library | | 106,000 | 114,000 | 121,000 | 128,000 |
| Building & Grounds | | 226,000 | 238,000 | 255,000 | 257,000 |
| Salary Increases (Cumulative) | | | 58,500 | 132,600 | 224,800 |
| Total Educational & General | | 1,749,900 | 2,196,200 | 2,702,500 | 3,129,700 |
| Auxiliary Enterprises | | 324,000 | 648,000 | 972,000 | 1,296,600 |
| Scholarship Aid | | 36,000 | 72,000 | 114,000 | 152,000 |
| Total Expense | | 2,109,900 | 2,916,200 | 3,788,500 | 4,577,700 |
| Estimated Balance (Deficit) | | (899,400) | (511,200) | 26,500 | 506,550 |

# EXHIBIT III

## HAMPSHIRE COLLEGE
### Gross Square Footage
### Covered Space

| | | |
|---|---|---|
| Houses | 4 x 129,435 | 517,740 |
| Library | | 61,500 |
| Administration-Service | | 8,865 |
| Humanities | | 18,735 |
| Languages | | 18,105 |
| Natural Sciences | | 40,095 |
| Social Sciences | | 6,600 |
| Health Services | | 6,000 |
| College Center | | 32,775 |
| Indoor Athletic | | 32,700 |
| Maintenance, Storage | | 10,000 |
| | | 753,115 square feet |

Note: A detailed breakdown of space by facility is included in the Appendix material.

# EXHIBIT IV

## HAMPSHIRE COLLEGE
### Cost Summary

| | |
|---|---:|
| Houses | $13,144,120. |
| Library | 2,029,500. |
| Administration/Services | 239,355. |
| Humanities Wing | 468,375. |
| Languages Wing | 633,375. |
| Natural Sciences Wing | 2,004,750. |
| Social Sciences Wing | 178,200. |
| Health Services | 162,000. |
| College Center (additional) | 1,048,800. |
| Recreational & Athletic | 1,316,600. |
| Maintenance, Storage | 220,000. |
| Site Development | 785,000. |
| Other Capital Outlay | 1,100,000. |
| Additional Land Purchase | 200,000. |
| | $23,530,075. |
| Professional Fees (10% of buildings, site development) | 2,223,000. |
| TOTAL | $25,753,075. |
| Contingency | 500,000. |
| Allowance for increase in costs (10%) | 2,625,300. |
| GRAND TOTAL | $28,878,375. |

# EXHIBIT V

## HAMPSHIRE COLLEGE
### Capital Financing
### 1967-72

Estimate of total capital funds required:

| | | |
|---|---:|---:|
| 1. Physical Plant | $21,445,075. | |
| 2. Land Acquisition (additional) | 200,000. | |
| 3. Site Improvement | 785,000. | |
| 4. Other Capital Outlay | 1,100,000. | |
| 5. Professional Fees | 2,223,000. | |
| 6. Contingency Fund | 500,000. | |
| 7. Allowance for Cost Increases (10%) | 2,625,300. | $28,878,375. |

Estimate of total capital funds available:

| | | |
|---|---:|---:|
| 1. Balance of Initial Fund | $ 2,543,400. | |
| 2. Federal Loans and Grants | | |
|     a. H.U.D. (Dormitories, Dining Halls) | 10,400,000. | |
|     b. H.E.F.C. (Other Facilities) | 1,000,000. | 13,943,400. |
| Leaving to be raised: | | $14,934,975. |

# EXHIBIT VI

**The Valley Center**
**for Cooperation in Education**

**Financial Needs**
**Ten Years: 1967-76**
**Capital Funds Needed**

1. Design and construction of physical facilities          $    500,000.

**Current Funds Needed**
**1967-76**

| | *Per Year* | *Ten-Year Total* |
|---|---|---|
| 1. Grants to five colleges —to stimulate continuing cooperation | $250,000. | $2,500,000. |
| 2. To undertake major cooperative projects | 250,000. | 2,500,000. |
| 3. Research and development in education | 350,000. | 3,500,000. |
| 4. Administration and General | 100,000. | 1,000,000. |
| | | 9,500,000. |

Total—Capital and Current Funds                          $10,000,000.

## EXHIBIT VII

### HAMPSHIRE COLLEGE

Total Capital and Current Funds Required for **Hampshire College** and **Valley Center** — 1966-67 to 1975-76

A successful demonstration of the results attainable through a cooperative enterprise of the kind proposed in this working paper is based on the simultaneous planning, building and funding of Hampshire College and the Connecticut Valley Center for Cooperative Development in Education. A summary estimate of the total resources needed for the demonstration follows.

| Year | Hampshire College | | | Valley Center | | |
|---|---|---|---|---|---|---|
| | Capital | Current | Total | Capital | Current | Total |
| 1 - 1966-67 | $   — | $ 190,000 | $ 190,000 | $300,000 | $ 950,000 | $ 1,250,000 |
| 2 - 67-68 | 5,593,245 | 500,000 | 6,093,245 | 200,000 | 950,000 | 1,150,000 |
| 3 - 68-69 | 7,553,565 | 1,000,000 | 8,553,565 | — | 950,000 | 950,000 |
| 4 - 69-70 | 7,322,865 | 899,400 | 8,222,265 | — | 950,000 | 950,000 |
| 5 - 70-71 | 6,060,440 | 511,200 | 6,571,640 | — | 950,000 | 950,000 |
| 6 - 71-72 | 2,348,260 | — | 2,348,260 | — | 950,000 | 950,000 |
| 7 - 72-73 | — | — | — | — | 950,000 | 950,000 |
| 8 - 73-74 | — | — | — | — | 950,000 | 950,000 |
| 9 - 74-75 | — | — | — | — | 950,000 | 950,000 |
| 10 - 75-76 | — | — | — | — | 950,000 | 950,000 |
| Totals | $28,878,375 | $3,100,600 | $31,978,975 | $500,000 | $9,500,000 | $10,000,000 |

Hampshire College    $31,978,975
Valley Center    10,000,000

*Grand Total* 1966-67 to 1975-76    $41,978,975

Less *Funds Available*

Balance H. F. Johnson Gift    $ 5,644,000
Federal Loans and Grants    11,400,000
   17,044,000

Balance to be raised    $24,934,975

# REFERENCES

Epigraph, Chapter 1. Martin Meyerson, "The Ethos of the American College Student: Beyond the Protests," *Daedalus,* Summer, 1966, p. 737.

1. As long ago as 1953 James B. Conant suggested among other things that there should be no expansion in the number or size of four-year colleges, that the programs of such colleges should not be expanded, that bachelor's degrees should be awarded after two college years, and that four-year colleges should become almost wholly corridors for entrance into graduate or professional schools. *Cf.* his *Education and Liberty* (New York: Vintage Books, 1965).

2. Professor Bell's remarkable study, *The Reforming of General Education* (New York: Columbia University Press, 1966), is far more than an examination of the Columbia College experience. It is a brilliant and original contribution to present discourse on higher education, with particular relevance to the undergraduate college and its questions. This section of the Hampshire College position statement reflects a substantial debt to Professor Bell. Among many other things, Daniel Bell points out in connection with research that a single experiment by two scholars at Columbia to confirm the existence of the neutrino cost a million dollars in federal support, and that American universities today are spending a billion and a half dollars per year on basic research alone, under government contract.

3. Bell comments that for the university-based colleges there are resultant difficulties different from those in independent institutions. The university college is likely to become the "stepchild" of the larger institution in terms of the teaching quality, funding, and prestige available to it. *Ibid.,* p. 103.

4. Wesley Lindow, Executive Vice-President, Irving Trust Company, and Sidney G. Tickton, Vice-President, Academy for Educational Development, "Yesterday, Today, and Tomorrow," a paper of the Academy for Educational Development, New York, 1966. Mimeo.

5. Daniel Bell, "The Disjunction of Culture and Social Structure: Some Notes on the Meaning of Social Reality," *Daedalus,* Winter, 1965, p. 210.

6. *Ibid.,* pp. 211-212.

7. *Ibid.,* p. 212.

8. *Ibid.,* p. 213. Italics and elisions added.

9. Kenneth Keniston, *The Uncommitted* (New York: Harcourt, Brace & World, Inc., 1965). *Cf.* also his "Faces in the Lecture Room," *Yale Alumni Magazine,* April, 1966, pp. 20-34. Professor Keniston, it should be said, is no gloomy student of American college youth. When it comes to prognosis, in his writing and in talk, Professor Keniston is far more sanguine about young people and colleges than this compressed sample of his views might suggest.

10. Bell, *The Reforming of General Education, op. cit.,* p. 308.

11. See Lionel Trilling, *Beyond Culture* (New York: The Viking Press, Inc., 1965), pp. i-xviii.

12. Miss Sontag (in *The Nation,* April 13, 1964) observes that a truly critical value is "a sensibility based on indiscriminateness, without ideas [and] beyond negation."

13. Bell, *The Reforming of General Education, op. cit.,* p. 311.

14. The influential work of the Physical Sciences Study Committee and Educational Services Incorporated, under the direction of Professor Jerrold Zacharias of MIT, expended more than $6 million in remaking a single high school course, physics, and in preparing teachers to teach it.

15. Aspects of curriculum and other changes in secondary education are described usefully in a number of reports. Among these is *Innovation and Experiment in Education,* A Progress Report of the Panel on Educational Research and Development of the President's Science Advisory Committee, Washington: GPO, March, 1964.

16. Regrettably little improvement in high school programs has occurred for students not planning on college.

17. See John I. Goodlad, *School Curriculum Reform,* a report to the Fund for the Advancement of Education, Ford Foundation, March, 1964.

18. Professor Zacharias has remarked, at least in conversation, that—had he the opportunity to "do PSSC over"—he would not again move toward a single course in "physics" but toward a sequence in "science."

19. It is important in this connection to note that no national reform effort comparable to those in natural science, mathematics, social science, and foreign language has succeeded in getting under way in one of the most basic of subjects: English.

20. *Toward Excellence in Physics: Reports from Five Colleges,* Committee on Physics Faculties in Colleges, American Association of Physics Teachers and the American Institute of Physics, New York: The Committee, 1964, p. 2.

21. *Ibid.,* pp. 2-3.

22. The Harvard-MIT accelerator cost a very great deal in millions of dollars, but the Palo Alto facility cost much more.

23. Dean Wiesner has consulted with Hampshire College leadership about this and other questions.

24. Seymour E. Harris, *Higher Education: Resources and Finance* (New York: McGraw-Hill Book Company, 1962), presents data and analysis which make the financial requirements and constraints of higher education painfully clear. For the field as a whole, Professor Harris suggests that total national operating educational and general budget will reach as high as $11,760,000,000 by 1970, contrasted with $3,600,000,000 for 1957-1958. The pressures on private liberal arts colleges are reflected in one study of twenty-four institutions where in 1953-1963 the average tuition increase was 124%.

25. Algo D. Henderson, "The Economic Aspects," in *Universal Higher Education,* edited by Earl J. McGrath (New York: McGraw-Hill Book Company, 1966), p. 204.

26. Julius A. Stratton, Commencement Address, Massachusetts Institute of Technology, June 12, 1964, in "The Contemporary University: USA," *Daedalus,* Fall, 1964, p. 1241.

27. *University of Oxford: Report of Commission of Inquiry,* Vol. I, "Report, Recommendations, and Statutory Appendix," (Oxford: Clarendon Press, 1966), p. 33. For a highly informative discussion of the Oxford financial position and the expensiveness of discrete operations even in one institution, see Chapter V, "Costs in a Collegiate University," Vol. I, pp. 155-188.

28. James M. Cass, "Changes in American Education in the Next Decade: Some Predictions," in *Innovation in Education,* edited by Matthew B.

Miles (New York: Teachers College Press, Columbia University, 1964), p. 618.

29. Derek J. Price, *Science Since Babylon* (New Haven, Connecticut: Yale University Press, 1961), provides a useful treatment of the kind of growth in science cited here.

30. Gerald Holton, "Scientific Research and Scholarship: Notes Toward the Design of Proper Scales," *Daedalus,* Spring, 1962, pp. 362-399. See, especially, Figure 4, pp. 86-87, "Connections among the contributions in an expanding part of basic physics."

31. P. B. Medawar, "Anglo-Saxon Attitudes," *Encounter,* August, 1965, p. 52.

32. Bell, *The Reforming of General Education, op. cit.,* p. 77.

33. *Loc. cit.*

34. George A. Miller, "The Psycholinguists: On the New Scientists of Language," *Encounter,* July, 1964, p. 30.

35. *Ibid.,* p. 29.

36. *INTREX: Report of a Planning Conference on Information Transfer Experiments,* September 3, 1965, edited by Carl F. J. Overhage and R. Joyce Harman (Cambridge, Massachusetts: The M.I.T. Press, 1965), p. 51.

37. The concern that this will not be the case, and that the information retrieval concept of libraries is relevant only for the sciences, has frequently been expressed. A recent expression was the address of Gordon N. Ray, opening the 85th annual conference of the American Library Association in New York City. See "Librarians Urged to Save the Book," *The New York Times,* Monday, July 11, 1966. Mr. Ray rightly emphasizes the virtues of the book itself as a highly flexible tool for information transfer. But he pays no attention to its limitations, such as those thoughtfully described by J. C. R. Licklider, *Libraries of the Future* (Cambridge, Massachusetts: The M.I.T. Press, 1965), pp. 4-8.

38. Licklider, *op. cit.,* p. 6.

39. Royce S. Pitkin and George Beecher, "Extending the Educational Environment: The Community as a Resource for Learning," in *Higher Education: Some Newer Developments,* edited by Samuel Baskin (New York: McGraw-Hill Book Company, 1965), pp. 174-195.

40. See John Keats, *The Sheepskin Psychosis* (New York: Delta Book Edition, Dell Publishing Co., 1966), 190 pp.

41. Considerable attention to the desirability of a flexible student leave or sabbatical program was paid in discussion at the Hampshire College Conference of Consultants, June 13-15, 1966. Mr. Philip Sherburne, president of the U.S. National Student Association, was one of those who favored as permissive an arrangement as possible.

42. Frederick Rudolph, *The American College and University: A History* (New York: Alfred A. Knopf, Inc., 1962, Vintage Books Edition, 1965), p. 92.

43. See Pitkin and Beecher, *op. cit.*, pp. 185-188.

44. Kevin Lynch, "The Pattern of Metropolis," *Daedalus*, Winter, 1961, pp. 95-98.

45. John Dyckman, "The Changing Uses of the City," *Daedalus*, Winter, 1961, pp. 123-125.

Epigraph, Chapter 2. Henry Steele Commager, "Social, Political, Economic, and Personal Consequences," in *Universal Higher Education*, edited by Earl J. McGrath (New York: McGraw-Hill Book Company, 1966), p. 16.

46. Albert E. Sloman, *A University in the Making: The BBC Reith Lectures, 1963* (New York: Oxford University Press, 1964), which, as he says, gets "down to brass tacks" in terms of the plans of the University of Essex, of which he was appointed first Vice-Chancellor in 1962.

47. C. L. Barber, Amherst College; Donald Sheehan, Smith College; Stuart M. Stoke, Mount Holyoke College; Shannon McCune, *Chairman*, University of Massachusetts, *The New College Plan: A Proposal for a Major Departure in Higher Education* (Amherst, Massachusetts: The Four Colleges, 1958), 56 pp. Reprinted 1965.

48. *Ibid.*, Prefatory statement, p. 2.

49. A synopsis of the 1958 Report may be found in the appendix material of this paper.

50. Letter, Charles R. Longsworth, Secretary, Board of Trustees, Hampshire College, Amherst, Massachusetts, to Members of the Educational Advisory Committee, October 15, 1965.

51. Robert C. Birney, Amherst College; Alice B. Dickinson, Smith College; Frederick C. Ellert, University of Massachusetts; Roger W. Holmes, Mount Holyoke College; Sidney R. Packard, *Chairman;* Charles R. Longsworth, Hampshire College, *ex officio, Report of the Educational Advisory Committee to the President of Hampshire College* (Amherst: Hampshire College, April 13, 1966), 52 pp. plus appendices. Mimeo. A synopsis of the 1966 Report may be found in the appendix material.

52. Italics added. The quoted material in these passages is drawn from John W. Gardner, "Agenda for the Colleges and Universities," Address to the California Conference on Higher Education, San Francisco, California, May 7, 1965. Mimeo.

53. Italics added.

54. Gardner, *op. cit.,* p. 10.

Epigraph, Chapter 3. Stephen Graubard, *Daedalus,* Fall, 1964, p. 1028.

55. Elting E. Morison, *Men, Machines, and Modern Times* (Cambridge, Massachusetts: The M.I.T. Press, 1966), p. 223.

56. Alfred North Whitehead, *The Aims of Education, and Other Essays* (New York: The New American Library of World Literature, Mentor Edition, 1929), p. 93.

57. *Ibid.,* p. 26.

58. *The New College Plan, op. cit.,* p. 9.

59. Morton White, *Religion, Politics, and the Higher Learning* (Cambridge, Massachusetts: Harvard University Press, 1959), p. 3. These papers are acute in their discussion of the need for more adequate application of the tools of philosophical analysis in public affairs, education, history, and other fields. That this need is unmet, Professor White avers, is a condition for which philosophers cannot escape their share of responsibility. In consultation with Hampshire College, Professor White has suggested that important uses of philosophical analysis (not in the context of usual courses in "types" of philosophy, etc.) could be developed in the general curriculum.

60. P. W. Bridgman, "Quo Vadis," *Daedalus,* Winter, 1958, p. 92.

61. *Ibid.,* p. 93.

62. William Arrowsmith, "The Shame of the Graduate Schools, A Plea for a New American Scholar," *Harper's Magazine,* March, 1966, pp. 51-59.

63. Letter, Elting E. Morison, Cambridge, Massachusetts, June 17, 1966, to Franklin Patterson, President, Hampshire College, Amherst, Massachusetts.

64. Jacques Barzun, "The New Man in the Arts," *The American Scholar*, Autumn, 1956, p. 442.

65. Bell, *The Reforming of General Education, op. cit.*, p. 311.

66. *Ibid.*, p. 312.

67. Edward B. Tylor, *Primitive Culture*, Third Edition (London: John Murray, Publishers, Ltd., 1891) p. 1.

68. Alfred L. Kroeber and Clyde Kluckhohn, "Culture: A Critical Review of Concepts and Definitions," *Papers of the Peabody Museum*, 47, No. 1a, Harvard University, Cambridge, Massachusetts, 1952. 223 pp.

69. *Ibid.*, p. 157.

70. David Riesman, "College Subcultures and College Outcomes," in *Selection and Educational Differentiation*, Report of a Conference, May 25-27, 1959, Berkeley, California (Field Service Center and Center for the Study of Higher Education, University of California, Berkeley, California, 1959), p. 3.

71. See James G. Rice, "The Campus Climate: A Reminder," in Baskin, *op. cit.*, pp. 304-317, for a helpful recent summary.

72. *Ibid.*, p. 307.

73. Quoted in Burton R. Clark, "College Image and Student Selection," in *Selection and Educational Differentiation, op. cit.*, p. 158. Professor Clark reports findings on college culture as seen in the "image syndrome" held by entering students at Antioch, Reed, Swarthmore, and San Francisco State College.

74. *Ibid.*, p. 160.

75. Rice, *op. cit.*, pp. 307-308.

76. Letter, Professor Kenneth Keniston, Yale University, New Haven, Connecticut, July 9, 1966, to Franklin Patterson, President, Hampshire College, Amherst, Massachusetts. We are indebted to Professor Keniston for advice which is reflected in much of this discussion.

77. *Ibid.*

78. Letter, Mr. Philip Sherburne, President, U.S. National Student Association, Washington, D.C., June 25, 1966, to Franklin Patterson, President, Hampshire College, Amherst, Massachusetts.

79. Byron Stookey, "Starting from Scratch: The University of California at Santa Cruz," *Harvard Review,* Winter, 1965, pp. 22-34.

80. An interesting discussion of American students vis-à-vis the ascribed purposes of higher education is Edgar Z. Friedenberg and Julius A. Roth, *Self-Perception in the University: A Study of Successful and Unsuccessful Graduate Students,* Supplementary Educational Monograph Number 80 (Chicago, Illinois: The University of Chicago Press, Janury, 1954), 101 pp. Friedenberg and Roth are preoccupied with socio-psychological factors in achievement and underachievement. One comment about passive-dependent young men and their behavior in college may suggest why it is not enough to think of students as rational beings alone: ". . . these young persons frequently behave as though they expected that, in school, at last, they might find an environment in which their passivity would not matter; much of their subsequent difficulty may be ascribed to disillusionment and rage at finding that this is not the case." p. 73.

81. Bell, *The Reforming of General Education, op. cit.,* p. 152. Professor Bell's usage of the prefix *meta-* is taken not quite as the usual construction of "among," "along with," "after," or "behind," but to denote the sense of depth, complexity, change, and connectedness in these fields as the object of education. Italics added.

82. Alfred L. Kroeber, *Anthropology,* Revised Edition (New York: Harcourt, Brace & World, Inc., 1948), p. 291.

83. Morison, *Men, Machines, and Modern Times, op. cit.,* pp. 84-85.

Epigraph, Chapter 4. Kingman Brewster, Jr., *Ventures,* Magazine of the Yale Graduate School, Spring, 1966.

84. A précis of each of these two reports is found in the appendix material of this paper.

85. For a list of consultants who have advised on the earlier and current approximations of Hampshire College's program, see appendix material.

86. Keniston, Letter of July 9, 1966, *op. cit.,* p. 2.

87. Letter, Professor C. L. Barber, Indiana University, Bloomington, Indiana, June 28, 1966, to Franklin Patterson, President, Hampshire College, Amherst, Massachusetts.

88. Charles R. Longsworth, Hampshire's Vice-President, has variously suggested:

    a vice-president in charge of revolution, "knowing what is happening in higher education and society and trying to get ahead of it."

    an RD Laboratory (not Research and Development, but Radical Departure) . . . "a special educational laboratory on the campus for the really wild things to be tried . . . where institutional or faculty reputations would not be lost; only made."

89. Julius A. Stratton in interview by Robert C. Cowen, "Quality *vs.* Quantity in the Colleges," *The Christian Science Monitor,* July 28, 1966.

90. *Ibid.*

91. *Report of the Educational Advisory Committee to the President of Hampshire College, op. cit.,* p. 6.

92. *Education at Berkeley: Report of the Select Committee on Education* (Berkeley, California: University of California, Academic Senate, March, 1966), pp. 39-40. Hereafter referred to as *The Muscatine Report,* after the Committee chairman, Professor Charles Muscatine.

93. Morton White's Review of James A. Perkins', *The University in Transition* (Princeton, New Jersey: Princeton University Press, 1966), *The Sunday New York Herald Tribune, Book Week,* March 6, 1966, pp. 12-13.

94. *The New College Plan, op. cit.,* p. 10.

95. *Report of the Educational Advisory Committee to the President of Hampshire College, op. cit.,* p. 10.

96. *Ibid.,* p. 11.

97. *Ibid.,* pp. 11-12.

98. *Ibid.,* pp. 27-33.

99. Rudolph, *op. cit.,* pp. 305-306.

100. *Ibid.,* p. 442.

101. *Ibid.,* p. 452. Quoted from Irving Babbitt, *Literature and the American College: Essays in Defense of the Humanities* (Boston: Houghton Mifflin Company, 1908).

102. *Loc. cit.*

103. *Ibid.*, p. 455.

104. *Education at Amherst: The New Program,* edited by Gail Kennedy (New York: Harper & Brothers, 1955), 330 pp. This account is of particular interest because it represents an in-operation evaluation seven years after the inception of the new curriculum when, as President Charles W. Cole remarked in a foreword, the college had "had time enough to learn a great deal about the effectiveness of the new curriculum, but not time enough drastically to modify its intent," p. xi.

105. Bell, *The Reforming of General Education, op. cit.,* p. 38.

106. *Education at Amherst, op. cit.,* pp. 309-310. Italics added.

107. See, for example, the use Professor Gabriel A. Almond, a political scientist, has made of sociological concepts and analysis in comparative national studies, e.g., with Sidney Verba, *The Civic Culture* (Princeton, New Jersey: Princeton University Press, 1963).

108. See especially E. H. Gombrich, *Art and Illusion* (New York: Pantheon Books, Inc., 1960), for a discussion of the concept of "convention" in aesthetic experience.

109. See Bell, *The Reforming of General Education, op. cit.,* pp. 157-163. Bell draws on Thomas Kuhn, *Structure of Scientific Revolution* (Chicago, Illinois: The University of Chicago Press, 1963), Joseph J. Schwab, and Paul F. Brandwein, *The Teaching of Science as Enquiry* (Cambridge, Massachusetts: Harvard University Press, 1964), and others.

110. *The New College Plan, op. cit.,* pp. 8-9.

111. *Ibid.,* p. 9.

112. Bell, *The Reforming of General Education, op. cit.,* pp. 192-193.

113. Again, description here is indebted to Professor Bell.

114. *Ibid.,* p. 197. Italics added.

115. *Ibid.,* pp. 208-209.

116. *Ibid.,* p. 166.

117. *Ibid.,* pp. 170-171.

118. *Cf.,* for example, Franklin Patterson, *Man and Politics,* Occasional Paper No. 4, Social Studies Curriculum Program, Educational Services Incorporated (Cambridge, Massachusetts: Educational Services Incorporated, 1965).

Epigraph, Chapter 5. Abbott Lawrence Lowell, from Aaron Yeomans' biography, *Abbott Lawrence Lowell 1856-1943* (Cambridge: Harvard University Press, 1948), pp. 160-161.

119. Professor Meyerson's essay, "The Ethos of the American College Student: Beyond the Protests," in *Daedalus*, Summer, 1966, pp. 713-739, is a most perceptive assessment of where students and their colleges stand today.

120. Professor Bruner dealt with curriculum generated around these questions in his Presidential Address to the Seventy-Third Annual Convention of the American Psychological Association in September, 1965. An adaptation of the text of that address is in Jerome S. Bruner, *The Growth of Mind*, Occasional Paper No. 8 of the Social Studies Curriculum Program of Educational Services Incorporated (Cambridge, Massachusetts: Educational Services Incorporated, 1966).

121. Bell, *The Reforming of General Education, op. cit.,* p. 163.

122. Schwab, *op. cit.,* p. 39.

123. Quoted in Bell, *The Reforming of General Education, op. cit.,* p. 164. Professor Bell remarks of his colleague: "This is how *he* teaches it; but regrettably, not all do."

124. *Ibid.,* pp. 164-165.

125. *Cf. Unified Science Program,* A bulletin of the College of Literature, Science, and the Arts, and the College of Engineering, The University of Michigan, Ann Arbor, Michigan, August, 1964, 2 pp. This is a two-year sequence for highly selected freshman and sophomore students with marked proficiency in mathematics. It includes physics, chemistry, and mathematics.

126. *Cf. The Muscatine Report, op. cit.,* p. 128, with regard to a new one-year Contemporary Natural Science (CNS) course at Berkeley for non-majors, covering "principles of physical, chemical, and biological science, together with their implications for society."

127. *Report of the Educational Advisory Committee to the President of Hampshire College, op. cit.,* p. 24.

128. *The New College Plan, op. cit.,* pp. 17-18.

129. "The Freshman Seminar Program" (multilithed report circulated to

the Faculty of Arts and Sciences of Harvard College, February 1963), p. i.

130. *Ibid.,* p. 97.

131. *Ibid.,* pp. 97-98.

132. C. L. Barber, *More Power to Them: A Report of Faculty and Student Experience in the Encouragement of Student Initiative* (Amherst, Massachusetts: The Committee for New College, 1962), 75 pp.

133. *Ibid.,* pp. 56-57.

134. *The Muscatine Report, op. cit.,* p. 135.

135. *University of Oxford, Report of Commission of Inquiry, op. cit.,* Vol. I, pp. 101-102.

136. *Loc. cit.*

137. Quoted in Bruner, *op. cit.,* p. 14.

138. White, *Religion, Politics, and the Higher Learning, op. cit.,* pp. 71-72.

139. *Ibid.,* p. 73.

140. *Ibid.,* p. 74.

141. *The New College Plan, op. cit.,* p. 25. The way this was put in 1958 leaves some doubt that the Committee then had entirely "dethroned the course" in their own minds as a customary unit of knowledge!

142. *Report of the Educational Advisory Committee to the President of Hampshire College, op. cit.,* p. 44. The résumé and quotations in this portion of the text are from pp. 44-45 of the *Report.*

Epigraph, Chapter 6. Susanne K. Langer, *Philosophy in a New Key: A Study in the Symbolism of Reason, Rite and Art* (Cambridge, Massachusetts: Harvard University Press, 1942), p. 103.

143. Edward Sapir, *Language: An Introduction to the Study of Speech* (New York: Harcourt, Brace & World, Inc., Reprint of 1921 edition in Harvest Book Series, 1949), p. 23.

144. Langer, *op. cit., p.* 18.

145. White, *Religion, Politics, and the Higher Learning, op. cit.,* p. 1. Discussion throughout this section is heavily indebted to Professor White's thinking, as Hampshire College understands it, but he bears no responsibility for the shortcomings it must certainly have.

146. Langer, *op. cit.*, p. 20.

147. *Ibid.*, p. 21.

148. Ernst Cassirer, *An Essay on Man* (New Haven, Connecticut: Yale University Press, 1944), p. 207.

149. *Ibid.*, p. 221.

150. White, *Religion, Politics, and the Higher Learning, op. cit.*, pp. 36-37.

151. Bridgman, *op. cit.*, p. 87.

152. *Ibid.*, p. 88.

153. Langer, *op. cit.*, p. 143.

154. George A. Miller and David McNeill, "Psycholinguistics," 198 pp. plus bibliography and charts, Mimeographed, May, 1966. This draft review of the entire field was generously made available to Hampshire College by Professor Miller of the Center for Cognitive Studies at Harvard University. Professor Miller was joined in its preparation by Professor McNeill of the University of Michigan; between them, they have produced a most useful and comprehensive résumé of the whole rapidly developing field of psycholinguistics. The twenty-three page bibliography of American, British, French, and German studies is extraordinarily helpful. Discussion in the present section is principally drawn from Miller and McNeill.

155. *The New York Times,* August 1, 1966. The *Times* of that date carried an important letter by Mr. McGeorge Bundy to the Federal Communications Commission, as well as the supporting briefs with regard to proposals for satellite uses for educational and commercial television.

156. *Ibid.*, Mr. Bundy's letter.

157. President Pusey is quoted by David O. Ives in "TV Comes to Harvard," *Harvard Today,* Spring, 1966, p. 30.

158. *The Revolution in the Schools,* Ronald Gross and Judith Murphy, editors (New York: Harcourt, Brace & World, Inc., 1964), 250 pp.

159. William Clark Trow, *Teacher and Technology: New Designs for Learning* (New York: Appleton-Century-Crofts, 1963), 198 pp.

160. Bell, *The Reforming of General Education, op. cit.*, p. 267.

161. *Report of the Educational Advisory Committee to the President of Hampshire College, op. cit.*, pp. 34-36.

Epigraph, Chapter 7. Robert Frost, "The Master Speed," *Complete Poems of Robert Frost* (New York: Holt, Rinehart and Winston, Inc., 1936), p. 392.

162. *The American College: A Psychological and Sociological Interpretation of the Higher Learning*, Nevitt Sanford, editor (New York: John Wiley & Sons, Inc., 1962), p. 17.

163. Donald N. Michael, *The Next Generation: The Prospects Ahead for the Youth of Today and Tomorrow* (New York: Random House, Inc., Vintage Books, 1965), p. 83.

164. Kenneth Keniston, "Faces in the Lecture Room," *op. cit.*, p. 33.

165. Richard B. Sewall, "The Undergraduate and His Culture," *Ventures,* Magazine of the Yale Graduate School, Spring, 1966, p. 12.

166. *The New College Plan, op. cit.*, p. 30.

167. Sewall, *op. cit.*, pp. 12-13. Professor Sewall was Master of Ezra Stiles College, Yale University.

168. See the *Carnegie Quarterly*, Summer, 1966, pp. 6-7, for a brief report of the program at Brandeis University.

169. *The New College Plan, op. cit.*, pp. 31-32.

Epigraph, Chapter 8. Dael Wolfle, "Diversity of Institutional Goals," *Science,* Vol. 150, p. 969, 19 November 1965.

Jean Gottmann, *Megalopolis: The Urbanized Northeastern Seaboard of the United States* (New York: The Twentieth Century Fund, Inc., 1961), pp. 3-16.

170. *Ibid.*, p. 5.

171. *Report of the Committee on Cooporation to the President of Amherst College, Mount Holyoke College, Smith College, University of Massachusetts,* June, 1956, p. 4.

172. *Loc. cit.*

173. *Ibid.*, p. 19.

174. Rudolph, *op. cit.*, p. 491.

175. Stuart Stoke, "Some Perspectives on Cooperation, with Implications for Amherst, Mount Holyoke, and Smith Colleges, and the University of Massachusetts," 1962.

Epigraph, Chapter 9. Adlai Stevenson, "Extend our Vision . . . to All Mankind," *The National Purpose* (New York: Holt, Rinehart and Winston, Inc., 1960), pp. 30-31.

# APPENDICES

# APPENDICES

## APPENDIX A

Synopsis
of
Report of the
COMMITTEE ON COOPERATION
to the Presidents of
AMHERST COLLEGE
MOUNT HOLYOKE COLLEGE
SMITH COLLEGE
UNIVERSITY OF MASSACHUSETTS

1956

INTRODUCTION

The committee had its inception in a grant made by the Fund for the Advancement of Education. In February 1955 funds were provided to relieve one teacher from each of the four institutions of a part of his regular work to study the problem of cooperative educational activities among the four institutions. The committee so formed was instructed to report its findings and recommendations to the presidents.

After initial misgivings about the possibility of accomplishing anything significant, the committee began to believe that if a thoroughgoing plan of cooperation among the four institutions could be devised and put into effect, it might be of more than local importance. It might indicate a pattern of action which could be successfully followed by other groups of colleges and universities. Of particular importance to the committee's thinking was the relationship between a public university and the private colleges and the effect cooperation might have in softening the criticism of the private colleges for their failing to meet the demand created by the increased number of college applicants.

## 1. Undergraduate Instruction

The first concern of the committee is cooperation at the undergraduate level. There are many handicaps to effecting cooperation. The interests of five groups must be coordinated. They are: the administrations, the departments, faculty committees on educational policy, the faculties as a whole, and the trustees. Requirements for general education and for majors and honors in each of the colleges must be observed, and an efficient mode of supervision of activities must be established. There are also practical impediments, including differences in accounting systems, the problem of transportation, discrepancies in calendars and class scheduling, and differences in salary scales and tenure provisions.

In spite of these obstacles, the committee is convinced desirable and workable proposals can be devised. Four possible modes of cooperation are suggested. They are: (a) joint appointments to supplement the work of departments in two or more institutions; (b) allocation of advanced or special courses to one of the four institutions; (c) the concentration of all work in one subject at one institution at the advanced level and, provision by the same institution at the intermediate and lower levels on the other campuses; (d) elementary and some intermediate courses on all campuses, with the advanced courses being distributed among the other institutions or at one institution but taught by members of the various faculties.

## 2. Cooperative Graduate Work

The committee feels that it is advantageous to cooperate in the offering of graduate work. Institutions offering the master's degree are expected to continue to do so. The cooperation in master's degree programs could be patterned after the suggestions for undergraduate cooperation. The Ph.D. degree should generally be given by the University although other institutions could retain or add programs.

General control of the program would rest with the University, under the Graduate Council, augmented by two representatives from each of the other institutions. The individual graduate departments would propose course offerings. The council would determine the makeup of the graduate departments. Development and operation of the program should lead to the establishment of a corporation which would not grant degrees nor give courses but would have administrative responsibility. The faculties of all the institutions might be utilized if approved by the appropriate department-head and president, thus increasing the teaching resources available. There would be some interchange where two or more institutions give the same degree, or there are specialized courses in one location, or one school owns special equipment. This interchange should not be great.

### Advantages of Development of a Cooperative Graduate Program

(a) The ability to offer a full graduate program with a qualified staff.
(b) The opportunity to satisfy top teachers who might otherwise leave for positions where they could teach graduate students.
(c) Attraction of more and better graduate students.
(d) The possibility of offering graduate assistantships even where the particular institution does not offer a graduate program itself.

### Disadvantages of Development of a Cooperative Graduate Program

(a) A slight increase in teaching staff at the other colleges although they will be compensated for the time of those who teach graduate courses.
(b) A partial loss of time in the services of some outstanding teachers.
(c) The time-consuming work involved in making formal arrangements for cooperation.
(d) The possibility that in some cases when a faculty member becomes involved in graduate teaching there may be a deterioration of his undergraduate teaching.

After inquiries among the four faculties, the commmittee concludes that for the time being cooperative enterprise would be directed primarily to fostering the growth of Ph. D. programs at the University by the sharing of courses and personnel.

### 3. A Graduate Program for Teachers

The University expects to expand its program in the professional education of prospective teachers who have completed a liberal arts degree. Practical consideration indicates that the number of students the other institutions can recruit for this project will be small.

### 4. Transportation

Transportation of students from one institution to another is one of the major difficulties in the way of cooperative action. It is assumed that institutions will prefer to provide supervised transportation.

## 5. Area Studies

One of the major criticisms of our American colleges is that they have developed curricula to deal almost exclusively with the history and culture of the West. The committee proposes introducing a cooperative program of various studies in the non-Western world and that possible ways of instituting a cooperative program be investigated by a representative or representatives of the four institutions.

## 6. FM Radio and Educational Television

A joint program of radio and television would be a means of participating in adult education, would improve committee relations, and would provide the means to experiment with some new approaches to instruction. After investigating the possibilities, the committee concludes that open or closed circuit television is too expensive, but that FM broadcasting is feasible. A sub-committee was formed which made recommendations which were subsequently transmitted to Presidents Cole, Wright and Mather.

## 7. Coordination of Lecture Programs, Concerts and Art Exhibits

The committee recommends joint enterprise in planning for lectures on several bases. The committee recommends sharing information about desires and intentions concerning concert programs in order to avoid conflicting dates and duplication in major features. The committee recognizes the possibility of reducing expense and broadening the selection of art exhibits should they be secured cooperatively. Recommendations were made for action to explore the possibilities.

## 8. A Joint Calendar

The committee recommends the publication of a joint calendar of major events for each semester of academic year.

## 9. Remedial Reading

The committee proposes that representatives from the four institutions study the remedial reading situation and make a recommendation for action to the presidents.

## 10. Speech Therapy

The committee proposes that the speech departments of the four colleges send qualified students from Smith and the University to Mount Holyoke for a course in the technical aspects of speech therapy. Further development of the program, including graduate work, depends on building a larger staff and building more housing at the University.

## 11. Adult Education

The four institutions have cooperated in the field of adult education for forty years through the Committee on University Extension in the Connecticut Valley colleges. The committee has supplied many needs but has attempted to not duplicate courses from elsewhere. There is a great need for adult education in the sciences. Therefore, the committee proposes that the four institutions explore the possibility of offering science instruction in evening classes as their special contribution to adult education.

## 12. Audio-Visual Aids

The committee suggests that there are financial savings and improved service to be gained through a central depository for materials. The committee suggests that the Director of Audio-Visual Aids at the University be invited in cooperation with representatives from other institutions to propose a plan to the presidents.

## 13. Joint Appointments of Statisticians

The committee recommends the joint appointment of a statistician to serve the four institutions as advisor on statistical procedure in research projects, to advise on statistical procedures in the presentation of information to the public by the institutions, to advise in correlating instruction in statistics, and to make analyses for the benefit of the administration and faculties of the institutions.

## 14. Cooperative Recruitment of Staff

Because of the impending shortage of good teachers it was suggested that the information about available personnel be pooled to the advantage of all. It was felt that such pooling could avoid the waste inherent in duplicated time, effort and expense. A coordinator would be important to the implementation of this recommendation.

## 15. Implementation of the Report

The majority of the recommendations cannot be realized without the enlistment of someone to encourage and coordinate the work of planning and implementation. He must be empowered to deal with complex and delicate problems including scheduled transportation, salaries, etc. The committee recommended and the presidents agreed to appoint an administrative officer. The committee closed its report with the following statement:

> We are not advocating cooperation just for the sake of cooperation, nor merely as a response to such pressures. We are advocating it as a safeguard for the future. At this stage no one can tell how far these joint activities may develop. Certainly they will grow only so far as it is apparent that they afford real advantages to the participating institutions.
>
> If joint activities eventually attain any considerable proportions, particularly in the field of graduate work, it will be advantageous to set up a separate corporation (as was the case with the Hampshire Inter-Library Center) for their operation. Some of the advantages accruing to a separate corporation are: (1) it can receive and use funds from foundations and other donors; (2) it can make agreements for the cooperating institutions with other organizations or individuals more easily than separate agreements can be reached; (3) it is able to take the initiative in developing new forms of cooperation without arousing the jealousy that might come from extensive leadership on the part of one of the member institutions; (4) it can serve as an arbiter among the members; (5) it can simplify the administrative tasks of the member institutions; (6) it can oversee the operation of cooperative enterprises better than member institutions; (7) it is free from a great deal of the institutional inertia of its constituents; (8) it can provide more continuity and persistence to cooperative efforts than can be secured from an opportunistic approach, and probably more than a single individual unless he served for a long time; (9) it might prove a convenient holding and operating corporation for affiliated enterprises such as the proposed FM radio station, HILC, funds for graduate or faculty research, a visiting scholars program, etc.
>
> Our final recommendation, therefore, is that if, eventually, the major proposals made in this report are put into effect a separate corporation to administer them should be established.

At the time of the report's publication the following recommendations had been approved by the presidents:

1. That committees be formed to study the possibility of cooperation in instruction at the undergraduate level in the following subjects: Astronomy, Botany, Classics, Geology-Geography, German, Italian, Physics, Russian, and Spanish.

2. That the presidents recommend to their trustees that establishment and operation of an educational FM station in conjunction with the Lowell Institute Cooperative Broadcasting Council be undertaken by the four colleges; and that efforts should be made to seek outside financial aid for the station's creation and maintenance.

3. That the chairmen of the lecture committees be invited to consider the suggestions made in the report for coordinating the programs of the four institutions.

4. That the chairmen of the concert committees also be invited to consider ways of coordinating their plans for concert series.

5. That representatives from Amherst, Mount Holyoke and the University be appointed to confer with Mr. Parks of Smith on the possibility of securing an art exhibit to be circulated among the four institutions.

6. That a joint calendar of major events be published for each semester of the academic year.

7. That a committee be appointed to study the possibility of a joint program for remedial reading and to make a recommendation to the presidents by next January.

8. That a committee be formed to study the following proposals for cooperation in speech therapy: (a) the joint appointment of a speech therapist for students in the four institutions; (b) the establishment of joint courses at both the undergraduate and graduate levels.

9. That a coordinator in charge of the administration of these various cooperative experiments be appointed.

Recommendations which the committee made which were still being considered by the presidents were the following:

1. That a letter be sent to the other departments of liberal arts and the sciences inviting them to consider similar possibilities of cooperation through (a) the offering of joint courses in fields where enrollments are small and (b) joint appointments to supplement their staff in areas where a full-time member of the department is not needed.

2. That where there are any two or more departments in the four institutions which are interested in working out a cooperative program for the Master's degree they be encouraged to do so.

3. That committees be appointed to study the possibility of a joint program for the Ph.D. in two or three subjects; and, in the event workable plans are formulated, that a subvention be sought for the purpose of getting these joint departments established.

4. That the possibility of instituting a cooperative program in the field of area studies, particularly the non-Western world, be studied either (a) by one person on released time, or (b) by representatives of the "Curriculum" or "Educational Policies" committees of the four institutions.

5. That the four institutions should explore the possibility of offering science instruction at the college and graduate levels in evening classes as their special contribution to adult education.

6. That the Director of Audio-Visual Aids at the University be invited, in co-operation with representatives from the other institutions, to study the possibility of establishing a central collection of materials and equipment.

7. That a statistician be jointly appointed to serve the four institutions.

8. That a central file pooling all information available in the four institutions which would be of use in the recruitment of staff be established.

9. That, if eventually the major proposals made in this report are put into effect, a separate corporation to administer them should be established.

# APPENDIX B

## Synopsis
## of
## THE NEW COLLEGE PLAN
## A proposal for a Major Departure in Higher Education
## (November 14, 1958)

FOREWORD — Letter of Transmittal

I. THE NEW COLLEGE PROPOSAL—An Introduction and Summary View

American higher education is facing a crisis in qualitative and quantitative terms. Solving the crisis will require great resources and great imagination. Amherst, Mount Holyoke, Smith and the University of Massachusetts can make a contribution to the solution cooperatively by sponsoring a new departure in liberal education of the highest quality.

The new college would provide economies, particularly in the efficient use of teaching resources, and yet would provide an education comparable to that of the "prestige" colleges. Unless privately endowed institutions meet the challenge of maintaining high academic standards in the face of increasing costs, they may not retain their roles as educational leaders. New College proposes to restructure liberal education to help meet the challenge of maintaining high quality in the face of rising costs.

### 1. *A new role for the course*

American higher education fosters the assumption that a subject is closed to a student unless he "takes" the course. Thus, the typical college strives to be a university in miniature. New College dethrones the course as the unit of knowledge, reduces the number of courses, and devotes the savings in faculty time to teaching the student to teach himself. It also dethrones the idea of institutional completeness by demonstrating the advantages of mutual cooperation wherever institutions are located near together. Each teacher will give one lecture course at one time; students will have a three-course program. Time saved will be for seminars and independent study.

### 2. *Training in independence*

The goal of liberal arts colleges is to prepare students for a lifetime of self-education. New College believes the average student in better colleges is capable of more independence, but must be given proper training and opportunity. New College will provide that training and those opportunities and test the result with rigorous field examinations in the junior and senior years.

### 3. *Common intellectual experience*

Students will share a common experience by taking two college-wide courses during a month-long midwinter term. One course will deal with some aspect of the Western cultural heritage, the other with some aspect of non-Western cultures.

### 4. *Teaching disciplines without departments*

Departmental organization working within the course system is chiefly responsible for proliferation of courses. New College will be divisionally organized, but recognize that the intellectual life of a college is structured by specialized disciplines. The training of faculty members will be exploited rather than ignored; each of the faculty will decide what he will teach, in consultation with his colleagues, and in response to his own interests and those of his students. Course offerings will be 100 per year. Each teacher will teach one lecture course at a time. The goal is free development of the curriculum in response to changing intellectual interests.

### 5. *Cooperation within the sponsoring institutions*

One of New College's great advantages is in utilizing some of the teaching resources of the four supporting institutions. Students will be required to take at least one semester away during their college career. If a discipline is not represented on the New College faculty at all, the student will not be able to concentrate in the field, although he can study the subject at one of the other colleges. In some cases a student may be able to organize a program of concentration at or with one of the other colleges. New College will avail itself of information about educational technology and take advantage insofar as possible of films, television and language laboratory facilities.

### 6. *Programs of concentration*

"Completeness" will not depend on the course offering, but on the student. Teachers will have time to help the student organize his program

because their course load will not be large. Programs in concentration will
be developed frequently on an *ad hoc* basis, with the approval of a faculty
committee drawn from the three divisions. Field examinations will periodically be set by outside examiners.

### 7. *Plans for the College as a community*

The goal is to carry into the rest of the life of the College the attitudes
promoted by the curriculum. It is hoped that intellectual and social interests
can be combined. Because of the strong emphasis on group life, it is important that each student have a place where he can work and be alone if he
chooses.

Recreation, athletics and social life should avoid the domination of
compulsive organization, while encouraging the free development of individual and group activities. There will be no fraternities or sororities, and
no highly organized intercollegiate athletics.

### 8. *Economies*

The first interest of the New College Committee was to provide for
liberal education of the highest quality. However, educational and economic
advantages can be made to go hand in hand. Savings are expected to be
in operating costs, not in capital outlay. The chief factor making savings
possible is the 20:1 ratio of students to faculty. If this ratio can be approxi-
mated, the College can operate on tuition and fees except for the need to
find scholarship funds. Other savings can come through the library, where
faculty research needs can be met with inter-library loans and Hampshire
Inter-Library Center, in avoiding some specialized scientific facilities, in
eliminating a formal athletic program, and unforced arrangements for
recreation.

The high cost of acquiring and developing a site and of building facilities
cannot be avoided.

## II. Curriculum and Its Rationale

### 1. *The academic program*

Each student takes three courses in the fall and spring terms of 14 weeks
each, and two college-wide courses at midterm. Freshmen have two fall
term freshman seminars in the humanities and social sciences, and a year-
long required science course. In the spring freshmen participate in lecture-
student seminars which combine lectures and seminars and train students

to work more and more independently. Freshman seminars will average twelve students; freshman lecture-student seminars will average twenty-four students. Upperclass lecture-student seminar courses, averaging forty-two students, are the staple of the curriculum after the freshman year.

Distribution requirement to be met by end of junior year: Each student to have four semesters in two different humanities, four in two different social sciences and three in science. Concentration programs occupy half and not more than two-thirds of regular course work the last two years. One field examination during junior year, two field examinations or one examination and a thesis during senior year. All juniors or seniors participate in at least one faculty-supervised advanced seminar averaging ten students.

No language requirement. Elementary languages will be taught, but not for credit.

Grades will be fail, satisfactory, distinction. Examinations will be de-emphasized and student work in projects and seminars will be important in evaluating performance.

## 2. *Establishing and sustaining the pattern of student initiative*

Student initiative is established first by the freshman seminar, which will require a large investment of faculty time. Thereafter, the lecture-student seminar courses will reinforce independence.

## 3. *The first-term freshman seminars in humanities and the social sciences*

Fall freshman seminars teach methodology by exploring limited subjects. Each teacher will select a subject and show a group of thirteen students how he works, and how they can work in his discipline. Subjects will be limited in scope. Students will be assigned independent work to encounter fundamental problems of topic and discipline.

Teachers will have to teach composition as it relates to their field (there may be a need for remedial work in composition). Oral reports will be part of the regular pattern.

## 4. *Science courses*

Freshman science seminars to be similar to the seminars in humanities and social sciences. Students will participate actively in operations of science chosen to be limited in scope and chosen to lead to a general understanding of scientific method and history.

A sophomore course on science and society will be an elective. Natural, biological and social scientists to join together to discuss the impact of science on modern society.

### 5. The freshman's transition to greater independence

The first midwinter term will consolidate attitudes inculcated by the fall freshman seminars. Freshmen will work with upperclassmen who are more experienced and with faculty who are almost as unfamiliar with the topic as the student. Life of the mind becomes real rather than an abstraction.

Second semester freshman year science seminar can be larger and more open-ended so the student is left to resolve questions for himself. Freshman lecture-student seminars to deal with larger subject-matters. Instructors will sometimes leave, sometimes listen, sometimes be absent. They will give advice on techniques for successful student-led group efforts.

### 6. The upperclass lecture-student seminar course

Rely on assumption that freshman year established independent study as a style of life at New College. Independent work associated with lecture courses will require much faculty time and thought to work out collateral projects, to visit student groups at intervals, to check and read papers and to advise students. The unique thought is the relationship between independent work and the lecture course. Tying these together should save faculty time and increase the possibility of student initiative. High quality of lecture preparations is a key determinant in the success of the lecture-student seminar course.

### 7. Programs of concentration

Differing needs and interests to be met by a great variety of programs ranging from the comparatively well-defined program for conventional goals to programs that cut across disciplinary and divisional lines.

Part of the student's self-education is the designing of his own program. Essays outlining a program of concentration required by each student at the end of sophomore and junior years; to be approved by a faculty panel representing the three divisions.

### 8. Field examinations and theses

Field examinations will make possible flexible programs in independent work while maintaining standards. Examinations will be larger than any course, but not so large as to make cogent testing impossible.

Field examinations may fall within one discipline or may be distributed across disciplines and divisions.

A senior thesis not universally required. If undertaken, it may be substituted for one of the two field examinations at the end of the senior year.

Course examinations can be dropped for students who are making the course part of their program of concentration.

### 9. *The advanced seminar*

The pattern of lecture-seminar courses will be varied by seminars organized in the manner which is customary for advanced departmental majors. Assume careful guidance on the part of the faculty to enable the student to reach high levels of scholarship.

### 10. *Courses in neighboring colleges*

The requirement that students take at least one semester course at a neighboring college during their college career will: a) enrich their programs and b) give them educational experience in a different institutional setting. The possibility of such interchange will increase the prestige of the new institution assisting in recruiting able students. Adjusting credits should not be a difficult problem.

### 11. *The midwinter term*

The midwinter term will supplant regular courses and projects. The College, with its guests, will turn itself into a conference.

The subjects will be of vital importance to the whole community; one, organized around a Western topic and the other a non-Western topic. The particular subjects to be dealt with in the two courses will be determined by faculty interest. Interdisciplinary efforts will be stressed.

Half the faculty will be involved in any one midwinter course. It is proposed that teachers who participate be given extra compensation. The other half of the faculty will be free to pursue their own studies from the beginning of Christmas vacation to the second week of February.

The president and dean should participate in the midwinter program.

Outside lecturers will be engaged from neighboring institutions and beyond. The visits of younger scholars will: a) provide a way for the New College faculty to see people being considered for teaching appointments and b) an opportunity to judge the work of younger colleagues.

The two month-long courses will be equivalent to a single term course.

There will be required reading, papers, discussions and examinations. The courses may develop so they can be offered during the summer, to other students, to teachers, to alumni.

## 12. *Foreign and ancient languages and literature*

The language requirement has been eliminated; persons without aptitude taking required language courses gain too little to justify the cost to them and the College.

New College will promote the study of philology and of foreign and ancient literature. New College will encourage all applicants to acquire a reading competence in at least one foreign language. Elementary non-credit courses will be offered by part-time instructors from without the New College faculty. Language laboratory facilities will be available.

The New College faculty will offer intermediate and advanced work in literary and philological subjects. There may be seminars to study subjects in the language of the culture, and upperclass courses in literature read in the original.

## 13. *The treatment of individual differences*

New College students will normally stay for four years. Advanced standing may be granted and a student allowed to begin his field examinations in his sophomore year. In general, however, students will be encouraged to take additional examinations and additional programs rather than to graduate in less than four years.

### III. The Institution as a Community

The educational goals of the New College curriculum can be realized most fully if they are promoted all along the line.

## 1. *Admissions and the character of the student body*

New College is aimed at making the average student more resourceful. The admissions goal is to recruit a student body similar to those at first-rate colleges.

If it is difficult to secure a full quota of students it may be advisable to suffer a financial deficit rather than suffer the failure of the program because of poor students.

Recruiting may be helped by the prestige of the supporting institutions and by the dearth of good coeducational colleges in New England.

At a later date, after the College is proven, the program may be tried with less talented students.

Scholarship help must be available to make possible a well-balanced student body.

2. *The quality of New College will depend on the faculty*

In order to attract a good faculty New College must offer:

a. Salaries at least equal to the sponsoring institutions.

b. Tenure in accordance with AAUP and AAC recommendations.

c. Help in the purchase or rental of homes and apartments.

d. Research and study leaves.

It is important not to attract just experiment-minded people.

An important recruiting factor will be provision for research opportunities to offset the very heavy teaching demands at New College. Such opportunities are provided for half the faculty during midwinter term. Most leaves of absence will probably extend from before Christmas to the following September.

New College should subsidize summer research work.

Each faculty member should have an individual office.

Approximately 10% of the faculty should be visiting teachers from other parts of the country to enrich, criticize and learn from the New College program. Part-time visitors from the neighboring faculties should be encouraged on the same basis.

Emphasis on student initiative makes possible the use of paid student teaching assistants for faculty and administration.

Faculty to be initially recruited to teach part-time in one of the four supporting institutions and spend part-time in planning and preparing for the opening of the new college.

Faculty already in existing colleges can be engaged from time to time to teach courses at New College where suitable people are not immediately available. Wherever possible, the advice of existing faculties should be enlisted in procuring the New College faculty.

3. *Administration*

The faculty should have a dominant role at New College. A senate should be substituted for the usual board of trustees. Membership would include the president, dean, treasurer, division chairmen, three members at large elected by the faculty, three persons chosen by the senate to represent the public interest, three alumni and, initially, the presidents of the sponsoring institutions or their delegates.

The president would be chosen from and by the faculty for a five-year term.

A board of counselors, who are outside specialists, will advise the senate and treasurer on financial affairs. Alumni and friends will raise funds.

If the usual arrangement of a board of trustees and a president whom they appoint is adopted, the president should have the advice of a powerful faculty standing committee, and a third of the trustees should be persons professionally concerned with education.

If the board of trustees system is adopted, the trustees should delegate to a College Council many responsibilities for the operation of the College. The Council would represent all interested groups in the community and would be formed in a variety of ways according to the problem at hand.

Faculty committees should be kept to a minimum.

The division chairmen will do much of the work usually done by department chairmen.

The dean will work in the usual ways.

Under the dean will be a director of student activities to organize athletics, student affairs and other recreation.

The faculty will formulate educational policy.

The librarian and treasurer will have status as voting members of the faculty.

Student government should help organize social life, enforce discipline and be concerned with the solution of academic problems as well as extra-curricular matters.


4. *The library*

Self-education, emphasis on depth, seminar work, individual projects demand ample resources and training in how to use them.

Some factors which will help solve the library problem are:

a. a limited curriculum

b. membership in the Hampshire Inter-Library Center

c. decision not to offer graduate work

d. borrowing privileges for New College faculty at the sponsoring institutions' libraries

e. according borrowing privileges to a New College student enrolled on a neighboring campus.

The neighboring libraries cannot make substantial contributions to regular undergraduate needs at New College.

Changes in book production and other technological advances may help solve the library problem. Such things are:

a. microfilm for out-of-print books

b. increase in the variety of paperback editions

c. duplicated excerpts from uncopyrighted books

d. anthologies created for the occasion by offset or mimeograph.

The librarian and his staff should have academic as well as technical interests. The librarian should be in charge of the College bookstore.

### 5. *Working facilities: the library, study centers, and laboratories*

The working life of the College will be centered in the library, the study buildings and the dormitories. The study buildings are for seminars, student seminars, and independent projects. This space should be close to the library reference room, the reserve desk and delivery desk.

There should be a large number of seminar rooms, some equipped with television monitors.

Study spaces would not be assigned. Library lockers would be provided for books and material.

There must be ample and well-constructed individual study spaces away from living quarters. Study buildings should have casual arrangements for easy social and intellectual interchange.

Auditoriums for large classes and the administration to be housed in a building near the library.

Science laboratories to be connected to the library by covered passages. Students enrolled in science courses at neighboring colleges to take laboratory work there, but New College to have adequate facilities to support its own courses.

### 6. *Living facilities*

Dormitories and dining halls should form subgroups, with the dining halls being served from single kitchens. Dormitory units would have less than 75 students to encourage group loyalty and student responsibility. There should be open lounge space. Single rooms for all students who want them. Living facilities for married students in a trailer park.

## 7. *Social activities, religious life, recreation and athletics*

Social life, religious life, recreation and athletics are to be determined by flexibility and student initiative. No sororities or fraternities; no highly organized intercollegiate athletics. No extracurricular activities will have "tenure."

College should provide a small meditation chapel.

Sports will be encouraged which can be played informally and which provide skills to be continued after college. Intramural teams will be formed according to student interest. Skills will be taught by proficient students who will be paid. "Game weekends" will be focused on intramural games and championships and can be associated with other group activities such as the theater, music and a dance.

No required physical education program.

Recreation activity and athletic activity will take place in the Activities Center, which will include:

a. fieldhouse type space

b. a stage

c. walls for exhibitions

d. snack bar

e. woodworking and metalworking shop

f. multipurpose rooms to function as music studios, sewing rooms, game rooms

g. offices for student organizations and for the director of student activities and his assistants

h. special exercise room

i. a swimming pool

j. showers

k. a stock room

l. student health office

m. simple kitchen facilities for student use

Playing fields and tennis courts and an outdoor amphitheater will be nearby.

Facilities for bowling, billiards and pool should be made available, but a charge should be made for their use.

All income from recreational and athletic activities will go to the College. The goals of the Activities Center are:

a. To permit a great number of student activities to be supervised by a small staff.

b. To avoid hardening of differences between student groups by having them all come to the same building.

c. To avoid building up of empires within buildings that are "owned" by one group or one discipline.

### 8. *The campus and its architecture*

The dominant central building will be the library with its associated study center. In one direction from the library will be student living areas and in the other direction the recreation center, amphitheater and playing field. Automobile traffic should circle the central living and working areas.

Forthright modern architecture rather than a period style is favored. Flexibility of use of space is important. Maintenance costs should be considered at every point.

### 9. *Cooperation by the sponsoring colleges*

Cooperation among Amherst, Mount Holyoke, Smith and the University of Massachusetts is increasing. Possibility for cooperation in the future is only beginning to be appreciated. Perhaps the largest single opportunity is the cooperative sponsorship of new institutions such as New College.

# APPENDIX C

## Synopsis
### of
## The Report of the Educational Advisory Committee
### to the
## President of Hampshire College

### May 2, 1966

*Introduction*

Committee suggests discussion of its proposals with the president. The *New College Plan* of 1958 was used as a "starting point." Nine most important proposals:

1. The freshman seminar and student discussion groups in other courses.

2. A four-divisional organization of the curriculum (with appropriate divisional examinations for majors and non-majors).

3. Emphasis upon independent projects and studies (including the "interim").

4. The abolition of any language requirement either for entrance or graduation (but abundant language study and use throughout College).

5. A virtually classless student body.

6. A small faculty, with assistants, and a relatively small number of courses.

7. A greater emphasis on academic counseling of students.

8. Appropriate provision for continuous curricular development and evaluation.

9. An administrative structure "to insure proper representation in decision-making by all elements in the Hampshire College community."

*The Hampshire College "Image"*

The College is founded on the principle that the best learning is that in which the student progressively acquires the ability to teach himself. Hampshire differs both from a university and a traditional college, in its view of teaching, in its curricular organization, in its emphasis on independent study, in its flexibility, and in its character as a laboratory for educational experimentation—especially experimentation in the methods by which a student best learns to teach himself. The life of the College includes visiting residence by talented outsiders, imaginative use of all media of communication, and opportunities to study and work in the world beyond the campus. The College is committed to a willingness to change.

*Divisional Organization*

Divisions may be argued for because departmentalization is an open-ended curse, but this is negative thinking and insufficient cause for going divisional. A positive reason for divisional organization for undergraduate education is that such organization allows a specialty to be treated but also to be fitted into a broad background. The *New College Plan* of 1958 proposed three divisions: *humanities, natural sciences, social sciences*. This did not provide suitably for studies of language, logic, mathematics, epistemology—for semantical and syntactical concerns. The current report suggests four divisions: *The Humanities, The Natural Sciences, The Social Sciences,* and *The Languages* (including mathematics and logic). Central concern of the fourth division would be communication, involving: a) study of three uses of language: analytic development of calculi and syntax, synthetic development of empircal statements and their semantic functions, and creative employment of language; b) history of language; c) foreign language study. Subjects represented and faculty who are appointed should be selected for their ability to contribute, beyond specialization, to the larger disciplines. The first love of faculty must be teaching.

1. *The Humanities Division*

    a. Thirteen professors with two courses each plus four or five majors.

    b. Ten (Group I) freshman seminars of twelve students per semester.

    c. Four (Group II) non-major courses of thirty students per semester.

    d. Twelve (Group III) major "lecture" courses per semester.

    e. Suggested faculty:

(*Disciplines*:)
1) Musicologist
2) Art historian
3) Literature scholars (3)
4) Philosopher
5) Historian
6) Comparative religion scholar
7) Historian of science

(*Cultures*:)
8) Orientalist
9) Classicist
10) Hebrew culture scholar
11) Near East scholar
12) Renaissance scholar
13) Scholar of Modern Age of Revolutions

Also a writer, musicians, an artist, and a dancer in residence.

f. This division should show how different cultures have dealt with the question of values; it should use study of the arts as well as of history, philosophy, and religion to this end. Performance is key to appreciation and students should be involved in production as well as study.

g. Goals of the division:

1) Provide an introduction to liberal education through the freshman seminar.

   Group I courses, e.g.:
   Revolt in Western Music
   Savonarola and His Enemies
   Etc.

2) Give non-majors appreciation of one or two major answers to the value problem.

   Group II courses, e.g.:
   Plato and Aristotle
   Erasmus
   Etc., built around great humanistic figures

3) Provide intermediate and advanced program for Humanities majors.

Group III courses (intermediate) would be relatively like such courses in conventional liberal arts programs (e.g., Nineteenth Century English Poetry, etc.); the advanced program would consist entirely of independent studies under tutorial direction.

2. *The Natural Sciences Division*

This division should have four types of course offerings to meet four distinct student needs:

a. *Unified program of mathematics, physics, and chemistry for the prospective scientist.* (*Cf.* Unified Science Program of University of Michigan) First two years, "half the student's work." Sophomores as research assistants to faculty scientists.

b. *A science program for non-science students.* Three or four courses per year; cross-field in type; probably full year in duration.

c. *Seminars in particular disciplines, for science students.* Designed to present methodology within framework of specific problem arising out of faculty interest. Could be freshman seminars; six to eight such per semester.

d. *Upper-level science courses in specific disciplines.* Some available at other colleges. Twelve to fifteen courses per semester; one per full-time faculty member. Each such course would assume the background of the unified science program.

The minimum faculty: 15—biology, 4; chemistry, 3; mathematics, 5; physics, 3. Teaching load: 2 courses and six student tutorial hours per week.

3. *The Social Sciences Division*

The intention is to offer a coherent program dealing with the study of man in society, including origins, organization, ideology, behavior, systems, and methodology. Assumptions: a) current state of knowledge permits definition of such study; b) education for general knowledge is still possible; c) the division will offer sufficient alternatives to accommodate diverse student interests; d) there are excellent scholars who share this frame of reference. The course areas break down as follows, with an example course in each:

—Origins, e.g.:
*Pre-literate Cultures*

—Study of Social Organization, e.g.:
  *The Family*

—Ideology, e.g.:
  *Social Values*

—Methodology, e.g.:
  *Non-parametric Statistics*

—Social Behavior, e.g.:
  *Behavior Analysis*

—Social Systems, e.g.:
  *Political Parties*

This division would include as faculty an anthropologist, a sociologist, a philosopher, a mathematician, plus economists, psychologists, and political scientists. Each of the six areas of courses should provide a freshman seminar. The specific disciplines are *implicit* in the course areas and courses, not explicit in the program. The offerings described provide not more than half the normal topical coverage found in the undergraduate major; tutorial and independent study will account for the other needed half. No special courses for non-social science majors foreseen.

4. *The Languages Division*

Mission: to promote understanding of variety of languages developed as instruments of human communication and as tools of artistic and intellectual achievement. Scope: the primarily formal structures (calculi of the mathematician and logician) ; the empirical communications of the natural and social sciences; the informal uses in everyday life; the artistic uses. Plus: the historical development of language, and through linguistics, the semantic, syntactic, and aesthetic factors. Argument: curricular innovation in this mission-scope direction is crucially needed and, at Hampshire, possible. Suggestions for courses (a few selected) :

Group I—Freshman seminars
  —Game theory
  —Grammar and culture

Group II—For non-majors
  —Finite mathematics
  —Computer linguistics
  —History of languages

Group III—For majors
  —Symbolic logic
  —Linguistic analysis: Metaphysics
  —Topology

Proposals with regard to foreign language instruction: that none be "required," but that active offerings be made, and *for credit*. Desirable to use summers for a "total" approach; also adequate mechanical aids. Staff includes: coordinator of language instruction, director of language laboratory, and part-time persons for aid in elementary language instruction. Unanswered: whether (and, if so, what kind) tests of foreign language background and proficiency should be required for admission to Hampshire.

## *Other Proposals*

1. The "Interim" Plan

   Three or four week period between fall and spring semesters. Free rein to student study and other interests. Half of faculty present. Range: independent projects, faculty-directed projects, non-academic work, no formal evaluation. Reverse of inter-semester suggested by the *New College Plan* (1958).

2. The Library

   Should be geared to highly independent study.

## *Summary of Implications of Proposals*

1. Faculty

   Not more than 50, if possible; salaries, etc., comparable to nearby institutions; load of two courses plus six hours of counseling per week; faculty assistants as needed; minimum pedagogical and administrative machinery; real faculty participation in administration.

2. Students

   Freshman seminars; student discussion groups in lecture courses; three courses per semester; divisional examinations; open-ended calendar; adequate academic counseling; continuous evaluation (no grades as such); opportunities to serve as paid teaching assistants; encouragement of off-campus experience, as approved by College, in specific instances; assistance in continuing education.

*Topics Where No Final Conclusions Were Reached*

1. Admissions

2. Graduation requirements

3. Administrative arrangements

4. A device for insuring continuation of the College's "experimental nature"

5. A specific uniqueness for the College. Possible suggestions include subjects not now taught in the Valley.

6. Relationship to other four institutions

# APPENDIX D

OFFICE OF THE COORDINATOR
9 Moore Laboratory of Chemistry
Amherst College, Amherst, Massachusetts 01002

OFFICE OF THE COORDINATOR
9 Moore Laboratory of Chemistry
Amherst College, Amherst, Massachusetts  01002

Four-College Cooperative Program                    September 1, 1965

To:  Presidents Gettell, Lederle, Mendenhall and Plimpton

From:  Robert B. Whitney, Four-College Coordinator

Subject:  Annual Report for 1964-65

It is my privilege to submit the following report on my first year's activities as Four-College Coordinator on a half-time basis. The year has been busy, interesting and enjoyable. As the job has unfolded itself it has seemed to me to consist of four parts—*communications,* helping in the exchange of ideas and information among the four institutions and between them and the outside world; *promotion,* furthering the interests of the Four-College enterprises and particularly in attempting to secure the cooperation of faculty members; *steering,* trying to see that directives are carried out in a way consistent with the policies and interests of the four institutions; and *evaluation,* studying the results of the various Four-College activities and trying to ascertain the reaction of faculty and administrative persons to them.

In order to indicate the present scope of Four-College activities, a copy of "Four-College Cooperation: Information for Faculty Members" is appended to this report. There are 27 areas in which some cooperative work is in progress.

The activities of the Coordinator have centered around 45 different meetings with twenty Four-College groups (those arranged by the Coordinator are marked with an asterisk).

| | |
|---|---|
| *Presidents | 4 |
| *Deputies | 8 |
| Asian-African Committee | 8 |
| Business Officers | 5 |
| WFCR Directors | 5 |
| *History of Science Committee | 3 |
| *American Studies | 3 |
| Massachusetts Review Directors | 2 |
| HILC | 2 |
| Registrars | 1 |
| *Lecture Committee Chairmen | 1 |
| Student Activities Personnel | 1 |
| *Four-College Seminar Committee | 1 |
| Four-College Alumni | 1 |

Agenda and minutes were prepared for many of these, and an important part of the communications function of the Coordinator (as it seemed to me) was the distribution of these documents to a list of approximately 25 individuals, comprising the Presidents, the Deputies, the Business Officers, and the Deans of the four institutions.

Special mention should be made of the valuable discussions which the Deputies held with such experts as Provost Oswald Tippo and Dean I. Moyer Hunsberger on the future of the relation of the University to the other Colleges, Mr. Horace W. Hewlett, President of the Western Massachusetts Broadcasting Council, on new developments in communications, the Editors of *The Massachusetts Review*, Dean Edward C. Moore of the Graduate School of the University on the Cooperative Ph.D. program, and on the new computer developments at the University, and with Professor Herbert Spiro, Chairman of the Asian-African Committee.

Dr. Walter T. Schoen, Phillips Intern in Educational Administration, connected with Smith College, was a valuable help to the Deputies and the Coordinator in collecting resource information. (A project which Dr. Schoen and the Coordinator had hoped to complete during the year, namely the revision of the Book of Agreements, was not accomplished. Perhaps this is just as well since so many changes are now occurring. Also, the previous Coordinator, Professor Stuart M. Stoke, had put it into excellent condition and had given it wide distribution.)

*Progress during the past year*

The appearance of the four institutions to the outside world was brightened in a significant way by *The Massachusetts Review* which achieved a new level of recognition in terms of subscriptions and critical acclaim, (and which incidentally abolished its old deficit, and acquired a small new one), and by WFCR which instituted successful local programming on a significant scale, broadcast four leading musical series (live), received an encouraging volume of fan mail and substantial financial contributions from an appeal to listeners. It should be noted also that WFCR has a very effective new station manager, Mr. Albert Hulsen, and that an expanding service to the four institutions has been the preparation of edited copies of the WFCR tapes of local lectures and concerts, for later use by the performers or their colleagues.

Small but worthwhile steps toward smoother and more effective cooperation were:

Establishment of more nearly coincident yearly class schedules, establishment of more convenient bus schedules resulting in a very large increase in patronage of the buses, improvement in Four-College registration procedures, working out of library rules, especially for graduate students, to the satisfaction of all of the Librarians, and the working out of new forms for faculty borrowing.

The Coordinator records but claims very little responsibility for these items.

*Old Programs in Need of New Decisions*

The Asian-African Committee, with a large amount of money still to be spent, and with almost completely new personnel begins the next to last year of its operation under the Ford Foundation grant. Many objectives of the subsidized program which began five years ago have been realized to a reasonable extent. The unusual turnover in personnel in Four-College Asian-African fields (itself a tribute to the success of a part of the program) leaves the four institutions with a sizeable task in getting the maximum benefit out of the generous funds remaining and in planning for the transition two years hence in such a way that this important field will not be neglected. The meeting of the Presidents with the Asian-African Committee on October 5th, 1965, should establish some directives.

The Four-College Astronomy Department, now under the temporary chairmanship of Professor Robert Gluckstern of the University Department of Physics, will need a revision of its administrative set-up as the University implements its plans in this field.

The Hampshire Inter-Library Center, which now is in need of additional funds if it is to carry out adequately the successful program of the past thirteen years, should, in the Coordinator's opinion, be maintained even though the University research library gives promise of growing into a much larger collection. HILC performs a number of unique functions, which should be valuable for many years to come (see minutes of the Deputies' Meeting, May, 1965).

The History of Science enterprise has just completed its first year with Dr. Harold Fruchtbaum. He will be teaching four different one-semester courses, one at each institution (and in addition doing extra work at Amherst College in connection with honors students, guest lecturing and preparing for the new Problems of Inquiry program). This will hopefully be better than the past year's program in which the same elementary course was repeated at each of the four institutions, and one advanced course only was given, at Amherst College. Since Dr. Fruchtbaum is what he calls an "external" historian of science, instead of an "internal" one, it seems that extensive prerequisites are not needed for his courses. Indications are that at least some of the institutions would like to see expansion in this important field. In any case it was the understanding of the History of Science Committee that the third year program would be different from the second, and a study of this should be undertaken at a fairly early date.

### Student Exchange

A complete tabulation of students taking courses at other colleges than their own was sent out somewhat after the middle of each semester. The following is a resume. The grand total of courses taken by students at other colleges was 467 for the past year as compared with 422 for 1963-64, and 365 in 1962-63. Of the 467 during the past year, 337 were undergraduate interchange courses, 30 were enrollments in "cooperative" courses, 28 were course enrollments by cooperative Ph.D. candidates, and 72 were enrollments by other graduate students.

### Faculty Exchange (numbers of semester courses are given):

a) Overtime borrowing:

| | |
|---|---|
| Amherst to Asian-African Program — | 2 |
| Mount Holyoke to Amherst | 1 |
| Mount Holyoke to Smith | 1 |
| Smith to Amherst | 2 |
| Smith to Mount Holyoke | 5 |
| University to Mount Holyoke | 3 |
| University to Smith | 5 |

b)  Released-time borrowing:     University to Asian-African Program  2

c)  Joint appointments:

> History of Science (all four colleges) (1 person)
> Chinese (Smith and the University) (1 person)
> Astronomy (all four colleges) (5 persons)

*New Ventures*

In the early stages of planning are a program of cooperation in regard to student activities (which incidentally should probably involve some form of Four-College evening transportation), and a Four-College Faculty Seminar program. One meeting of the committee which the Presidents appointed indicated some rather fundamental differences of opinion as to how this should be carried out in detail. One such seminar, that in Latin-American Studies, will be subsidized to the extent of $800 during the coming academic year. It is hoped that foundation support can be secured for an expanded program.

Last but not least in July the establishment of Hampshire College was announced and Four-Colleges, Inc., had its incorporation meeting. The incorporators of the latter are the four Presidents, the four chief Business Officers and the Coordinator. In addition to these nine persons as directors, the incorporators elected Mr. Robert McCartney, Secretary of the University, as a director and secretary of the Corporation, and Mr. George B. May, Comptroller of Amherst College, as a director and treasurer of the Corporation. The final issuance of legal papers by the state is expected to take place in September. It is hoped that the existence of this corporation will gradually simplify and make more efficient several of the existing Four-College ventures and will allow for the establishment of new ones in the course of time.

Hampshire College represents the culmination of one of the early great dreams of Four-College cooperation. The evolution of the plans of the 1958 New College report (prepared by Shannon McCune, now president of the University of Vermont; Cesar Barber, now at the University of Indiana; Stuart M. Stoke, now retired and Donald Sheehan, Smith College) is welcomed and will present many interesting problems and possibilities for ingenious schemes in cooperation.

The Coordinator would like to express his gratitude to the Presidents, the Deputies (Professor William E. Kennick of Amherst College, Miss Florence S. Kimball, Registrar of Mount Holyoke College, Professor George W. de Villafranca, of Smith College, and Dr. William C. Venman, Assistant to the Provost at the University), and the Business Officers for the frequent help which they have given him. The Secretaries of the Boards of Trustees of the four institutions (Mr. J. Alfred Guest, Amherst, Miss Mary Tuttle, Mount Holyoke, Miss Florence Macdonald, Smith College and Mr. Robert J. McCartney, University of Massachusetts) as well as Mr. Horace W. Hewlett, Secretary of Amherst College have given valuable advice and help. In the complexity of the rapidly expanding University situation, Provost Tippo, Dean Hunsberger and Dean Moore have been most generous in sharing their wisdom and knowledge. Finally I should like to thank my predecessors Professors Sidney R. Packard, and Stuart M. Stoke for all that they started, as well as for the helpful advice which they gave me when I began the job.

> Respectfully submitted
> ROBERT B. WHITNEY
> *Coordinator*

# APPENDIX E

## Four-College Student Interchange
## 1962-63 to 1965-66

|  | Interchange Course Enrollment | Cooperative Course Enrollment | Total Graduate Course Enrollment | Cooperative Ph.D. Students |
|---|---|---|---|---|
| 1962-63 | 253 | 123 | N. A.* | 21 |
| 1963-64 | 320 | 25 | 89 | 32 |
| 1964-65 | 336 | 30 | 90 | 43 |
| 1965-66 | 578 | 45 | 120 | 101 |

*Not available.

*Interchange course enrollment*—undergraduate enrollment in courses on campuses other than the students' own.

*Cooperative course enrollment*—undergraduate enrollment in courses taught cooperatively by two or more of the four institutions.

*Total graduate course enrollment*—graduate enrollment in courses on campuses other than the students' own. Includes cooperative Ph.D. enrollment.

*Cooperative Ph.D. students*—number of students enrolled at the beginning of the first semester.

# APPENDIX F

## Estimates of the Resources of the Four Connecticut Valley Colleges
## Amherst, Mount Holyoke, Smith, University of Massachusetts

| | Amherst | Mount Holyoke | Smith | University of Massachusetts | Totals |
|---|---|---|---|---|---|
| # Faculty | 155 | 175 | 235 | 750 | 1,315 |
| # Vols. library | 550,000 | 300,000 | 477,000 | 300,000 | 1,627,000 |
| # Departments | 24 | 24 | 32 | 60 | 140 |
| # Courses | 203 | 250 | 250 | 1,000 | 1,703 |
| Endowment | $73,000,000 | $22,800,000 | $37,600,000 | $846,600 | $134,246,600 |

# APPENDIX G

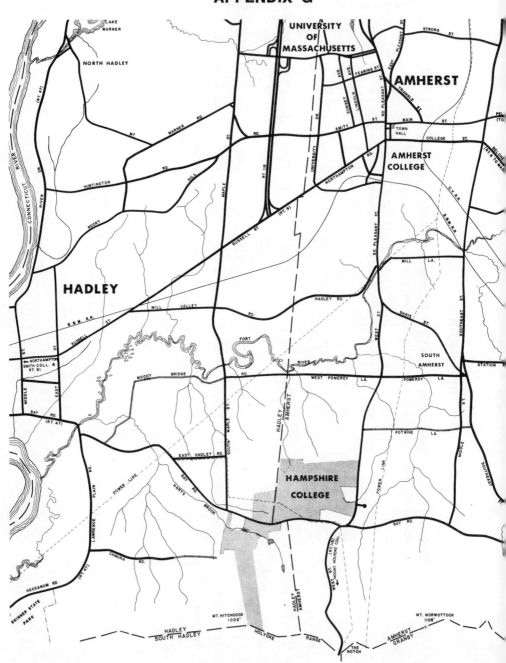

AMHERST – HADLEY AREA
SITE OF HAMPSHIRE COLLEGE

MAY 1966   SCALE
NORTH
NOTE: MANY MINOR ROADS ARE OMITTED
SOURCES: U.S.G.S., FIELD SURVEYS, AERIAL PHO
PREPARED BY T. S. BACON, PLANNING CONSUL
AMHERST, MASS.

# APPENDIX I

## Estimated Square Footage and Cost of Hampshire College Physical Facilities and Campus

### One House — 360 Students

| Facility | Gross Square Feet | Assumptions |
|----------|-------------------|-------------|
| Living/study | 100,800 | Gross 280 square feet per student, 360 students, bedroom-study, toilets, social, service, library. |
| Dining/kitchen<br>Dining room<br>Kitchen | 10,260 | One dining room each house; 18 square feet per seat; one kitchen for four houses. |
| Instructional Space<br>Lecture hall (1)<br>Seminar/classrooms (2) | 4,200<br>3,375 | 14 square feet net per station; 200 stations.<br>15 square feet net per station; two rooms, 75 stations each. |
| Administrative offices<br>Master and Secretary<br>Proctor | 375<br>250 | Net 250 square feet.<br>Net 167 square feet. |
| Faculty offices (16) | 2,880 | Net 120 square feet/office |
| Residential<br>Master<br>Proctor<br>Faculty (duplex) | 2,000<br>750<br>2,800 | |
| | 129,435 | |

## One House — 360 Students

| | Gross Square Feet | $/S.F. | Cost |
|---|---|---|---|
| *Living/study | 100,800 | 25 | $ 2,520,000. |
| *Dining/kitchen | | | |
| Dining | 10,260 | 32 | 328,320. |
| Kitchen | 1,745 | 40 | 69,800. |
| *Instructional Space | | | |
| Lecture hall | 4,200 | 27 | 113,400. |
| Seminar/classrooms | 3,375 | 27 | 91,125. |
| *Administrative | | | |
| offices | 625 | 27 | 16,875. |
| *Faculty offices | 2,880 | 27 | 77,760. |
| Residential-non-student | 2,750 | 25 | 68,750. |
| | | | $ 3,286,030. |
| | | x 4 houses | $13,144,120. |

*Includes furnishings.

## Library

*Square Footage*

| Facility | Net Square Feet | Assumptions |
|---|---|---|
| 1. Stack space | 20,000 | 10 vols./s.f.; 200,000 vols. |
| 2. Reading, browsing | 10,000 | 500 spaces, 20 s.f./space |
| 3. Faculty research offices | 5,000 | 50 @ 100 s.f. |
| 4. Service | 6,000 | 20% of total stack and reading (Excluding faculty offices) |
| Net S.F. | 41,000 | |
| Gross S.F. x 1.5 | 61,500 | |

## Library

*Cost*

*61,500 S.F. @ $33/S.F.     $2,029,500.

*Includes furnishings.

## Schools

*Humanities*

| Facility | Net Square Feet | Assumptions |
|---|---|---|
| Dean's office Secretary | 300 | |
| Seminar/Conference room | 300 | |
| Faculty offices | 600 | 100 S.F. net (3) 150 S.F. net pooled offices (2) |
| Classroom | 900 | 15 S.F. per station; 60 stations |
| Music practice rooms | 640 | 8 @ 80 S.F. each |
| Dance practice rooms | 2,500 | 50 stations @ 50 S.F. each |
| Experimental theatre | 2,500 | 2,500 S.F. |
| Graphics | 1,750 | 50 stations @ 35 S.F. each |
| Sculpture | 2,500 | 50 stations @ 50 S.F. each |
| Photography, darkroom | 500 | |
| Net S.F. | 12,490 | |

*Humanities*

Gross S.F. x 1.5              18,735

*Humanities Cost*

*18,735 S.F. @ $25        $468,375

---

*Includes furnishings.

## Schools

### *Social Sciences*

| Facility | Net Square Feet | Assumptions |
|---|---|---|
| Dean's office Secretary | 250 | |
| Seminar/Conference room | 300 | |
| Lecture room | 2,250 | 150 stations, convertible, 15 S.F./station |
| Laboratory space | 1,600 | |
| Net S.F. | 4,400 | |
| Gross S.F. x 1.5 | 6,600 | |

### *Social Sciences—Cost*

| | | |
|---|---|---|
| *6,600 S.F. @ $27/S.F. | | $178,200 |

*Includes equipment and furnishings.

## Schools

*Languages*

| Facility | Net Square Feet | Assumptions |
|---|---|---|
| Dean's office<br>Secretary | 250 | |
| Seminar/Conference room | 300 | |
| Language Laboratory | 1,000 | 50 stations @ 20 S.F. |
| Language Lab. office | 120 | |
| Linguistics Laboratory | 1,600 | |
| Classrooms | 4,050 | 270 stations @ 15 S.F. each |
| Intran Center<br>    Director's office<br>    Secretary | 250 | |
| Television studio | 1,000 | |
| Engineering room | 300 | |
| Computer center | 600 | |
| Offices | 600 | 200 S.F. each (3 double offices) |
| Unspecified reserve | 2,000 | |
| Net S.F. | 12,070 | |
| Gross S.F. x 1.5 | 18,105 | |

*Languages—Cost\**

| | |
|---|---|
| 18,105 S.F. @ $35/S.F. | $633,675 |

\*Includes equipment and furnishings.

## Schools

*Natural Sciences*

| Facility | Net Square Feet | Assumptions |
|---|---|---|
| Dean's office | 250 | |
| Secretary | | |
| Seminar/Conference room | 300 | 15' x 20' |
| Faculty offices | 1,680 | Ten 12' x 14' |
| Lecture/Classroom | 3,000 | 200 stations, two 100 capacity rooms, 15 S.F./station |
| Laboratories | | |
|   Biology    ) <br>   Chemistry  ) <br>   Physics    ) | 17,500 | Lab space, storage, preparation, 350 students @ 50 S.F./station |
| Preparation, shop, stock, mechanical, etc. | 4,000 | |
|     Net S.F. | 26,730 | |
|     Gross S.F. x 1.5 | 40,095 | |

*Natural Sciences—Cost*

| | |
|---|---|
| *40,095 S.F. @ $50/S.F. | $2,004,750 |

*Includes equipment and furnishings.

## Health Services

| Facility | Net Square Feet | Assumptions |
|---|---|---|
| Outpatient facilities, nurse's office, doctor's office | 4,000 | 20 beds @ 150 S.F./bed<br>3 offices @ 150 S.F./bed<br>Examination; treatment |
| Net S.F. | 4,000 | |
| Gross S.F. x 1.5 | 6,000 | |

### Cost

| | | |
|---|---|---|
| *6,000 S.F. @ $27/S.F. | | $162,000 |

*Includes equipment and furnishings.

## Administration — Service

| Facility | Net Square Feet | Assumptions |
|---|---|---|
| President's office | 400 | |
| Secretary | 120 | |
| Dean | 225 | |
| Secretary | 120 | |
| Vice-President | 225 | |
| Secretary | 120 | |
| Admission | 600 | 1 office 10' x 10'<br>1 office 10' x 15'<br>Work space 10' x 20'<br>Reception waiting 10' x 15' |
| Registrar | 400 | 1 office 10' x 10', waiting area, secretarial, clerical |
| Development | 300 | 1 office 10' x 12'<br>Secretarial, work area |
| Business Mgr./Comptroller<br>(Purchasing officer)<br>(Personnel officer) | 650 | 3 offices 10' x 12'<br>Secretarial, clerical work area |

## Administration — Service

| Facility | Net Square Feet | Assumptions |
|---|---|---|
| Conference/Board room | 600 | Divisible into two rooms 15' x 20' |
| Buildings and Grounds | 800 | 1 office 10' x 15'<br>1 office 10' x 12'<br>Secretarial, work area |
| Student government | 400 | 1 office 10' x 10'<br>Work, meeting space |
| Reception/waiting | 200 | |
| Institutional R & D | 250 | 1 office 10' x 12'<br>Working area |
| Dean of Students | 500 | 1 office 12' x 15'<br>1 office 10' x 15'<br>Secretarial |
| Net S.F. | 5,910 | |
| Gross S.F. x 1.5 | 8,865 | |

### Administration—Service Cost

*8,865 S.F. @ $27/S.F.                    $239,355

*Includes furnishings.

## College Center

| Facility | Net Square Feet | Assumptions |
|---|---|---|
| *Shops* | | |
| Coffee | 2,000 | |
| Snack bar | 2,000 | |
| Book and record | 2,000 | |
| Barber | 400 | 2 chairs |
| Woodworking, metal-working | 2,000 | |
| Gallery | 2,500 | |
| Auditorium/Theatre | 8,000 | 800 seats, 10 S.F. per seat; divisible into smaller units |
| Production area | 2,500 | |
| *Offices* | | |
| Director S.A. Secretary | 300 | |
| Asst. Dir. S.A. | 150 | |
| Net S.F. | 21,850 | |
| Gross S.F. x 1.5 | 32,775 | |

*Cost*

| | | |
|---|---|---|
| *32,775 S.F. @ $32/S.F. | | $1,048,800 |

*Includes equipment and furnishings.

## Recreational — Athletic

| Facility | Net Square Feet | Assumptions |
|---|---|---|
| **A. Indoor** | | |
| Swimming pool | 6,300 | 42' x 75' plus apron, lounge |
| Locker rooms, showers | 4,000 | Two 50' x 40' |
| General exercise | 4,000 | |
| Spectator | 1,500 | |
| Covered space | 6,000 | Geodesic dome or inflated bubble |
| Net S.F. | 21,800 | |
| Gross S.F. x 1.5 | 32,700 | |
| **B. Outdoor** | **Gross S.F.** | |
| 12 tennis courts | 86,400 | 60' x 120' |
| 2 basketball courts | 9,000 | 50' x 90' |
| 4 badminton/volley-ball courts | 7,200 | 30' x 60' |
| 4 softball fields | 250,000 | 250' x 250' |
| 1 baseball field | 122,500 | 350' x 350' |
| 4 touch football, soccer fields | 324,000 | 225' x 360' |
| | 799,100 | |

### Recreational facilities—Cost

*Indoor*

| 32,700 S.F. @ $30/S.F. | $1,131,000 |
|---|---|

*Outdoor*

| Tennis courts $10,000 each | 120,000 |
|---|---|
| 799,100 less 86,400 = @ $4,000/acre | 65,600 |
| Cost | $1,316,600 |

## Maintenance, Heating, Storage

| Facility | Gross Square Feet | Assumptions |
|---|---|---|
| Storage, Buildings and Grounds Equipment, Personnel area, Central Heating (?) | 10,000 | |
| Gross Square Feet | 10,000 | |

*Cost*

10,000 S.F. @ $22/S.F.                                        $220,000

## Site Development

| | | |
|---|---|---|
| Grading, seeding, planting, and drainage | 50 acres @ $3,300/acre | $165,000. |

*Roads*

| | | |
|---|---|---|
| Main and secondary access | | 160,000. |
| Interior service | | 125,000. |
| Parking | 500 spaces @ $300/car | 150,000. |
| Outdoor social space | | 85,000. |
| Lighting | | 100,000. |
| | | $ 785,000. |

*Other Capital Outlay*

| | | |
|---|---|---|
| Library books | 100,000 @ $6/book | $600,000. |
| Vehicles, maintenance equipment | Lump sum | 50,000. |
| Language laboratory equipment | | 100,000. |
| Audio visual, TV equipment | | 250,000. |
| Computer | | 100,000. |
| | | $1,100,000. |

*Fees*

| | | |
|---|---|---|
| Architects, landscape architects, engineers | 10% of total cost of building site development | $2,223,000. |

*Additional Land*

| | |
|---|---|
| Purchase land | $ 200,000. |

# APPENDIX J

## MASTER PLAN STUDIES

## HAMPSHIRE COLLEGE
## Amherst, Massachusetts

## I  SITE EVALUATION

Sasaki, Dawson, DeMay Associates, Inc.
July 1966

Mr. Charles R. Longsworth
Vice President
Hampshire College
Amherst, Massachusetts

Re: Hampshire College

Dear Mr. Longsworth:

Please find enclosed, *Master Plan Studies—Hampshire College Site Evaluation."*

This report summarizes our analysis of the College's existing land-holdings and evaluates their potential for economic campus development. Major issues of college-community relationships and a preliminary schematic plan for the South Amherst area are also discussed.

As a progress report, the study presents the best information and evaluation available at this time. Some of the material is incomplete, however, and will be refined as the Master Plan Studies continue.

In our opinion, the site is very well suited to the development of Hampshire College. The site offers a handsome setting, prime building sites for economic development, good accessibility and an opportunity to plan rewarding community relationships.

Sincerely,

Sasaki, Dawson, DeMay Associates, Inc.

RICHARD F. GALEHOUSE

RFG:cs
Enclosure

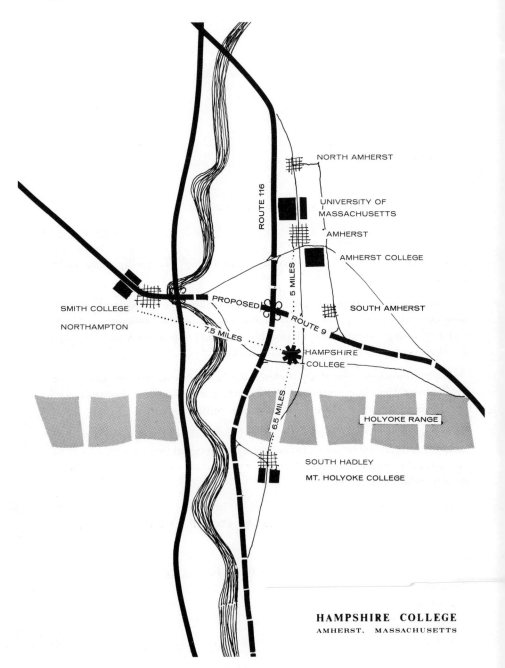

NORTH AMHERST

UNIVERSITY OF
MASSACHUSETTS

AMHERST

AMHERST COLLEGE

ROUTE 116

5 MILES

PROPOSED

ROUTE 9

SOUTH AMHERST

SMITH COLLEGE

NORTHAMPTON

7.5 MILES

HAMPSHIRE
COLLEGE

6.5 MILES

HOLYOKE RANGE

SOUTH HADLEY

MT. HOLYOKE COLLEGE

**HAMPSHIRE COLLEGE**
AMHERST, MASSACHUSETTS

MAJOR ELEMENTS OF THE SITE

▨ TREE COVER          ⬆ VIEWS
⣿ ORCHARDS
▥ 8% + SLOPE

HAMPSHIRE  COLLEGE

AMHERST,  MASSACHUSETTS

0     400'   800'        1600'

Labels within map: CONNECTICUT VALLEY, AMHERST COLLEGE, EAST SLOPE, WEST SLOPE, HIGHLAND, HOLYOKE RANGE, 0 TO 8% SLOPE, 8% + SLOPE

# I. HAMPSHIRE COLLEGE SITE: DESCRIPTION & ANALYSIS

## A. Regional Location

Hampshire College is centrally located in the Connecticut River Valley, five miles south of the town of Amherst, Massachusetts. The site is within seven miles or fifteen minutes driving time of its sponsoring institutions: Smith, Mount Holyoke, Amherst and the University of Massachusetts. Frequent interchange between these institutions and the bountiful educational, cultural and recreational resources of the Valley is one premise on which the Hampshire College program is based. The College's strategic location will afford this accessibility.

## B. Size, Topography, Vegetation

The Hampshire College property covers 434 acres in the southern parts of Amherst and Hadley. The land varies from gently rolling farmland and orchards to the precipitous slope of the Holyoke Mountain Range. Bay Road separates the farmland to the north from the mountains to the south. The site is further divided under two political jurisdictions; the western portion lies in Hadley, the eastern in Amherst.

### SUMMARY OF LAND HOLDINGS AND SLOPE CHARACTERISTICS

|  | Land in Amherst | Land in Hadley |
|---|---|---|
| **North of Bay Road** | | |
| Open land—land under 8% slope* | 120 | 34 |
| Wooded land—land over 8% slope | 128 | 6 |
| Subtotal | 248 | 40 |
| **South of Bay Road** | | |
| Open land—land under 8% slope | | 32 |
| Wooded land—land over 8% slope | | 114 |
| Subtotal | | 146 |
| Total Acres (July 1966) | | 434 |

*Land of 0-8% slope is most suited to economic building and open space development. Wooded land which requires clearing and land which requires extensive grading places a premium cost upon campus development.

The prime developable area on the site is presently considered to be 120 acres of open land north of Bay Road in Amherst. There are practically no limitations imposed by slope except where the land rises from Bay Road on the east side.

A pocket of poorly drained land exists on the northeast portion of the Amherst parcel. Other sluggish drainage areas have been noted in the scrub woods, near the Amherst-Hadley line north of Bay Road. These pockets of poorly drained land are not considered prime building sites.

The tree cover on the campus north of Bay Road is generally not of significant value. There are, however, individual specimen trees and twenty acres of apple orchards which are a distinctive and positive asset. At present, the orchards are leased and maintained by a fruit grower. Continuation of this arrangement might be considered after the campus is developed.

Most of the land south of Bay Road above 300' elevation (approximately 90 acres) is not suited to economic building and open space development because of steepness and forests. The scenic value and recreation potential of this land is important to the College. The mountain is an important part of the visual background to the main campus north of Bay Road. Adjacent properties on the mountain side owned by Amherst College, the Federal Government and the town of Hadley will probably remain undeveloped for the foreseeable future.

The general orientation of the site is north toward Amherst. From the mountainside south of Bay Road one sees the magnificent Valley of the Connecticut River. Lower, on prime building land north of Bay Road, the view is less far reaching but sweeps a full 360° to surrounding hills and mountains.

## C. Soil and Subsoil Conditions

An investigation of subsurface soil conditions was made by a soils engineer to determine the feasibility of economic building development. The detailed findings of the geological reconnaissance, based on 7 to 12 foot test pit excavations, are found in Exhibit I.

The Hampshire College site falls in an area once covered by a glacial lake which stretched from southern Connecticut to northern Vermont. A beach line marking one edge of the lake has been found on the property south of Bay Road. As it receded, the lake left extensive deposits of clays and plastic silts in the Valley. The reconnaissance confirmed that though these unstable soils occur beneath the site, they are confined to a very small portion to the west and northwest below 220' elevation. The majority of the site is covered by glacial till or till with outwash deposits consisting of stratified sands and gravels. To quote from the engineer's report:

> "The site from the standpoint of soils and foundations is excellent. Buildings could be supported on economical shallow spread footings throughout the site. In small areas at the lower elevations along the western border and at the northwest corner of the site cohesive lake deposits underlie alluvial sands. If buildings of more than two stories were to be constructed in these areas additional explorations should be made to determine thickness, extent and consolidation characteristics of the clay soils. In all other areas the soil at the site could support high rise structures on shallow footings after stripping organic materials.

> "It is our opinion that bedrock will not be a problem at this site for shallow excavations in the order of 10 feet or less. If deeper excavations are planned, then the possibility of encountering bedrock in the cuts must be considered.

> "The earthwork required for site grading and road construction will be economical as it is not expected that rock excavation will be required. Also there are sands and gravel deposits on the site to utilize as fill and even for base courses under paved areas."

### D.  Existing Structures, Rights of Way

At present, there are four farms and a single house existing on the site. One farmhouse on West Street is being converted into temporary headquarters for the College administration. Two other houses and three acres surrounding each are held in life tenancy. The remaining structures which border West Street and Bay Road are old, in poor repair and do not appear to be of any significant historic or architectural value.

There are three rights of way crossing the site; The Hadley Water Supply District, Western Massachusetts Electric Company, and American Telephone and Telegraph Company. A pipeline to the Hadley Reservoir is located south of Bay Road. A power line easement crosses Bay Road one-third of a mile from the corner of West Street and angles northwest. AT&T's buried cable cuts the southeast corner of the property.

None of the rights of way are expected to limit development opportunities, but all must be considered in future site planning.

### E.  Utilities

A small water line along West Street is the only utility presently serving the Hampshire College site.

In anticipation of future requirements, the Town of Amherst has undertaken a program to enlarge most of its water mains to twelve inches and

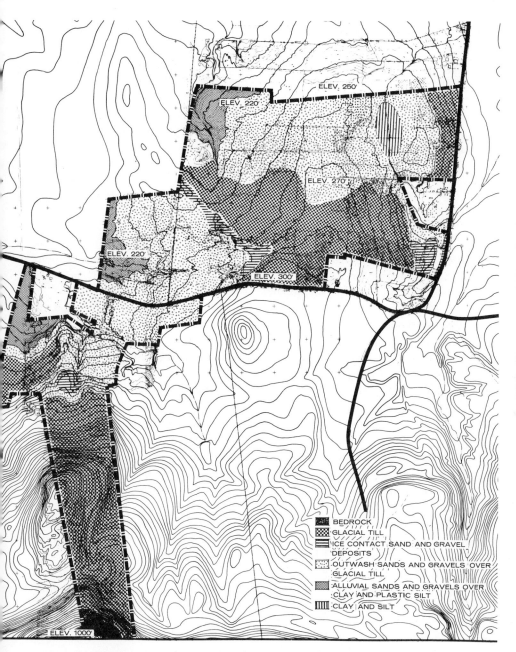

ELEV. 250'

ELEV. 220'

ELEV. 270'

ELEV. 220'

ELEV. 300'

ELEV. 1000'

BEDROCK

GLACIAL TILL

ICE CONTACT SAND AND GRAVEL
DEPOSITS

OUTWASH SANDS AND GRAVELS OVER
GLACIAL TILL

ALLUVIAL SANDS AND GRAVELS OVER
CLAY AND PLASTIC SILT

CLAY AND SILT

SOIL AND SUBSOIL CONDITIONS

HAMPSHIRE COLLEGE

AMHERST, MASSACHUSETTS

SOURCE — HALEY & ALDRICH
CONSULTING SOIL ENGINEERS

0      400'    800'              1600'

extend sewer facilities into South Amherst from the pumping station on West Street. Both water and sewer facilities will be placed east of the campus in or near West Street. A new million gallon storage tank, with a twelve inch connecting line is planned for a site south of Bay Road east of the College.

This planned distribution system for sewerage and water will provide the capacity necessary to serve Hampshire College.

## F. Program

A preliminary program of space requirements for the College has been compiled and tested against the amount of readily developable land on the campus. There seems to be adequate land of suitable quality for the accommodation of 1,440 students, the faculty and supporting staff.

Lacking a definitive program at this time, it was assumed for the purposes of testing site size that structures would be no more than three stories high. At a two-story average approximately 310,000 square feet or 7 acres of ground are covered by buildings.

In the program, parking and playfields are the most extensive users of space. Daily parking requirement for 760 cars can be accommodated on 9 acres. The capacity may need to be increased for special occasions. Field parking offers a convenient simple solution to the overflow problem except in mud or snow seasons.

The playfield requirements for tennis, outdoor game courts and large playfields for general use require 18 acres.

## G. Land Acquisition

Acquisition of additional land should be considered in light of the following questions: First, does the college have sufficient developable land for its future space requirements; second, are certain select parcels needed for optimum campus development?

There is sufficient buildable land on the Amherst parcel to accommodate the requirements of 1,440 students. However, institutions are long-lived and some consideration will have to be given now to the probable growth and objectives of the College in the decades ahead. Development pressures in Amherst continue to mount, and open land now surrounding Hampshire College will be completely developed in the near future.

The most desirable direction for additional acquisition of acreage would be to the north and northwest of the Amherst parcel. This land is contiguous and has very good development potential.

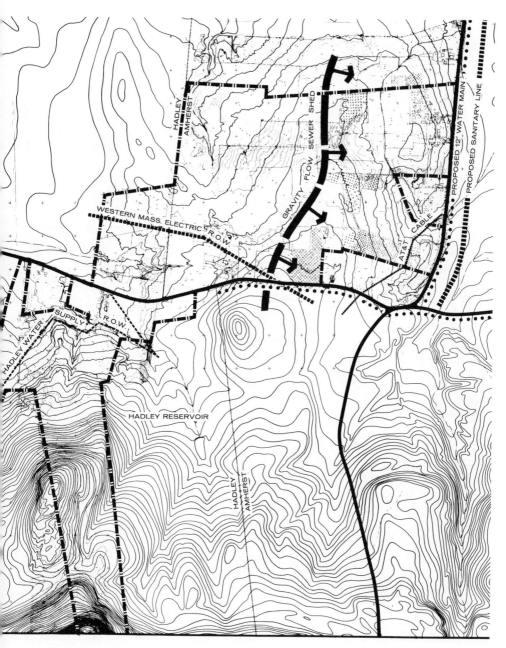

UTILITIES AND RIGHTS OF WAY

HAMPSHIRE COLLEGE

AMHERST,  MASSACHUSETTS

SOURCE — PLANNING BOARD
TOWN OF AMHERST

0      400'    800'              1600'

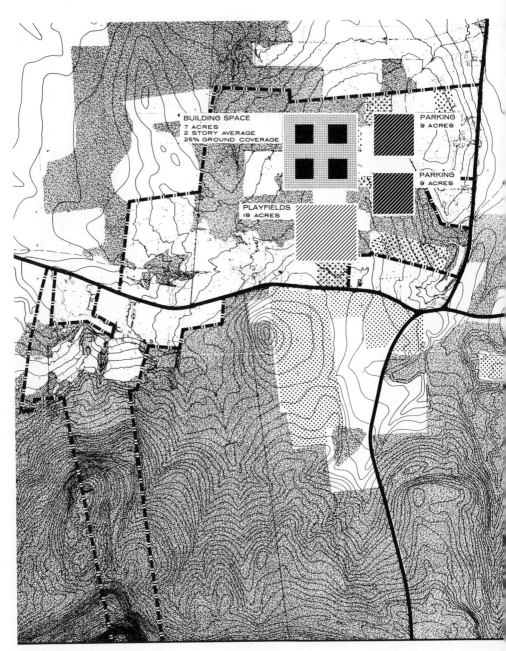

BUILDING SPACE
7 ACRES
2 STORY AVERAGE
25% GROUND COVERAGE

PARKING
9 ACRES

PARKING
9 ACRES

PLAYFIELDS
18 ACRES

PROGRAM SPACE REQUIREMENTS

■■■ BUILDING SPACE
▨▨ PARKING
/// PLAYFIELDS

HAMPSHIRE COLLEGE
AMHERST, MASSACHUSETTS
0      400'    800'              1600'

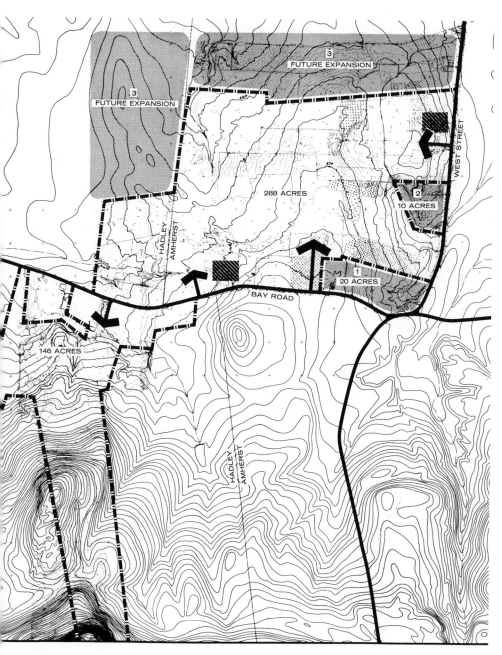

## FUTURE EXPANSION AND DEVELOPMENT

↑ POTENTIAL SITE ENTRANCE POINTS

▦ RECOMMENDED PURCHASE

▧ 3 ACRES LIFE TENANCY

### HAMPSHIRE COLLEGE

AMHERST, MASSACHUSETTS

At this time we strongly recommend the acquisition of the Warner, Ives and Kielbasa properties on Bay Road and West Street. These properties comprise only 30 acres and do not, therefore, increase the total aggregate of developable land significantly. They are, however, visually prominent and strategically located along the principal approaches to the campus and are critical to the control of these approaches.

## II.  RELATIONSHIP OF HAMPSHIRE COLLEGE TO THE COMMUNITY

A Master Plan is being prepared now for the Town of Amherst, and Hampshire College has an unusual opportunity to contribute to its development. The land of South Amherst between Fort River and the Holyoke Mt. Range is still open. By articulating its ideas to the town and the Planning Board, the College can be instrumental in the planning and development of the area. Continuing interest in new development which will supply housing and service-commercial facilities is consistent with the College's concern to be a part of the vital and beautiful community.

### A.  Existing Development in South Amherst

At the present time South Amherst is largely rural, but it is developing rapidly. There are a total of thirteen subdivisions in South Amherst, most of which have been started in the last few years. Major new trunk lines for sewer and water are being planned. The growth of the University and the presence of Hampshire College will increase all development pressures on remaining open lands.

The South Amherst community is marked by natural boundaries to the north, east and south: Fort River, Lawrence Swamp and the wall of the Holyoke Mountain Range. More intensive older development in South Amherst occurred along South East Street and South Pleasant Street, with a natural locus of activity at South Amherst center. Newer development is moving southward along the roads and penetrating the open agricultural land.

The entire area is zoned for low density residential use with one small commercial center at the intersection of Pomeroy Lane and West Street. Some non-conforming light industrial and commercial uses are scattered through the area.

## B.  Principal Development Problems

In addition to the overall need for comprehensive planning for the entire South Amherst community, certain key development problems have emerged. The most important development considerations are: first, the location of Route 9 through South Amherst; second, the location of additional service commercial centers in South Amherst; third, the disposition of major areas of land with great conservation and recreation potential; fourth, of more concern to the College, the control of the foreground and approaches to the College along Bay Road and West Street.

### 1. *Proposed Route 9*

The proposed Route 9 will be a four lane, limited access divided highway passing through South Amherst.

The major objective of the highway is the provision of high volume-high speed access to generators in Amherst: the University, Amherst College and the community itself. A secondary objective is the provision of improved access for through traffic.

The highway will have a major impact on traffic flow through Amherst and will significantly influence patterns of land use in Amherst and Hadley.

Two alternative alignments for Route 9 have been advanced by state and local officials. A northern alignment (Alternate A) generally follows the course of the Fort River from east to west across Amherst; a southern alignment (Alternate B) runs between Lawrence Swamp and Bay Road and crosses West Street near the northeast corner of the campus.

Exhibit II contains a detailed evaluation of these two alignments. On most counts, the northern alignment would most effectively serve the community. However, it splits the extensive land holdings of Amherst College. Should this alignment seriously inhibit the long range development of the College, another alignment would have to be found.

Hampshire College's concerns lie in three major areas: first, safe and convenient access into the college and to its sister institutions in the Valley; second, the impact of the highway on the development of the campus and surrounding land use; and third, the impact of Route 9 on the landscape.

From a transportation standpoint either the northern or southern alignment would serve Hampshire College equally well. On several counts, however, the southern alignment would have a negative impact on the college. It is uncomfortably close to the northern boundary of the campus passing through lands which might be considered for future expansion. The southern alignment of Route 9 coupled with the extended Route 116 would tend to limit access into the college from the north and west and create a barrier to close integration with the surrounding community. Finally, the road would be both audible and visible from the campus detracting from the quality of the present landscape.

Two additional alignments are suggested in an attempt to minimize the limitations of the alignments already proposed. Both skirt the south side of Lawrence Swamp, circumvent Mt. Pollux (Alternate C to the north, Alternate D to the south) and generally follow the south bank of the Fort River to Route 116 extended. An extension of East Street is shown as a by-pass to South Amherst Center. Interchanges indicated at the East Street extension, West Street and Route 116 would provide good accessibility to Hampshire College.

Either Alternate C or D offer multiple advantages: less disruption to existing development than Alternate A; better alignment in relation to Hampshire College than Alternate B; good alignment in the east of South Amherst in a belt of low lying land less desirable for residential development, and in the west in a valley formed by Fort River.

## 2. *Location of Additional Service-Commercial Centers in South Amherst*

At the present time the only commercial zone in South Amherst is at the junction of West Street and Pomeroy Lane. A test of developable land in South Amherst shows that a population of 15,000 persons could be accommodated if all land is residentially developed as presently zoned. Clearly, additional service-commercial facilities will be required. The present business zone is centrally located and its controlled expansion seems warranted. Activity in this business zone would be reinforced by the nearby interchange of Route 9 as shown on the schematic plan for South Amherst.

Additional service-commercial facilities might also be located at Bay Road and West Street. At this corner the facilities could provide more immediate support to Hampshire College. Their controlled development in this latter location is critically important.

Under current Amherst zoning, additional service-commercial facilities can be introduced as part of an integrated higher density development plan by permit from the Zoning Board of Appeals.

## 3. *Conservation and Recreation Areas*

Lawrence Swamp, Fort River and the Holyoke Mountain Range have unusual potential for development in conservation and recreation uses in the Amherst community. Fortunately, the town is slowly assembling large

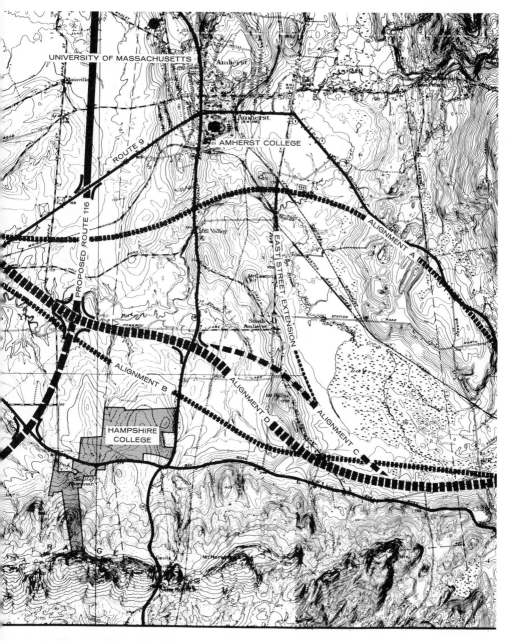

ROUTE 9 ALTERNATE ALIGNMENTS

SOURCE — DEPARTMENT OF PUBLIC WORKS &
SASAKI, DAWSON, DEMAY ASSOCIATES

HAMPSHIRE COLLEGE
AMHERST, MASSACHUSETTS
0      1/3     2/3      1 MILE

portions of Lawrence Swamp to conserve it and to protect Amherst's water supply.

Amherst College, Hampshire College, and the Federal Government own large portions of the north slope of the Holyoke Mountain Range. Additional acreage of the Holyoke Mountains is under consideration for a State Park.

The recommended alignment of Route 9 along the Fort River could aid in the development of the river for conservation and recreation purposes. For example, damming the Fort River just north of the College could create a small chain of lakes.

All three areas contribute positively to the quality of the environment of Hampshire College. The Holyoke Mountain Range is a dominant element in the visual background of the College and offers potential ground for skiing, rock climbing and hiking. Lawrence Swamp and Fort River are prominent on approach to the campus from the north and east. Depending on their development as recreation or conservation areas they may be enjoyed and used by members of the College.

Any assistance the College can lend to insure the development of these areas for recreation or conservation will be in their own and the community's best interests.

### 4. *Control of Approaches to Hampshire College*

Consideration of the immediate edge of the college to the community is a concern to most institutions. Many institutions with frontages on public streets have seen the opposite side of the road develop in an uncontrolled manner. Hampshire College should look to the control of its foreground and approaches along West Street from the north, and Bay Road from both the east and west.

On the north side of Bay Road the college owns .6 miles of frontage from West Street west towards Hadley. Approximately .4 miles of frontage on the south are in direct college control. Mr. Atkins, the owner of the largest remaining frontage on the south side of Bay Road, has apparently expressed willingness to develop his lands in cooperation with the College.

The west side of West Street is in College ownership except for the Warner and Ives properties. Their purchase by the College is recommended. A subdivision has already been started on the east side of West Street. Control of the remaining frontage poses a real problem. Ultimate control over the land use would be achieved by ownership. Barring this Hampshire College might extend its influence by one or more of the following methods: tradi-

tional zoning controls; realignment of local roads; incorporation or association with property owners.

Planning, zoning and building controls are already being exercised in the
town of Amherst, and have been effective in setting the standard of general
orderliness. However, these are less effective in guiding the pace and quality
of new development. A master plan for the whole community is being prepared but, in the meanwhile, the street frontage may be developed in uses
incompatible to the College.

The intersection of Bay Road and West Street is badly aligned with poor
sight distances. It will undoubtedly become more dangerous over time as the
volume of traffic increases. Preliminary appraisal, which can be verified in
the detailed design period ahead, suggests that redesign of the intersection
could create a Common in the tradition of the New England community.
The Common would fall on College property, thereby insuring direct control
over the intersection and immediately surrounding uses.

The College may find it feasible to participate in a land corporation
which would have among its powers the purchase and improvement of land.
(See Exhibit III). Another alternative might be an association of property
owners in the given area. This relatively new concept, permissible under
zoning ordinances, allows local authorities with limited eminent domain
powers to plan and implement neighborhood plans.

By taking the initiative at an early stage, Hampshire College can better
insure the satisfactory development of its environs.

PROPOSED SOUTH AMHERST COMMUNITY

≣ EXISTING SUBDIVISION
▨ COMMERCIAL SERVICE CENTER
▧ POTENTIAL HOUSING AREAS

HAMPSHIRE COLLEGE

AMHERST, MASSACHUSETTS

0    1/3    2/3    1 MILE

## EXHIBIT I

## LETTER FROM SOILS ENGINEER
## CONCERNING HAMPSHIRE COLLEGE SITE

5 August 1966
File No. 66-1580

Sasaki, Dawson, DeMay Associates
23 Main Street
Watertown, Massachusetts

Attention: Mr. Richard F. Galehouse

Subject: Proposed Hampshire College
Amherst-Hadley, Massachusetts

Gentlemen:

This letter presents the results of our soils and foundation investigation of the site of the proposed Hampshire College in Amherst-Hadley, Massachusetts. The study was undertaken at the request of Mr. Richard Galehouse. A brief report on the geological reconnaissance of the site, performed on 8 and 9 June 1966, was sent to you on 13 June 1966. The test pit program, recommended at that time, was approved by you in your letter of 19 July 1966 and the test pits were excavated on 28 and 29 July 1966 as soon as a backhoe became available.

The soil and rock conditions at the site and the locations of test pits are shown on the enclosed map. Logs of test pits are also enclosed. A total of twenty one test pits were excavated, examined and logged during the two days of field investigations.

The test pits confirmed the general conclusions reported in our letter of 13 June 1966. They also disclosed that while glacial lake clays and plastic silts do in fact occur beneath the site they are confined to a very small portion of the overall site area. This was the major uncertainty remaining after completion of the geological reconnaissance.

The principal subsurface units are as shown on the legend on the enclosed Soil and Rock Map. In order of deposition from bottom to top they are as follows:

1. Bedrock
2. Glacial till
3. Ice contact deposits (sand)

4.   Outwash over glacial till
5.   Alluvial sands and gravels over cohesive lake deposits
6.   Post glacial shallow pond deposits

Bedrock outcrops are rare and were only observed south of Bay Road. A small linear zone of diabase breccia outcrops at the locations shown on the Soil and Rock Map between TP19 and TP20. A red-brown arkosic sandstone outcrop was observed at the crest of the ski-slope hill and of course a portion of the massive basalt scarp of Mt. Hitchcock is included within the bounds of the site at the extreme southern limit. No bedrock was encountered in any of the test pits with the exception of TP21 and at this location it is not certain as to whether the excavation penetrated a highly weathered boulder in the till or the actual weathered upper surface of rock. It is our opinion that bedrock will not be a problem at this site for shallow excavations in the order of 10 feet or less. If deeper excavations are planned, then the possibility of encountering bedrock in the cuts must be considered.

The rock underlying the site north of Bay Road is believed to be part of the Triassic sedimentary rocks, sandstones, siltstones and shales which occupy the Connecticut basin in this area. South of Bay Road both diabase, basalt and sedimentary rocks occur.

The till at the site is conspicuous for its fine grain and general absence of cobbles and boulders. It is classified as a dark red-brown sandy silt with a trace to little coarse sand and gravel. It is slightly plastic, very dense and relatively impermeable. The till is directly overlain throughout much of the site by outwash sands and gravels and by a few ice contact deposits.

The ice contact deposits consist of isolated kames, a kame terrace and an ice channel filling. In general, they are believed to consist primarily of fine sand although coarse to medium sands may occur in their upper layers.

The outwash deposits over till consist of stratified sands and gravels. The gravel strata are often coarse and contain many cobbles. The origin of this granular blanket over the till is obscure. It appears, however, to have been laid down by a stream flowing generally east-west and whose course moved continually downslope keeping pace with the receding ice.

The alluvial sands and gravels over cohesive lake deposits are found at lower elevations along the western border and in the northwest corner of the site. From the test pit data and topographic considerations the upper limit of this deposit is taken at Elevation 220. Clay was actually encountered in only one test pit, TP18. Here the material was a uniform stiff gray clay. It was not varved, but rather a number of thin layers of silty fine sand were found scattered randomly throughout the stratum. It is believed that silt and clay occur as a wedge shaped deposit feathering out to zero thickness at El. 220 and increasing in thickness downslope i.e. to the north, northwest and west.

The small shallow pond deposit in northeast corner of the property consists of interbedded clayey silts and clayey sands. It is a thin post-glacial deposit formed by washing of fine materials from the adjacent slopes into a small undrained depression in the outwash. The 6.5 feet of plastic material noted in TP6, taken in the approximate center of the deposit is believed to represent about the maximum thickness of cohesive soils to be found in this unit. The clayey silt was relatively stiff.

A few areas of sluggish drainage were observed in which shallow organic soils have accumulated, possibly as thick as 3 feet. No significant deposits of organic soils however occur within the bounds of this site.

The site from the standpoint of soils and foundations is excellent. Buildings could be supported on economical shallow spread footings throughout the site. In small areas at the lower elevations along the western border and at the northwest corner of the site cohesive lake deposits underlie alluvial sands. If buildings of more than two stories were to be constructed in these areas additional explorations should be made to determine thickness, extent and consolidation characteristics of the clay soils. In all other areas the soil at the site could support high rise structures on shallow footings after stripping organic materials.

The earthwork required for site grading and road construction will be economical as it is not expected that rock excavation will be required. Also there are sands and gravel deposits on the site to utilize as fill and even for base courses under paved areas.

If you should desire additional or more detailed information, do not hesitate notifying us.

Very truly yours,

HALEY & ALDRICH, INC.
JAMES F. HALEY
DONALD E. REED

JFH:mp
Enclosures

## EXHIBIT II

## PRELIMINARY EVALUATION OF THE
## ALTERNATIVE ALIGNMENTS FOR THE
## PROPOSED ROUTE 9 IN AMHERST

July 26, 1966

Mr. Charles R. Longsworth
Vice President
Hampshire College
Amherst, Massachusetts

Re: Hampshire College

Dear Mr. Longsworth:

At your request we have summarized our preliminary evaluation of the alternative alignment for the proposed Route 9 so that this information could be made available to the community.

The primary objective of our evaluation has been to order and weigh the principal criteria for judging the alternative alignments. No recommendation is made for either alignment.

We hope that this preliminary evaluation will help to clarify some of the issues involved and stimulate more detailed study of those elements which are critical to a final determination.

Sincerely,

SASAKI, DAWSON, DeMAY ASSOCIATES
RICHARD F. GALEHOUSE

RFG:ms

## PRELIMINARY EVALUATION OF THE ALTERNATIVE
## ALIGNMENTS FOR THE PROPOSED ROUTE 9 IN AMHERST

Two alternative alignments have been proposed for the new State Route 9 through Amherst. A northern alignment would depart from the existing Route 9 in east Amherst, follow the Fort River to North Pleasant Street and continue west to a connection with Route 116 in west Amherst near the existing Route 9 - Route 116 interchange. A southern alignment would depart from the existing Route 9 in Belchertown and generally follow a course west-northwest between Lawrence Swamp and Bay Road, cross West Street immediately north of Hampshire College, connect with the Route 116 extension about 1.6 miles south of the existing Route 9 - 116 interchange. The proposed Route 9 will be a 4 lane divided highway with access at only a few major north-south streets in Amherst.

The three main objectives for constructing the new highway appear to be:

1. Provision of high volume - high speed access to generators in Amherst: the University, Amherst College and the community itself.

2. Provision of a high volume - high speed road for traffic passing through Amherst to destinations east and west.

3. Provision of improved east - west inter-community access.

As part of planning studies for Hampshire College, preliminary evaluation has been made of the alternative alignments at the community level and college level. The proposed Route 9 will have a major impact on traffic flow through Amherst, and will significantly influence future patterns of land use, in Amherst and Hadley. In addition, the proposed Route 9 will exert direct and immediate influence on the development of Hampshire College.

Considerations of the various criteria at both levels are presented for consideration.

### The Amherst Community

The concerns of the Amherst community should include: first, the functional effectiveness of the road; second, the impact on land use and the local economy; third, the impact on the landscape; fourth, the impact on the "sense of community"; and fifth, construction feasibility.

### 1. Functional Effectiveness

If the primary objective of Route 9 is to provide improved regional access to the generators of traffic in the Amherst community, the northern alignment would be preferable. It is adjacent to Amherst College, the most densely developed portion of the community and the central business district, and it would provide the closest access to the principal traffic generator—the University.

If Route 9 is intended primarily as a bypass for through-traffic, the southern alignment would be preferable. Were this the case, a route south of the Mt. Holyoke range might even be more desirable.

The Massachusetts Department of Public Works' current study should provide fairly conclusive evidence on the functional effectiveness of the alternative alignments.

## 2. *Impact on Land Use and the Economy*

A northern alignment of Route 9 appears to have more negative impact on existing land use than a southern alignment. More homes and developed land would be immediately affected. Amherst College's holdings would be divided with a possible deleterious effect on future development of the College.

On the other hand, a northern alignment of Route 9 would probably serve the area's economy better, by supporting existing business in Amherst Center, and the newly developing commercial interests in Amherst and Hadley at the present Route 9 - Route 116 interchange. Detailed cost benefit analysis could be made of the alternative alignments to give correct emphasis to the highway's economic impact.

In the long run perhaps, the effect of the highway on Amherst College may be the most important single factor in considering the impact on land use because the educational institutions in Amherst are the basic source of the community's livelihood. High priorities should be given to the plans and interests of Amherst College.

## 3. *Impact on the Landscape*

The northern alignment in the Fort River Valley is shorter in length than the southern alignment and for a certain distance follows a natural cleft in the physiographic features of the community. The road might be more easily fitted into the landscape in the river bottom than on side slopes at the foot of Holyoke Range in South Amherst.

The southern alignment crosses rolling and poorly drained land in Lawrence Swamp and consequently, the road bed would have to be elevated or diked. Following no topographic line of cleavage impact on the landscape might be unduly obtrusive.

The community would be well advised when a general course for the highway has been chosen, to seek the services of a landscape architect in the review of the State's design of alignments and interchanges.

### 4. *Impact on the Sense of Community*

The Fort River Valley is a natural boundary and a recognized division between Amherst and the South Amherst communities. A northern alignment would not appear to inhibit easy interchange within the South Amherst community or access to Amherst Center.

The southern alignment visually and physically splits the South Amherst community. As a limited access road, there would be no cross access between the point of departure from the existing Route 9 to West Street. The southern alignment tends, therefore, to isolate a long wedge of the community along Bay Road.

### 5. *Construction Feasibility*

Overall construction costs for the northern route may be less than the southern route. The shorter length of the northern route should be weighed against probable higher land acquisition costs, some poor soil conditions in the Fort River Valley and difficult intersections.

The northern alignment will have much greater immediate relief to traffic congestion on community roads since the new Route 9 can be tied to the community's principal north-south road, Route 116, with only a short extension of 116.

A southern alignment will depend for the foreseeable future on the utilization of existing N. Pleasant Street for access to Route 9 from Amherst Center.

### *Hampshire College*

Hampshire College's concerns lie in three major areas: first, access to the college and its sister institutions; second, the impact of the highway on the use of the college's land and the impact on land use in the immediate community; third, the impact of Route 9 on the landscape.

### 1. *Access*

Because of its unique program of sharing facilities with Mount Holyoke, Smith, Amherst and the University of Massachusetts, safe and convenient access to these institutions is of prime importance to Hampshire College.

Either route provides equally good access to the other colleges, as well as the regional transportation system and Amherst. Were the northern route chosen, a complete interchange would be built at Route 116 and in the future an interchange at the intersection of Bay Road and Route 116. This, in all probability, would unload more traffic on Bay Road than if the southern route were chosen. With a southern alignment, traffic to and from the college would travel West Street, from a ramped intersection at Route 9 and a complete interchange at 116 and 9.

## 2. *Impact on Land Use*

The alignment of Route 9 will influence the location of the main entrance(s) to the college and the development of the community in the immediate environs of the college.

A northern alignment for Route 9 makes all sides of the campus accessible, with a possible future east-west extension to Potwine Lane north of the present holdings. The southern route tends to limit potential entrances to the east, from West Street, or to the south, from Bay Road.

A southern alignment of the road with Route 116 to the west could be viewed as creating a "buffer" to the north and west of the college or a real and psychological wall preventing close integration to the community. It would place increasing pressure for non-residential development along West Street in the vicinity of the college.

## 3. *Impact on the Landscape*

A southern alignment of Route 9 will be both visible and audible to Hampshire College. These considerations, when combined with those previously stated concerning the road's impact on the landscape of South Amherst, would make the road seem a negative presence in the vicinity.

## EXHIBIT III

## LAND CORPORATIONS IN MASSACHUSETTS

The formation of a land corporation falls under legal regulations governing the formation of any business corporation in the Commonwealth of Massachusetts. Pre-incorporation actions involve the execution of a written agreement of association defining rights, provisions and purpose of the corporation. In the case of a land corporation, whose intent is to purchase, improve, subdivide land and develop housing, the delineation of the location and area of land prior to corporation would probably be mandatory. The advance commitments of investors in an undertaking which depends on a large initial investment would practically necessitate this. Otherwise, the procedure follows precisely defined steps and must comply to all the regulations of the normal business corporation. A final note: the advantages of forming a corporation with centralized management and limited liability should be carefully thought out for the disadvantages, including administration and taxes, might eventually predominate.

Control over land and development exists in other guises, but none is as powerful as ownership. Governmental control by police power tends too often to set minimum standards or rigidly conventional rules. Planning zoning and density controls are the accepted means of insuring general orderliness and protecting the neighborhood environment. However, these have seldom been used effectively to guide the pace and quality of new development. Taxation, with its incidence on land and improvements, can be carefully adjusted to insure control to some extent, but benefits to some are detriments to others. Public ownership whether complete, partial or temporary would be applicable in highway and flood control areas or land reserved for open space and might be used in conjunction with other methods for the directed development of the area surrounding Hampshire College.

# APPENDIX K

## The Future of Library Automation*

The rapid growth of student population, the inter-disciplinary character of most academic endeavors have placed great demands on libraries serving higher education. At the same time rising costs of books and increasing library operating expenses make it difficult to add to the staff or to improve inadequate physical facilities in spite of constantly rising budgets.

Librarians have long ago recognized that no one institution can or should store all the books that its patrons may need and they have developed a strong tradition of regional cooperation. It is apparent that to continue the level of service libraries must render, the area of cooperation must be extended. Much of the processing work in college libraries is similar from a procedural viewpoint and deals with almost identical elements of bibliographic information. Data Processing equipment could be employed to carry out the clerical functions incident to the acquisition of books, accounting and budgetary control, preparation of statistical data, catalog preparation and maintenance, circulation control, etc.

To the extent that there exists overlap in the acquisition of material, the cost of acquisition and cataloging could be shared by cooperating institutions.

A cooperative library data processing institution could evolve in the following manner:

Under the leadership of a committee of librarians representing their institutions, a study should be made of the existing practices and agreement reached on a common classification scheme, bibliographic standards, etc. The degree of overlap in acquisitions and holdings between the libraries should be investigated. Each library might start independently of the others with the use of data processing equipment in acquisition. With a minimum of equipment, such as the installation of a typewriter-key punch or paper-tape punch, bibliographic information could be captured in machine-readable form. Upon receipt of the book ordered, cataloging would be performed at each library from Library of Congress proof sheets and the same data processing equipment used to prepare the necessary catalog cards. The machinable data would be processed for accounting and budgeting information on a computer at one of the institutions. Periodically, the acquisitions of each institution or of all cooperating libraries could be processed on a computer to prepare a catalog in book form. If it represents the acquisitions of all the libraries and indicates the location of each item, this would be the first new product of the computer: A union catalog.

While at first limited to new acquisitions, it could be printed in multiple copies, distributed throughout the campus of each institution, and thus facilitate utilization of the resources of the libraries of the area.

As a by-product of the acquisitions process, each institution would also obtain a machinable book-card which would facilitate the installation of a recording device to charge out books in circulation.

In due course, consideration must be given to the conversion of the holdings of the libraries into machine readable form. Depending on the degree of overlap, determined by the study, one of the libraries could convert its catalog by key punching. The other libraries would match their holdings by punching a minimum of information from the shelf-list. Unmatched items would have to be updated to indicate location. Thus by cooperating the libraries could at minimum expense create a union catalog of their holdings.

It is hoped that in the near future the Library of Congress will make machinable information available. At first this will be a relatively small portion of the total acquisition but will undoubtedly continue to expand. Complete compatibility with LC format is therefore essential.

Within 3-5 years the cooperative system should be at the point where the traditional catalog, as well as the book catalog, can be abandoned in favor of a computer-stored catalog. This catalog would be accessible from remote points (dormitories, classrooms, laboratories, faculty offices) via terminal units equipped with keyboards and Cathode Ray tubes which would display the desired information. Searching via terminal would be under control of the computer program which would also instruct the user in how to use the system, offer alternatives, etc. The information would always be as up-to-date as the latest transaction processed. Circulation recorders would likewise be on-line, and thus show availability of a book at time of inquiry saving the user unsuccessful trips to the library. At that time it is to be expected that cooperation will extend beyond processing to acquisitions and the librarians may be able to agree on acquisitions policies making it unnecessary for several of them to buy the same expensive books not likely to be frequently used.

Parallel with this development is to be expected the increased use of non-book material: journal articles, conference proceedings, etc. Computers will be used to perform Current Awareness services for faculty and students. SDI (Selective Dissemination of Information) is an existing computer program comparing interest profiles of people to index profiles of documents. In case of a "match" notices are prepared and sent to the individual, calling his attention to an item in his sphere of activity. Retrospective searches to prepare bibliographies can be made of the data banks which have been stored.

In the next 5-10 years substantial changes will occur in the publishing field and information will be marketed in different "packages": in book or journal form, on microfilm or microfiche or on magnetic tapes or chips. It will therefore be possible not only to search the catalog remotely but to ask for the desired information to be displayed and printed out over the telephone wire. The library will eventually come to the user rather than forcing the user to make the effort to go to the library which often requires several trips.

The impact on scholarship when one can surround oneself with a substantial portion of the world's recorded knowledge is not difficult to envision.

The proposed evolutionary development of a cooperative college library system can be implemented in its initial phases with commercially available data processing equipment.

To make a start we would like to offer our assistance in conducting a seminar for interested library personnel to acquaint them with the possibilities and limitations of equipment, set the stage for the initiation of studies to arrive at agreement on system specifications and compatible procedures.

*This statement is excerpted from a letter to Hampshire College by Steven E. Firth, International Business Machines Corporation, August 29, 1966.

# APPENDIX L

## Modification of "Recognition of Candidacy for Accreditation" to Permit Application for College Housing Loans for New Institutions

*(The following is an excerpt, with minor modifications, of a statement by Prof. Livingston Hall, Secretary, Simon's Rock, Inc., Great Barrington, Massachusetts, to the New England Association of Colleges and Secondary Schools, on June 9, 1966.)*

The definition of educational institutions eligible for College Housing Loans from the Federal Housing and Home Finance Administration was amended in 1965 to include institutions which had not yet commenced operations. Any public or private non-profit educational institution is now eligible if it "offers, or provides satisfactory assurance to the Administrator that it will offer within a reasonable time after completion of a facility for which assistance is requested under this Title, at least a two-year program acceptable for full credit towards a baccalaureate degree."

The U.S. Office of Education has confirmed the fact that such "satisfactory assurance" from its Office can be obtained for a new institution only upon certification from its Regional Association.

At present the New England Association does not appear to have any sort of candidacy for accreditation for which new schools which have not yet begun operations are eligible. Its "Recognition of Candidacy for Accreditation" requires that the institution must be (1) authorized to grant degrees, and that (2) "one class must be enrolled; and normally (3) one year of operation must be completed."

The Middle States Association of Colleges and Secondary Schools has already done this. In April, 1966, it granted certification of satisfactory assurance to Eisenhower College, Seneca Falls, New York. This is a new college, chartered in New York January 28, 1965. It will not enroll its first class until the fall of 1967, and building construction did not begin until the spring of 1966. It now has only a provisional charter, and it is without present degree granting authority. (Degrees may be conferred upon its graduates by the University of the State of New York, only if in the judgment of the Regent they have duly earned the same.)

The initial step under the Middle States Accreditation Program for a new institution is to become a "Correspondent of the Commission." In order to give the Association sufficient information to entitle the new institution

355

to a "satisfactory assurance" to the Office of Education, the institution must go on to the second step in the Middle States Association Program, by becoming a "Candidate for Accreditation." The requirements of the Middle States Association for this are comparable to those of the New England Association for its "Recognition of Candidacy for Accreditation." But the Middle States Association does not require either authorization to grant degrees or the enrollment of one college class, before it will certify the institution for a College Housing Loan.

The Conditions for Recognition could be rewritten to eliminate the absolute requirements of authorization to grant degrees, and of enrollment of one class. The first part of the second paragraph on "Recognition of Candidacy for Accreditation" might be changed to read as follows:

"The conditions for recognition in this category are as follows:

1. Any unaccreditated institution, old or new, may be considered for recognition under the following provisions:

    (a) The institution must have been in existence as a non-profit educational institution for a period of not less than one year;

    (b) the institution must either (i) have enrolled one class, and normally have completed one year of operation, and be authorized to grant degrees; or (ii) its basic structure, management, resources, and program must provide satisfactory assurance that within a reasonable time after its admission to Recognition of Candidacy for Accreditation it will offer at least a two-year program acceptable for full credit toward a baccalaureate degree, and will be eligible to apply for authorization to grant degrees; and

    (c) the institution must be developing in accordance with the general standards of NEACSS."

If some modification along these lines is made, the New England Association might also wish to consider establishing a new preliminary status such as "Correspondent of the Commission," as the Middle States Association has done. While not crucial in determining eligibility for federal funds, this might be a desirable means of establishing an initial consultative relationship between a new institution and the New England Association.

# APPENDIX M

## Architects, Landscape Architects and Planning Consultants, and Architectural Consultant to Hampshire College

*Architects*

Hugh Stubbins and Associates
806 Massachusetts Avenue
Cambridge, Massachusetts

*Landscape Architects and Planning Consultants*

Sasaki, Dawson, DeMay Associates, Inc.
23 Main Street
Watertown, Massachusetts

*Architectural Consultant*

Pietro Belluschi
1 Fairfield Street
Boston, Massachusetts

# APPENDIX N

## Hampshire College
## Biographical Data
## Trustees and Administrative Officers

### Trustees of Hampshire College

*Harold F. Johnson*

Harold F. Johnson is chairman of the Board of Trustees of Hampshire College. He is retired from the practice of law, as a partner in Coudert Bros., Paris, France, and New York City from 1932-1942, and as a consultant, administrator and advisor to the United States State Department, to the United States Ambassador in Paris, France, and as a member of the Economic Mission to Turkey for the World Bank. Mr. Johnson is a graduate of Amherst College and of Harvard Law School, and is a member of Phi Beta Kappa.

*Charles W. Cole*

Charles W. Cole, vice-chairman of the Board of Trustees of Hampshire College, is president-emeritus of Amherst College. He was president from 1946-1960. In 1960-61 he was a vice-president of the Rockefeller Foundation and from 1961-1965 was United States Ambassador to Chile. Dr. Cole has written or edited a number of books and articles on European history and economics. He is active as a consultant to educational institutions and as an historian. Dr. Cole is a graduate of Amherst College, holds an M.A. and Ph.D. from Columbia University, and is a member of Phi Beta Kappa.

*Franklin Patterson*

Franklin Patterson is the first president of Hampshire College. He was appointed in 1966. From 1957-1966 he was director of the Lincoln Filene Center for Citizenship and Public Affairs at Tufts University and was a professor of government and education. During the same period he had leaves of absence to serve as co-director of the Social Studies Curriculum Progam of Educational Services Incorporated, and as staff director of the Carnegie Commission for Educational Television. Previous responsibilities include the chairmanship of the Department of Secondary Education at New York University, associate national education director of the National

Conference of Christians and Jews, and history teacher and curriculum co-ordinator in the Pasadena City Schools, Pasadena, California. He has taught at Vassar College, Claremont Graduate School and the University of Michigan. Dr. Patterson is the author of a number of books and pamphlets on civic affairs, curriculum development, political action and education. He is a graduate of Occidental College and has a Ph.D. from the Claremont Graduate School. He is a member of Phi Beta Kappa.

### Winthrop S. Dakin

Winthrop S. Dakin, treasurer of the Board of Trustees of Hampshire College, is a member of the Massachusetts and American Bar Associations and practices law in Northampton, Massachusetts. He is a newspaper columnist, Moderator of the Amherst Town Meeting, and chairman of the Massachusetts Board of Higher Education. Mr. Dakin is a graduate of Princeton University and of Harvard Law School.

### Richard G. Gettell

Richard G. Gettell is president of Mount Holyoke College, which he has served in that capacity since 1957. Dr. Gettell taught previously at Berkeley, Harvard, Wellesley, and Yale. Prior to his appointment at Mount Holyoke he was, successively, assistant to the publisher and chief staff economist of *Fortune* magazine, economist for Time, Inc., and chief foreign economist for The Texas Company. Dr. Gettell is a graduate of Amherst College and holds a Ph.D. from the University of California.

### John W. Lederle

John W. Lederle is president of the University of Massachusetts, the post to which he was appointed in 1960. Previously, Dr. Lederle taught political science and served as a dean at Brown University, and was a professor of political science and director of Institute of Public Administration at the University of Michigan. He is a member of the Michigan Bar and practiced law in Michigan prior to his appointment at Brown University. He has served as a public administrator as controller of the State of Michigan and head of the Michigan Department of Administration and as a legislative consultant to the United States Senate and the United States House of Representatives. Dr. Lederle is a graduate of the University of Michigan, from which he also has received a law degree and a Ph.D. in political science.

## Thomas C. Mendenhall

Thomas C. Mendenhall is president of Smith College, the post to which he was appointed in 1959. Prior to his presidency at Smith he was a professor of history and Master of Berkeley College at Yale University. Dr. Mendenhall is the author of several books on general European and English history. He received an undergraduate degree from Yale, after which he earned a Ph.D. at Yale and as a Rhodes Scholar to Oxford, B.A. and B. Litt. degrees. He is a member of Phi Beta Kappa.

## Elting E. Morison

Elting E. Morison is Sloan Fellows Professor of Industrial History at the Massachusetts Institute of Technology, where he has taught since 1946. Previous teaching experience was at St. Marks School and Harvard College. For the academic year 1966-67 he is Acting Master of Ezra Stiles College, Yale University. Mr. Morison is the author of several books, including *Turmoil and Tradition, A Study of the Life and Times of Henry L. Stimson,* and is the editor of *The Letters of Theodore Roosevelt.* He is a graduate of Harvard College, from which he also holds an M.A. degree.

## Calvin H. Plimpton

Calvin H. Plimpton is president of Amherst College. Prior to his appointment in 1960 he was assistant dean and assistant professor of clinical medicine of the College of Physicians and Surgeons at Columbia University. Previous teaching and medical experience was at Presbyterian Hospital in New York, Columbia University, and as professor of medicine and chairman of the department at American University of Beirut, Lebanon. Dr. Plimpton is a graduate of Amherst College and of Harvard Medical School. He also has an M.A. degree from Harvard University and a Med. Sc.D. from Columbia University.

## Administrative Officers of Hampshire College

*Franklin Patterson*
President

*Charles R. Longsworth*
Vice-President

Charles R. Longsworth is administrative vice-president of Hampshire College and secretary of the Board of Trustees. He was assistant to the president of Amherst College from 1960-1965. Previous experience was with Campbell Soup Company and Ogilvy, Benson & Mather Inc., New York advertising firm. Mr. Longsworth is a graduate of Amherst College and of Harvard Graduate School of Business Administration. He is a member of Phi Beta Kappa.

# APPENDIX O

## ADVISORS AND CONSULTANTS TO HAMPSHIRE COLLEGE PLANNING (THROUGH SEPTEMBER, 1966)

The administration of Hampshire College expresses its gratitude to the following persons and committees, as indicated below, for important contributions to the thinking that resulted in this working paper.

> To the Committee on Cooperation, the New College Committee, and the Educational Advisory Committee, whose written recommendations and, in some cases, letters and consultations, provided a rich inheritance for Hampshire College:

### COMMITTEE ON COOPERATION (1956)

Charles J. Hill                 Bruce R. Morris
Gail Kennedy                    Stuart M. Stoke

### NEW COLLEGE COMMITTEE (1958)

C. L. Barber                    Stuart M. Stoke
Donald Sheehan                  Shannon McCune

### EDUCATIONAL ADVISORY COMMITTEE (1966)

Robert C. Birney                Frederick C. Ellert
Alice B. Dickinson              Roger W. Holmes
                 Sidney R. Packard

> To the participants in the Academic Conference held in Amherst in June 1966. Their stimulating discussions and follow-up papers cast many new lights on the complex problem of designing a college:

### PARTICIPANTS IN JUNE 1966 ACADEMIC CONFERENCE

C. L. Barber                    Donald McNassor
Samuel Baskin                   Elting E. Morison
Jerome S. Bruner                Arthur Penn
Benjamin H. DeMott              Esther Raushenbush

Charles Eames                         Arleigh Richardson, III
Elizabeth Hall                        Peter Schrag
Sister M. Jacqueline                  Philip Sherburne
Ulysses Kay                           Morton G. White
Kenneth Keniston                      Laya Wiesner
Jonathan King                         Kent Wilson

To the following, whose thoughtful and generous contributions, although made informally in correspondence and conversation, were significant and influential:

Nelson W. Aldrich
Dean A. Allen
Rae D. Anderson
Arnold B. Arons
Howard W. Atkins
William E. Aubin
Edward S. Babbitt
Jervis J. Babb
Theodore S. Bacon, Jr.
George B. Beitzel
Robert Berkey
Robert J. Bernard
John M. Bevan
J. Seelye Bixler
Roy R. Blair
Marshall I. Bloom
William A. Bodden
John R. Boettiger
Nathan Boortz
Laura Bornholdt
Julio L. Bortolazzo
Frank Bowles
Gordon B. Bridges
Howard Brooks
Ralph A. Burns
John L. Callahan
John B. Carroll
John R. Coleman
Edward Colin

Pauline R. Collins
George H. Colton
Henry S. Commager
James B. Conant
Theodore Conant
Robert L. Conway
Richard W. Couper
Steven Coy
G. Armour Craig
Merrimon Cuninggim
Paul B. Davis
Casimir deRham, Jr.
John S. Dickey
Richard P. Dober
George B. Dunnington
Donald R. Dwight
Anne C. Edmonds
Robert L. Ellis
Everett H. Emerson
Clarence H. Faust
Gerald W. C. Fee
Alan D. Ferguson
Steven E. Firth
Norman C. Fletcher
Frank C. Foss
William E. Frenaye
Robert W. Gage
Hendrik Gideonse
Harold B. Gores

Martin C. Gowdey
Gerald J. Grady
Jean D. Grambs
Walter Gropius
Minot Grose
Robert F. Grose
J. Alfred Guest
Hartford N. Gunn, Jr.
Livingston Hall
Van R. Halsey, Jr.
Chester Hammond
William C. Havard
Joseph Havens
Morrison C. Haviland
Henry T. Heald
Robert H. Heidrich
Herbert M. Heston
Horace W. Hewlett
DeWitt Howell
Philip T. Ives
Kenneth W. Johnson
Margaret L. Johnson
Edward L. Katzenbach
Henry W. Kendall
John P. Kendall
James R. Killian, Jr.
Harry W. Knight
Otto C. Kohler
Donald W. Korth, Jr.

Cooper H. Langford, III John Pemberton       Kenneth W. Thompson
Thomas J. Lantos       Rollin P. Posey       Burton D. Thuma
Charles T. Laugher     Paul N. Procopio      Oswald Tippo
Merritt C. Ludwig      Leo F. Redfern        Allen L. Torrey
Robert W. McEwen       Walter Orr Roberts    Frank A. Tredinnick, Jr.
Bruce G. McInnes       Anthony P. Sager      David B. Truman
Newton F. McKeon       John E. Sawyer        Marc Tucker
Robert W. McLaughlin   John P. Scanlon       John Volpe
Louis A. McMillen      Homer W. Schamp, Jr.  Philip Von Blon
Walter C. Markert      Peter Schrag          Frederick H. Wagman
George B. May          Emerson S. Searle     F. Champion Ward
William F. May         Oscar M. Shaw         John W. Ward
Hugh Montgomery        John Sheetz           John D. Warner
John A. Moore          Richard M. Simon      Vera Z. Washburne
Lewis S. Mudge         Kendrick Smith        Seward Weber
J. Guy Nassberg        H. Evan Snyder        Willard T. Weeks
Martin J. Neeb         John H. Spencer       Ruth Weinstock
Robert V. Norwine      Herbert J. Spiro      Nils Y. Wessell
Per Nylen              Eugene S. Staples     Robert B. Whitney
David Ogilvy           Stanley F. Teele      Jerome B. Wiesner
Richard Olmsted        Benjamin Thompson     Philip Will, Jr.
James E. Ostendarp     John M. Thompson, III Eugene S. Wilson
Manning M. Pattillo                          Jerrold R. Zacharias

Thanks and recognition are due the women whose faithful
and skillful efforts produced this paper:

Virginia H. Aldrich              Miriam C. Berry
Dorothy L. Anderson              Ruth G. Hammen
                    Sandra J. Saba